The Safety

P. E Fischetti

To Kent,
Best wishes

P E Fischetti.

pcfischetti.com

For my son Anthony

Prologue

During the post-Civil War era in the United States, organized sports slowly replaced war between states, cities, and towns as acceptable aggression between conflicting sides. What was called "football" at that time was the most combative of these aggressions.

The first attempt at college football was a rough combination of soccer and rugby at Rutgers University against Princeton University on November 6, 1869. The academic institutions were a twenty-mile, horse-drawn carriage ride apart in central New Jersey.

The rules were set by the home team. No player was allowed to pick the ball up and carry it forward, much less throw it forward. There were twenty-five players a side, colliding in large scrums while trying to kick the ball toward the goal line. Each crossing of the goal line was worth a point, and Rutgers won 6-4.

The following week, the two teams played again, this time at Princeton. With the home team setting the rules, Princeton came up with a new one that would change the game forever. Any player would be awarded a "free kick" when catching the football on the fly. This allowed for a team to gain precious field position from a player with great hands who was also a talented punter. Princeton won 8-0 because they reconfigured their defense by dropping a player from the line of warfare to intercept the unabated advancement of a kicked football. This new position would become "The Safety." Suddenly, this game of football that was replacing the idea of any ground war in the United States had introduced the air game.

The Safety is the last line of defense in football, and among the many responsibilities of the current position, the most important is defending against "the bomb." This became extremely important to the game during the Depression, as throwing the football became a new form of creativity for the football fan to observe and enjoy. Just as the Manhattan Project was developing the atomic bomb in the late thirties for the US military, the National Football League (NFL) started their own experiment for developing "the bomb" with a new air-weapon delivery position, the throwing quarterback (QB). It was an arsenal unleashed over the next two decades led

4

by the remarkable rookie QB Sammy Baugh in 19 37, when Washington unveiled an expanded passing attack that captured their first NFL title. Washington's owner, George Preston Marshall, had just moved his team from Boston to the nation's capital, where decisions about the Manhattan Project were being made. His reasons were purely financial; he wanted to be closer to the untapped potential of a professional football audience in the South.

In the 1940 NFL championship game, the great Chicago Bear QB Sid Luckman unleashed a highly potent missile-carrying system called the "T-Formation." Luckman used the new strategy to embarrass Washington 73-0, as their defense was scorched by air strikes and burned into oblivion. Some thought the championship game score in the paper was a typo, because Washington had beaten the Bears 7-3 during the regular season before facing the T-Formation.

In 1945, after a stellar college football career at Northwestern and then finishing his pilot's training course in the navy, Otto Graham was signed by innovative coach Paul Brown to play in the upstart All-American Football League (AAFL) for the Cleveland Browns. Graham went on to win four straight championships in the AAFL running Brown's groundbreaking precursor to the current "West-Coast Offense." When the popularity of the AAFL finally forced the NFL into a merger, Graham proved that Brown's air-attack offense was no fluke by winning a fifth straight championship in his first year in the NFL. He finished his NFL career by winning championships in 1954 and 1955.

With the advent of football on television in the early fifties, the "pigskin," or the football itself, became sleeker and less round, therefore making it easier to throw. Moving the quarterback under the center (the T-Formation) and allowing passes to be thrown from anywhere behind the line of scrimmage (instead of an old rule of at least five yards behind the line of scrimmage) made it harder for defenses to defend the pass.

Finding great athletes to shore up the last line of defense against these new offensive weapons became an obsession for NFL coaches by the early fifties. Up to this point, most players in football played both ways-offense and defense. "The Safety" was usually the quarterback on offense and played defense because he was very athletic, had good instincts, and had great hands to catch punts and interceptions. An experiment was tried with the position in the early fifties that was like splitting the atom. A new form of energy was released for the defense by dividing "The Safety" into two positions on defense: a free safety and a strong safety, manned by players playing only defense. This was the NFL's idea of developing an antiballistic missile (ABM) system, first proposed by the United States in the fifties to defend against a Russian nuclear attack.

Tom Landry, the future coach of the Dallas Cowboys for twenty-eight seasons (1960-1987), was the first defensive coach to come up with the idea of the 4-3-4 defense that utilized two safeties. After watching the great QB Johnny Unitas of the Baltimore Colts air-raid defenses with his golden arm in the mid-fifties, Landry's brilliance was to change the old 6-2-3 defense into a 4-3-4 defense by taking two linemen positions and turning them into the middle linebacker and strong safety positions.

The greatest coach in NFL history, Vince Lombardi, copied the intricacies of the 4-3-4 defense from Tom Landry when he started his first head coaching job with the Green Bay Packers in 19 59. They were both assistant coaches for the New York football Giants in the fifties.

Lombardi's first trade as coach of the Packers was for All-Pro free safety Emlen Tunnell from the Giants. Tunnell played his last three seasons for the Packers and Lombardi's first championship in 1961. He finished his career with seventy-nine interceptions, the most at the time in the NFL and still second all-time. He was replaced in 1962 by another future Hall-of-Famer, free safety Willie Wood. Coach Lombardi felt that it was critical to stop "the bomb" on defense.

He made it to the 1960 NFL championship game in his second year as head coach, but his offense fell ten yards short of the winning touchdown when time ran out. A veteran mad-bomber QB, Norm Van Bracklin, beat Lombardi's Packers in his last game. It was Lombardi's only loss in a postseason game.

Lombardi was a first-generation Italian American who played guard on the famous "Seven Blocks of Granite" college football team at Fordham University in the early thirties. Before accepting the Packer job in 19 5 9 at age forty-six, he labored for over twenty years as an assistant coach on the college and professional levels. His only previous head coaching experience was after college at St. Cecilia's High School in New Jersey.

After his disappointment in 1960, he went on to win five NFL titles over the next seven years in Green Bay, including a record three NFL titles in a row. The last two titles included winning a new game against the upstart American Football League (AFL) called the "Super Bowl." After his death from cancer in 1970, the Super Bowl Trophy, the most sought-after prize in sports, was renamed the "Lombardi Trophy"!

The fear of a country developing an ABM system was seen by the handful of nuclear-capable countries as a financial escalation impossible to sustain. The NFL had the same problem when the AFL started in 1960, based almost exclusively on throwing "the bomb." For seven years the NFL tried to ignore the mad-bombers being developed in the

AFL like quarterbacks Joe Namath, John Hadl, Darryl Lamonica, Lenny Dawson, George Blanda, and Jack Kemp.

Around the same time that an ABM treaty was agreed to in 1967 to avoid mutually assured destruction (MAD) between Russia and the United States, the NFL and AFL agreed to a merger and started the Super Bowl. It quickly became the biggest entertainment day in the world, but as crowds of fans grew, they wanted to watch more football and witness the thrill of more bombs. Monday Night Football started in 1971, followed by Sunday and Thursday Night Football.

Ironically, Coach Tom Landry started using different offensive formations, like the shotgun with shifting linemen and men-in-motion. The assistant coach who had developed the 4-3-4 defense to stop "the bomb" in the fifties changed his offense as head coach to promote the passing game in the sixties.

During the 1978 off-season, two games were added for each team to make a sixteen-game schedule. But then the NFL rules committee decided to join the offensive party. They changed two rules on defense to allow the passing game to expand into the stratosphere and therefore promote more scoring.

The first change meant that defensive linemen would have to play in virtual handcuffs taken into custody by the newly legal grabbing linemen on offense. The second forced defensive backs to play musical chairs as they watched receivers roaming the secondary without contact until the pass was thrown and the football nicely found a seat, likely in the hands of an untouched receiver. Inflated passing and receiving records would be added to the resumes of the players, which meant bigger contracts in the future. The final escalation of "the bomb" in the NFL was now complete.

Three years later, President Reagan decided to come up with an umbrella defense named the Strategic Defense Initiative (SDI), better known as Star Wars, to protect against the nuclear bomb. Suddenly, the safety provided by the ABM treaty was in doubt. In 2001, the United States officially withdrew from the ABM treaty.

The television show *24* became popular in 2002 and was based on hunting down terrorists who had small nuclear devices called "smart bombs" hidden in large cities. In 2003, the United States invaded Iraq because President Bush was convinced, they possessed "weapons of mass destruction" (WMDs). Currently, countries like Iran and North Korea, without diplomatic ties to the United States, possess or are feared to be making WMDs.

To defend against the "bomb" in the next decade, the idea is to stop the escalation of offensive weapons. A super- interceptor, a new defensive hero, or perhaps a superhero is

7

needed to bring sanity to this conflict. A balance is necessary to return the use of weapons to the ground, or In the game of football, just a dozen yards or so above it. A beacon of hope is needed to even the playing field; something bigger, faster, smarter, and bolder than before; somebody that gives us a fighting chance to keep the defense in the equation; a superhero that will rise in this decade for our protection-something quite simply known as "The Safety."

Part I
Before Now

The Finelli- Angelluci Family Tree 2012

Geraldo Finelli and Philomena Finelli

(Died 1/19/53)   (Died 1984)

Children

Gaetano (Guy I) Finelli / Pietro Finelli / Helen Finelli

(Died 8/21/93)

Phillip Angelucci & Rosina Angelucci

(Died 1955)   (Died 1967)

Children

Ernesto Angelucci / Rose Angelucci

(Died 9/4/2012)   (Died 7/7/2010)

Guy I Finelli married Rose Angelucci 1944

Children

Ernesto Angelucci married Helen Finelli 1951

Children

Anthony Finelli   Phillip Finelli   Joseph Angelucci   Philomena (Philly) Angelucci

(Born 1944)   (Born 6/7/53)   (Born 1952 Died 9/4/69)   (Born 6/7/53)

(Anthony, Phillip, Joseph, Philly are known as Double First Cousins. All with the same Grandparents)

Anthony Finelli married Florence Gray 1966   Phillip Finelli married Carol Werner 1986

Children   Children

Child w/ Leah Raines 1976)

Melissa Finelli   Joseph Finelli   *Alex Santucci   Grace Finelli   Gaetano (Guy)Finelli

(Born 1967)   (Cousin Joe-Born 6/4/70)   (Born 8/8/76)   (Born 11/2/91)   (10/04/94)

**Charlotte Roberts

(Born 8/8/83)

*Adopted by Dr. Gene Santucci and Laura Santucci

**Step-Sister to Alex, fathered by Dr. Gene Santucci   Alex Santucci married Sally Keegan 2012

(Died 8/15/91)

CHAPTER 1

BEFORE DAWN ON Monday, November 26, 2007, thirteen-year-old Guy James Finelli heard the creaking of the almost sixty-year-old subflooring above the ceiling in the finished basement as his father, Phillip, came down from the second-floor stairs. Each succeeding step across the living room area rug echoed more gently into Guy's sleepy consciousness as Phillip reached the kitchen to start the coffee for the workweek. His dad's morning task reminded Guy that reality on the other side of sleep was about to start.

The house, built in the Washington, DC, suburb of Silver Spring during the post-World War II housing boom, had its charming traits, but squeaky floors was not one of them. Guy kept his eyes closed, hoping to sneak out another thirty minutes of sleep before having to wake up at six o'clock for another week of eighth grade.

Guy slept most weekend nights in the basement, which was evolving into a serious teenage man cave. On his thirteenth birthday in early October, Phillip had presented him with a forty-two-inch HDTV to go with a killer couch from his grandmother's house for television- viewing heaven. He was hoping for an Xbox 360 at Christmas to complete the perfect playground triangle. For now, the entire basement was great for sleepovers with friends, Ping-Pong, gaming on the old Xbox, and even occasional homework and naps-but most importantly, watching sports, especially football.

The HDTV was left on without the volume and emitted an ever-so-slight buzz throughout the entire night that entered his subconscious during his sleep. On most nights it gave him a good feeling to know that *SportsCenter* would be there in the morning to help him wake up. This morning his subconscious created one final dream about his favorite football player, Washington's All-Pro safety, Sean Taylor.

He dreamed about Sunday's game against Tampa Bay and experienced it ending with a spectacular interception by Taylor to thwart a last-second comeback by Tampa Bay. Sean Taylor for three-and-a-half seasons had played for Washington with the force of a hurricane, reaching landfall with crashing waves of hits on all opponents in the path of his storm. The excitement created by his energy on the field equaled that of a superhero to young football players like Guy Finelli.

Presently another energy source seemed to be emanating from Guy's stomach as he was trying to enjoy the dream victory. The electrical pulse spread like that from a

11

slow-motion stun gun.

Finally, Guy rose into a minor consciousness as he located his right hand, feeling numb under his head and pillow. He managed to reach under his stomach to find his cell phone vibrating a wake-up alarm. The combination of facing a Monday morning and accepting a Washington loss was now a bit overwhelming.

He quickly recalled the fallacy of his last dream, because Sean Taylor was currently hurt with a knee injury that had kept him from playing Sunday in his native state of Florida. He was given permission to travel separately from the team and rehabilitate his knee in South Florida while staying in his house in Palmetto Bay.

Phillip sat in the kitchen at six in the morning, enjoying his morning coffee and reading the *Washington Daily*. The 2007 Thanksgiving holiday weekend had been a success for the family, except for Washington losing on Sunday. He noticed in the Metro section that the weather looked good enough for the coming week to sneak in a couple rounds of golf before the December cold settled in. He had only one nightmare real-estate settlement to complete before the Christmas season; otherwise, he could relax for the rest of the year and focus on a great holiday season with his family.

His wife, Carol, was struggling with the morning as she entered the kitchen in her robe, smelling the coffee and motioning for some hot oatmeal. She mumbled something about hearing their sixteen-year-old Grace in the shower already. After taking her first sip of coffee, she found her voice and asked about Guy's progress in getting up for school.

"Did he crash in the basement again? You know, if he keeps this up, his bedroom upstairs could become a great place to store some of my summer plants!" Carol was always looking to explore new territory in the house for her serious gardening hobby. She had already taken over Grace's former bedroom to use as a dressing room and its south-facing double windows for her plants. Now, apparently, Guy's room was going to be her new conquest.

"Hold on, Columbus!" Phillip laughed, "Guy crashes down there every weekend, but on school nights he makes it upstairs. I think I heard him moving already." Phillip poured a perfect amount of oatmeal into the boiling water, stirred it for a few seconds, turned off the burner, and put on the lid. "The oatmeal will be good in five minutes. I'm going to the basement to check on our boy."

As Guy Finelli began to accept the reality of the morning, he slowly turned his body and eyes toward the magnificent HDTV. His eyes were slowly coming into focus as he noticed an unfamiliar-looking female reporter standing in front of a house with palm

12

trees under a sky of morning darkness. She was reporting something from Palmetto Bay with serious eyes as the bottom of the screen ran a large banner that was just grabbing Guy's attention. He felt for the remote control under the couch to quickly turn up the sound. The reporter, Kimberly Manning, was mouthing the words that he finally understood from the banner-"Sean Taylor Has Been Shot in His House." Phillip kissed his lovely bride of twenty-one years and headed down the stairs. He saw Guy sitting up on the couch, wrapped in a blanket, staring at the television. Phillip came around to his side, saw his motionless face, and then looked at the screen as he asked, "What happened, son?"

After a quiet pause that seemed to take a lifetime, Guy stayed motionless but mumbled a response without volume. Then his voice found some air, and he stated with clarity and certainty, "They shot him, Dad...in his bedroom!"

Phillip nestled into a spot on the couch next to his son and held him. The numbness of the news was starting to settle into his consciousness. It was in stark contrast to the happiness they had felt together on draft day in April 2004.

Phillip had gone through a few of these shocks to his nervous system, starting at age ten with the Kennedy assassination, and then losing his cousin Joe at age sixteen and his friend Taylor at age thirty-six and his father at age forty. He knew that this would change his son's life forever.

As Guy laid his head on his father's shoulder, Phillip felt his son's energy being drained by raw emotion. They both loved football, but Guy was living it and wanting to achieve greatness. Now a building block of joy had been pulled out from under him. Phillip suddenly realized that since Guy was a toddler, this was the first time he had ever witnessed his son crying, but unfortunately, there was nothing he could do to make it better.

CHAPTER 2

B Y THE FALL of 1929, some sixty years after the first recorded game in 1869,

football had become a somewhat more civilized game. At the turn of the century, college football had become so violent that President Theodore Roosevelt threatened to outlaw the game if changes were not made. By 1906, the ideas of the forward pass and first downs were introduced to make the game less of two battle lines running into to each other on every play. As with any new initiative, the potential was unknown; and it was mainly seen as a gimmick used to bolster the status quo-the running game. There were many rule restrictions put on this new forward pass idea, including lining the field into squares to limit where one could throw the ball, having to be five yards behind the line of scrimmage, and penalties for two incomplete passes 1n a row.

On the less brutal idea side, only seven players were now needed on the line of scrimmage to run a play. This allowed three players to be legally in the backfield, with the quarterback or on the flank. Eventually, this led to the idea of the fullback and the right and left halfback, positions with new formations in the backfield. Suddenly, a new generation of great college coaches like Pop Warner and Knute Rockne started to mold the game. Soon there were new creations like the box and the single-wing formations.

One thing that did not change until the 1930s was the idea of HM's (hash marks). Taken for granted now when one looks at a present-day football field; HM's were finally installed to start each new play closer to the middle of the field. Until this change, there was a disadvantage for an offense to run a play wide, because wherever a play ended, the next play started-even if it was right next to the sidelines. This led to an awkward formation with the center closest to the sidelines and the rest of the line and backfield to his right or left.

New positions for the passing game, like a flanker (a halfback lined up as a wide receiver but a step off the line of scrimmage), a split end (an end lined up as a wide receiver on the line of scrimmage), or a tight end (a receiving end as opposed to a blocking end), would not happen until the ball was "marked" on a now-familiar HM by an official after each play.

• • •

Guy's grandfather, Guy Anthony Finelli (Guy I), was an unusual physical specimen at the age of seventeen in the summer of 1929. At five feet five and 135 pounds, he was over a half a foot shorter and weighed 70 pounds less than his immigrant Italian father, Geraldo. He had short but powerful legs from running ten miles a day to watch and then practice football after school with the semipro adult team for a couple years in the nearby town of Bound Brook, New Jersey starting in tenth grade.

His father had forbidden him from playing the crazy, violent game of football at Sommerville High School. He feared it would ruin his son's musician hands that he had nurtured from the age of five, learning to play piano, flute, and violin. At the movies on Saturdays, Guy I would accompany the piano player with the violin to add drama or background melody to the reels of silent movies playing to the Raritan crowd. He had made money for the family as a musician since he was twelve.

Guy, I had a long torso full of lean muscle from years of wrestling any of his cousins or friends for fun. He swam up and down or across the Raritan River in the summers as a kid for exercise or to cool off.

Sometimes he would race his friends, always winning, to see who could get to the famous Duke residence on the other side first. Once they made it to the stone wall, he would do hundreds of push-ups and sit-ups to impress the girls, especially if Doris Duke was playing nearby on the mansion grounds.

Besides his practice time spent as a musician, he would lift hundreds of pounds of materials onto his grandfather's and then his father's truck to supply their landscaping business before school or on the weekends.

Before his senior year in July of 1929, Guy I had decided to go against his father's will and tried out for the football team at Sommerville High School. Reluctantly, his father decided not to stop him. Guy's grandfather had died the previous month with Guy I at his side holding his hand and listening to his last breaths. His last words to him were *"Segui i tuoi sogni, mio figlio,"* a message felt through his powerful hands as well: "Follow your dreams, my son."

When Guy I first showed up for practice, Coach Joe Favarro had run out of team jerseys, so he wore his own old, sewn-together Princeton jersey sweater that his adult semipro friends had given him to practice with them. His cleats were taped up to keep them together, barely leather masses that covered his feet. He was assigned to the fourth team made up of freshmen and sophomores headed to make up the junior varsity squad.

In the locker room, he would arrive dressed in his dapper shirt and tie, with tailored pants to allow room for his massive thighs and muscular buttocks. During the day at school, Guy I was all business as he started his senior year, expecting to attend Princeton in the fall of 1930. He wore glasses with Coke-bottle-sized lenses and appeared ready to play at Carnegie Hall rather than being a football lineman. Carefully, he hung his perfectly pressed pants and shirt in his locker and then put his glasses away in a case. He could never afford to have them broken on the football field.

Unfortunately, without them, his visual acuity was dreamlike, fuzzy at best, and confusing at times. It left him mainly seeing images or colors. As long as the other team wore a differently colored jersey, he figured to have a fighting chance. Guy I had survived scarlet fever when he was three. It left him with terrible vision and poor health for his younger years. His adoring mother, Philomena, bought him a violin at age five because she was sure he would not be very athletic. It kept him from sports like baseball or tennis, but football, swimming, and wrestling required skills right up his alley. In helping with the family landscaping work in the morning, he developed short spurts of speed covering ten to twenty yards to do those chores quickly. His goal was to make it to school on time or do other fun things on the weekend.

Coach Favarro had heard rumors about this little lineman that had practiced with the semipro boys in Bound Brook for the past three years, but he did not believe the urban myths and figured that they used him for a warm body to run over for fun. He was curious to witness the rumors of his panther-like quickness to the ball and his lion-like strength to tackle the runner in the backfield.

Finelli reminded him of a peacock, with his fine clothes and colorful ties; strutting the hallways in school with his violin case in one hand and books in the other, slowly making his way to class, and talking to all the cute girls on his way. He seemed more like a lamb slowly grazing the grass in the field instead of a quick big cat leaping on his prey from out of nowhere.

"No player is gonna get on my field without earning his way!" Coach Favarro thought to himself. His eyes would be the only judge.

Finally, by the end of the August practice sessions, Coach Favarro had seen enough of Finelli to put him on the second team and give him a regular uniform. He had a senior-laden, talented squad led by his best athlete, Fillepe "Freckles" Ferraro, at quarterback and safety; and his massive tackle, Riccardo "Rock" Russo, at 240 pounds of muscle. He had to find the right time to put Finelli in the lineup without disrupting the

16

chemistry of his team.

After their last practice before the first game, "Rock" and "Freckles" came to the coach and asked to speak with him. Freckles spoke first: "Coach Favarro, Finelli has to be in the lineup against Flemington. He's unblockable on defense, and he can knock players off their feet on sweeps better than any guard I've seen. We're barely able to run our plays in practice!"

Freckles was an outspoken, forceful team leader and most likely-the greatest all-around player to ever put on a uniform for Sommerville High School. Besides being a great runner and passer at quarterback, he was a terror at safety. He would guess the plays nine out of ten times from his position and call out the direction of the play.

Running back punts was his forte. He would see the direction of the football and then, like a centerfielder in baseball, take a running start to the ball and catch it in midstride. To defenders running down to cover the punt, he seemed to come from the middle of nowhere.

To Coach Favarro, Freckles was everything he wanted in his captain and quarterback, but he had heard enough. He put up his hands to stop Freckles from foaming at the mouth about Finelli. "What do you think, Rock?" Coach Favarro asked quietly to his huge block of granite with a great sense of humor.

"Just put him next to me, and he'll make twenty tackles a game when I take on the double-team. I'll make him a star!" Rock smiled.

"Yeah... but who's he gonna block on offense? There are no cupcakes on that Flemington line, Rock."

"Coach...he's like one of them submarines that jackknives a battleship in two. He's underwater so you can't see him coming. Anyway, Freckles can dodge at least one guy coming at him if someone bowls him over... otherwise, I got his back." Freckles smiled and patted Rock on the back, hardly able to contain his excitement.

Coach showed no emotion as he pulled out a cigar and got it ready to light, his one vice after finishing a practice or a game. "We'll see, boys; Flemington didn't win the state championship last year because they got lucky... I got to spring Finelli on them when they're not looking, thanks, boys." Coach would soon find out in the first game at Flemington whether he had a tiger or a lamb as his secret weapon.

• • •

17

On Saturday, September 21, 1929, most Americans were hopeful about the future, with the new decade just three months away. The "Roaring Twenties" had created great wealth and made many Americans rich. The town of Raritan, New Jersey had assimilated a generation of immigrant Italians and now many first-generation Italian Americans. The fall football season for nearby Sommerville High School would show how these sons of immigrants could turn hard work into a championship. It was a time to learn how their dreams could aspire into opportunity and success. After the World War and the Roaring Twenties, this "seemed" to be a time of abundance in America. The stock market crash of 1929 was still five weeks away.

Most of the fans jamming the Flemington stands were certain that the beautiful fall weather would last forever and was an indication of another championship year for their boys.

The visiting boys of Sommerville High School had another idea in mind. "Freckles" Ferraro and "Rock" Russo were ready to crash the Flemington party and the early celebration of a certain victory. They had their secret weapon on the sidelines, Guy Anthony Finelli. Coach Favarro made sure he had Guy I stand next to him on the sidelines as the game started.

Things were going in Flemington's favor early when their defense intercepted a screen pass thrown by Freckles and returned it for a touchdown. Then, just before halftime, Freckles was tackled for a safety after a Flemington punt had pinned his team back inside the five- yard line. Being down 9-0 to the state champs in 1929 football was like being behind three or four touchdowns in the present-day game. Finelli had played sparingly in the first half, mainly on punt coverage and kickoff returns.

Three buddies were in the stands near the end zone, following Guy Anthony Finelli's every move: twelve-year olds Pietro Finelli and future World War II hero John Basilone, along with thirteen-year-old Ben Carnevale, a future US Basketball Hall-of-Farner. A worried father, Geraldo Finelli, had driven the boys in his truck to the away game but was walking in solitude behind the stands, unable to watch his first son potentially get hurt on the field. His fear came true when Guy I was knocked unconscious on the last play of the half covering a punt. He had made five tackles earlier in the first half covering punts, but Flemington made sure he was blocked on this play. He was sandwiched between two pieces of Irish beef that weighed over two hundred pounds each, wearing mustard-colored Flemington jerseys.

Rock Russo was not pleased with the cheap hit by the Flemington boys and let them know while he picked up his teammate and walked him to the bench. He shouted,

"Andare all inferno...you scumbags... inizieremo a dare la merda su di voi," with a vengeance.

Most of the Irish boys from Flemington understood the first two parts but missed out on the "We're going to kick the shit out of you!"

At halftime inside the locker room, Guy I was fully awake and seething inside, upset that he had not seen the double-team coming. The anger helped clear his head. He was now ready to explode on the football field.

Coach Favarro never asked him how he felt; he just noticed his elbows on his knees with his fingers spread apart, touching each hand like a spider web preparing to snatch its prey. His downward stare gave the coach his answer that his somewhat tame, panther-like player was ready to attack the Flemington boys in the second half.

Rock Russo took his soon-to-be best friend out to the field for the second half. They played the Flemington boys even for the third quarter, with neither offense able to gain more than one or two first downs. Finelli was starting to dominate, making ten solo tackles in twenty-five plays, five of which were behind the line of scrimmage. The Sommerville defense was starting to gain confidence, knowing that an animal had been unleashed on Flemington.

As the clock started to wind down in the fourth quarter, the Flemington coach thought he could put the game away with a trick play that would take advantage of Finelli getting into the Flemington backfield on every play. The ball was on their own twenty-five-yard line when the ball was snapped to the quarterback, who took three steps to his left and handed it off to his halfback going right. Finelli dove under a double-team and headed to snare the legs of the runner. As he drove him down to the ground, he noticed a laugh from the runner and Rock yelling reverse. The speedy right End had come around the backfield and took the flip of the ball from the halfback as he was going down. Finelli could not see any of it but instinctively rolled over to his feet and headed toward the left sidelines. Leaping over bodies at the scrimmage line, Finelli bowled over three blockers as he sprinted toward the Flemington caravan heading to the end zone. Freckles Ferraro from his safety position seemed to have the best angle to get through the blockers. He managed to slow down the caravan by holding up a lead blocker but fell back, failing to get his hands on the swift running end.

Geraldo Finelli had turned toward the field near the end zone, watching the excited Flemington crowd cheering for some reason. He could read the scoreboard and knew that his son's team was losing, and the boy running with the football was not wearing a Sommerville jersey. He could hear his son Pietro shouting out from the stands, "Guy, you can get him!"

Geraldo scanned the field and saw his short-legged son running like a bullet train across the field, angling for the ten-yard line. "Please, St. Anthony, let him be safe!" he said to himself.

Guy was moving like a lightning bolt with his head down, not watching the Flemington caravan rolling down the field. He was nearing the ten-yard line as he lifted his head and heard the End ahead of him. He completed a ninety-yard, cross-field sprint with a dive from the ten- yard for the back toe of the Flemington End, who had no idea that a short-legged panther with fuzzy eyesight was coming for the kill.

Suddenly, the Flemington End went from feeling the euphoria of scoring the winning touchdown to having his right foot struck in midair, with a hand of steel circling it like a shackle on a prisoner. He flew headfirst toward the goal line, landing on the one-yard line and barely holding on to the ball. Finelli rolled over after landing his prey and stood in front of the stunned Flemington crowd. He pointed towards the voices of his brother and friends, who were screaming in the stands, while the Flemington fans were awkwardly quiet.

The Sommerville defense was energized by the play as the crowd spoke in a whisper, wondering what animal had curtailed the celebration. Rock Russo grabbed Guy off of his feet as the team rallied in the end zone for a defensive huddle.

Instead of feeling doomed with the ball on the one- yard line and down by nine points, the team was oozing with confidence as Freckles Ferraro took control in the huddle and called the defense for the next play.

"Rock, come across the line, grab every lineman you can, and keep low." He looked at Finelli, who was not even breathing hard, just waiting for his next kill. "Guy, you dive high across the line to the left and get to the ball if they pitch it to our left; I'll be right behind you."

Luckily, Flemington followed Freckles's plan as they faked the ball to their left and came right toward a flying Finelli. Guy, I arrived as the quarterback and halfback were exchanging the ball. The ball popped into the air, and Freckles Ferraro was right behind Finelli to jump up and catch it, hurdle over the pile of players, and run ninety-five yards for a touchdown. He drop-kicked the extra point to make it 9- 7 with less than a minute left in the game.

Coach Favarro organized the kickoff team to make an onside kick. He had never practiced the play but told Freckles to kick the top on the ball toward the sidelines.

Flemington was in complete disarray and only had five linemen in their regular receiving formation. Rock Russo was on the outside, with Finelli right behind them as the ball was kicked in their direction. Russo led the charge, crushing three Flemington players, clipping them like a bowling ball crashing pin into each other. Finelli went for the only Flemington player left standing, crushing him in the chest as the ball was falling into his hands. As Finelli rolled off the dazed player, he felt the ball spinning back to him and curled around it like he was protecting a baby.

The ball was barely into Flemington territory as the official told the teams that there were thirty seconds left in the game. Freckles quickly got the team to the scrimmage line and yelled out a call for the Notre Dame Box-Set with a sweep to the right. Freckles called out, "Ready," which caused all four backfield players in a square to take two steps to the right; then "Set," which led a further dance to the left and back a step; and then "Hike."

The ball was snapped to Freckles, who turned left and faked to the first back and then flipped to halfback for the right sweep. With the Sommerville cavalry being led by Rock Russo and Guy Finelli, they downed every lineman in sight, grabbing ankles and pulling down jerseys. Finelli got in front of the charge and leaped into the outside linebacker, knocking him out with his knees; then he punched the cornerback and grabbed the safety's ankle as he tried to get past him.

The Sommerville halfback cut back at the forty-yard line, crossed the thirty-five, and then cut again to the middle of the field to get inside the thirty. He bounced off a defender, spinning to his right and keeping his feet to the twenty-five, and finally tripped up from behind as he fell to the twenty-three-yard line.

The referee ran up to mark the ball, amazingly near the middle of the field. The umpire judge was looking at his watch, only focused on yelling out the seconds left in the game-"Fifteen...fourteen...thirteen"- as Sommerville lined up confused at the scrimmage line.

Russo stood tall and yelled, "Tight formation," as the umpire continued the countdown, "Nine...eight...seven."

Finelli was next to the center and quietly whispered, "Hike the ball on three." The crowd went quiet with anticipation, thinking the game would be over with a home victory.

Pietro, John, and Ben were making the most noise, screaming, "Snap the football, snap the football."

The umpire raised his handgun to shoot a blank into the air to end the game, loudly shouting, "Five... four... three." The center looked back at Freckles through his legs and saw him back in punt formation. He snapped the ball back with great vigor and was

21

immediately bowled over by two Flemington linemen. Both Russo and Finelli flew out of their three-point stances and caught the flying linemen with vicious elbows and knees in their midsections to keep them from further penetration. The biggest and smallest of the Sommerville players had held off the insurgency as Freckles caught the ball ten yards deep on the thirty-three-yard line. His eyes never left the bloated pigskin as Flemington players penetrated from both the right and left sides. Freckles calmly took a short step with his right foot and a long step with his left as he dropped the football to land perfectly upright on the dirt of the field. Effortlessly his muscular right leg swung in motion and booted a masterpiece. His right foot compressed the football and sent it flipping end over end from thirty yards out, perfectly sailing through the wooden uprights in a moment of silence.

The referee ran forward with his arms in the air, as Rock Russo grabbed Finelli off the pile of the fallen state champions and lifted him on his shoulders. Russo was screaming with glee, "We won, you stupid bastards," as he reached Freckles, still admiring his kick while Flemington boys had rolled into him trying to block the kick. Russo, with Finelli on his right shoulder, grabbed Freckles on his left and raced to meet his oncoming teammates running in from the sidelines. The trio of great players was pummeled by their teammates, and Finelli saw a multitude of unfocused images as he descended off Russo's shoulder into the pile of celebration.

Eventually, he worked his way out of the pile, headed to the sidelines, and was interrupted by a strong hug from Coach Favarro, who had tears in his eyes as he said, "I should have known you would be a block of granite for me...I should have believed my eyes watching you in practice all summer...! should have..."

"Coach...Coach, we won; that's all that counts...and really, you did the right thing. It made me a better ballplayer. Listen...nobody will beat us this year, and nobody will score on our defense. Hell, Coach, we just started playing!"

Most of the fans stood in silence as though an instant Ice Age had overcome them, never having witnessed a comeback like the one that had just happened. In a small corner of the stands, there was mad pandemonium as Pietro Finelli, John Basilone, and Ben Carnevale led a small group of *Sommerville High School fans onto the field to join the pile of players celebrating with Freckles Ferarro on their shoulders.

Gaetano Anthony Finelli was near the sidelines, looking for his dad. As he walked around the stands where the tree line left a quiet nook of solitude, he saw Geraldo Finelli on his knees, resting on the backs of his heels, with his head bowed in silence. Guy patted him on the back and said, "Pop, are you OK?"

22

Surprised to be found in his solitude, Geraldo stood up quickly to hug his son with great passion. His talked softly in a deep baritone voice into his ear. "Gaetano... my boy... are you fine with your body? How did you learn to play so well, my son? You make the family so proud!"

Guy felt captured in his dad's broad shoulders. It felt like an eternity since he had nestled into his father's torso, where he remembered being thrown in the air and gently caught by his father's enormous hands as a young boy. Now he could only muster a nod as his voice choked with emotion. "I'm fine Pop... I'm great Pop...Thanks for being here."

Geraldo released the bear hug and grabbed his son by the shoulders. He fought back tears and looked straight in his eyes. "OK, now...we go eat!"

*The Sommerville High School Athletic Hall of Fame has members like Paul Robeson, the great African-American actor and All-American athlete at Princeton, and Ben Carnevale, a National Collegiate Basketball Hall-of-Famer and a NCAA pioneer as a coach, athletic director, and builder of the NCAA basketball tournament. But the best story of the athletic history at Sommerville High School is how the 1929 football team went on to an undefeated season and a New Jersey state championship. The defense was unscored upon during the entire season, a unique accomplishment in any sport. Three great players were on that squad and named to the school's all-time football team, but the team's smallest lineman became the only athlete in Sommerville High School football history to be named to the New Jersey All-State Football Team and win a New Jersey state football championship. He was elected to the Sommerville High School Athletic Hall of Fame after only one season of athletic competition.

CHAPTER 3

P HILLIP FINELL! SAT alone, keeping the fire going at full capacity, enjoying the last few minutes of November 22, 2012, the best Thanksgiving of his life. It was the first celebrated in the renovated Parkwood house, the house he grew up in. The intimate family room, at less than four hundred square feet, provided perfect comfort and went untouched during the renovations. The uniqueness of the room was that it presented a hint of grandness but felt like a small study as one sat with the fire ablaze.

The walls were covered by three-quarter-inch-thick mahogany paneling, along with the fourteen long- standing Pella windows that could open the room to nature. Overhead, the ceiling was adorned with a honey- stained, paneled pine that glowed with texture, and below your feet was a multicolored, half-inch-thick, polished floor of flagstone. But when you entered the room, your eyes were drawn to the back wall by the floor-to-ceiling Tennessee-stone fireplace with its twelve-foot-long slabs of sitting hearth. The two-inch-thick stone collected heat from the fireplace, making it a place of pleasure to remember celebratory memories of family history.

The flames of the ferocious fire swarmed the wood from a substantial white oak. Though the family had left a skeleton after devouring the Thanksgiving turkey, the fire would leave only embers of the beautiful white oak. The tree had shaded a lovely brick patio Phillip had built with his bare hands twenty-five years ago next to his previous house in Oakview. He had the massive, overgrown tree cut down before the move and brought the many years' worth of wood for winter fires with him to the Parkwood house for occasions just like this one.

Watching the flames seemed to freeze the holiday in time as Phillip sipped another glass of spiked apple cider, created by his wife, Carol, with her special ingredients, including Grand Marnier. As time melted down toward midnight, he tried to savor every last second of the day, reliving the highlights from the festive holiday celebration.

• • •

24

Prior to dawn on November 22, 2012, Phillip had woken up to a misty, cold Thanksgiving morning. He collected the *Washington Daily* from the front lawn to read about the big Washington-Dallas game being played that day in the late afternoon. He quickly went to the sports section to read about the rookie quarterback sensation, Marcus McNeil III, leading the hometown team back into the playoff hunt for the first time since 2007.

As he continued to sip his morning decaf Earl Grey tea, after taking his ten pills for high blood pressure and cholesterol, he considered his attire for the upcoming Turkey Bowl football game in two hours. He began to realize that this might be his last competitive football game as he approached the age of accessing his IRA funds without penalty, fifty-nine-and-a-half. Enjoying every second of playing with his two sons, brother, nephew, and new friends would be his goal.

The uncomfortable, wet weather would limit the turnout to only the diehard football athletes, a gang of seven, instead of the fifteen to twenty that had normally attended the game in decent weather conditions for the past thirty-two years. Only an ice storm and a trip to Florida had kept them from playing on Thanksgiving morning since he started the game in 1980.

He arrived at the field, always a half-hour early, to set up the gridiron with his nephew and college assistant coach, Joseph Finelli. The sculpted 285-pound Joe enjoyed a laugh as some young "millennium machos" challenged Phillip to play against them for two grand in cash during the setup. A friends-and-family game could suddenly turn immensely competitive. They offered to spot Phillip and his "gang of seven" two touchdowns because they had two women on their team.

Phillip laughed as he thought about how badly they would beat these hyperactive, energy-drink-stimulated twentysomethings with his almost sixty-year-old arm throwing to his two thoroughbred sons and his all-pro tight-end-looking nephew. He countered their demand by granting them leniency, offering them a two-touchdown lead if they agreed to a one-hand touch game. The "machos" laughed as they perceived softness and then shook hands, thinking they were about to steal two grand from the old man.

As they walked back to their group of a dozen or so players, they crossed paths with Phillip's two sons-Alex Santucci, baseball's MVP and world championship hero for the hometown Washington Presidents, and the eighteen year-old Guy James Finelli, a college freshmen and football sensation for the University of Maryland (UMD). Their laughing turned into a gulp of humility as they appeared stone-faced to their fellow "machos" to explain the challenge with a fake dose of confidence. The bravado in their teammates was only heightened when they heard about the two-touchdown lead given them by the

25

old man with "two girls" on his team. They hooped and hollered as they went on the field to start on defense against the Finellis.

The scoring started on the first play as Phillip spiraled a perfect bomb on a post pattern to Alex just past midfield, who easily caught the pigskin and outran his coverage into the end zone.

Guy scored on the extra-point play, which he followed up with an interception TD return on the machos' first pass play.

The bet was never in doubt after the first five minutes of the game.

Phillip threw seven more touchdown passes that stunned the "millennium machos." Every player on his team caught at least one touchdown pass, including Phillip himself when Guy took over as QB on the final series and Phillip played wide receiver. Playing on the left side, Phillip in succession caught a flanker's delay, a "Bobby Mitchell" screen, and a "Farrell's" move. In today's football, they are called a bubble screen, an inside pick, and a back-shoulder pattern.

On the game's last play, Phillip ran his patented, top-of-the-house (sideline comeback) pattern that had made him famous in high school. Fully extended, Phillip prepared to cradle the incoming missile from his son into his stomach. As it settled into his gut, he lightly dragged his two feet inbounds like a ballerina in the narrow blades of wet grass, just before the forbidden white chalk. Like a statue turning in the wind, he politely landed on his back, securing the cargo like a loaded mortar shell.

He lay curled on the ground, enjoying the moment as he looked skyward to witness the flameless sun working its way through the clouds. The mist of midmorning falling into his eyes added moisture to his sudden tears of joy. Phillip felt that surge of emotion, content that his football story was now completed as it had begun, with a simple neighborhood competition. At this moment, he sensed his purpose in life: support his wife and stay in good health to experience the coming football generation led by his son, Guy James Finelli. His last hours of competition on the football field had been just served to wet his whistle and taste the icing on the cake.

Fellow teammates Guy and Alex; his stepsister, Charlotte and their friend, Patty; Phillip's brother, Anthony; and his nephew, Joe, ended his isolation by completing a circle above him, celebrating, and then picking him up and pounding him with back slaps and hugs.

After the rout was over, Alex Santucci recruited the "machos" to volunteer for a Christmas fundraising event he was hosting with his wife, Sally Keegan, instead of collecting the two grand. The "millennium boys" happily agreed to volunteer for the famous couple with a chance to mingle with the Finelli clan, replacing their humiliation with a story for the ages-without mentioning the score of the game (73-0), of course.

The perfect day continued for Phillip as he hosted, along with his own family of Carol, Grace, and Guy; Carol's parents; Anthony, and wife, Florence; Joe, and wife, Brandy; Sally and Alex with his mother, Laura; and Turkey Bowl participants Charlotte and Patty, for a grand afternoon of eating and football watching and an early evening of dessert and digestion.

Drinks and appetizers started around two o'clock/ followed by a three-course meal an hour later that included spinach-cube soup, manicotti and meatballs, and finally, turkey with asparagus, sweet potatoes, corn pudding, cranberry sauce, and lots of stuffing.

The day turned serious as the Dallas-Washington football game came on at four thirty. Phillip put on his number forty-two (Charley Taylor's) jersey, and Guy his number twenty-one (Sean Taylor's) jersey to lead the serious cheering. Rookie quarterback sensation Marcus McNeil III led Washington to a big first half, only to barely survive an expected second half comeback by Dallas for their first win in Dallas on Thanksgiving. Phillip and Anthony celebrated like their touchdown plays in the morning and Washington victories many years ago.

Dessert was served after the game, including homemade pecan and pumpkin pies, along with Italian favorites- canolli, struffoli, and pizzelles.

Finally, Carol's parents, Laura, Charlotte, and Patty all left together and headed back to Bethesda. Anthony, Joe, and their wives walked home, only a few blocks down the road on Parkwood Drive.

After receiving a phone call from his first cousin, Bonnie Walton, around eight o'clock, Phillip, Carol, Grace, Guy, Alex, and Sally decided to visit his uncle, Pietro Finelli, at his retirement community. His uncle was affectionately known as "the Rock" in the family, because he was thought of as the family's foundation, very much like Saint Peter in the Catholic Church. He was ninety-six and a family icon, but more importantly, he was the younger brother of Gaetano Anthony Finelli, who was known as Guy I, the father of Phillip and Anthony. Guy I was five years older than Pietro and had died in 1993 at the age of eighty-one. He had been the oldest sibling and cousin in the Finelli family and relished the role of keeping the extended family together. Guy, I parented his boys like his contemporary, Vince Lombardi, coached, relentlessly pushing for perfection.

Pietro had a less volatile, quieter personality, and he had assumed the family leadership, passing along the values of his family's immigrant Italians to generations to come. He was loved for his warmth and wise counsel.

He had been in terrific shape, walking and swimming daily, until being diagnosed with congestive heart failure almost a year ago. It did not seem to stop him from leading a full life, until his brother-in-law, Uncle Ernesto, passed in early September. For the last month, he had been on oxygen full-time in his apartment.

Bonnie called Phillip to say that her father was feeling strong after the Washington win and wanted to see him and his family for a visit.

Alex and Sally led the six of them into Uncle Pietro's room as he sat up in his bed, supported by several pillows. His eyes immediately misted up as the newly married couple were the first to his bedside, with Phillip, Carol, Guy, and Grace close behind. Pietro reached out for Alex's hands and pulled him into chest.

"You were fantastic this season, the greatest I've seen since DiMaggio, Gehrig, and Ruth when I was a kid! And I'm so happy for you and Sally." He paused for a moment to catch some air, not wanting to waste a second of time. "You must have really enjoyed being in Italy after winning the championship. Did they recognize you?"

Alex was enjoying every second and did not want to interrupt such joy with his answer, so he shook his head no to keep listening.

"Did you make it to Lioni and Nuzco?"

He knew Pietro's energy would be limited, so he answered succinctly, "Yes, we spent a day going through each town. It was magnificent!"

Sally stood patiently at the bedside behind Alex, also wondering how much strength Pietro had left in the evening. Suddenly, she felt a need to get closer to him as Alex was suspended a few inches away from Pietro's face. She took Alex's elbow and slowly tugged him to the side as she put her hand on Pietro's shoulder. Alex turned, put his hand on Sally's back, and pulled her in toward Pietro. "The Rock" lifted both his hands, slightly shaking but still strong, and laid them on Sally's hips as she hugged him very tightly. She then stayed in his grasp and put her hands around his face, focusing on his tired but deeply intense eyes.

"I hope your babies are going to be as beautiful as you. When are they due? Soon, I hope!"

Sally continued to be locked in his focus and realized that Uncle Pietro knew! *But how?* She thought to herself. They were keeping quiet about the pregnancy until the ten-week mark, just before Christmas. She quietly responded to Uncle Pietro. "In late June, we hope. Did Alex tell you?"

"No, my dear, I can see you are full of life...enough for two beautiful children. Please let them know how much we love them. Gaetano and Rose will be so excited when I see them soon!"

She kissed him gently on his cheek and whispered in her ear.

"Please, Uncle Pietro, we need you to be here for a long time. You are the rock of the family. Besides, Washington is on a winning streak." Sally stood back up, still holding his hand, when he pulled her close again.

"Do you mind if I put my hands on them?"

Without hesitation, Sally leaned her stomach toward Pietro, took his hand under her blouse, and placed it on her womb. Pietro extended his left palm and tired fingers on her slightly extended abdomen. At the same time, he intertwined his right hand with Alex's giant right paw, while he closed his eyes and said a prayer to himself. Finally, he pulled his hands back and folded them on his chest, still with his eyes closed.

Sally turned to Alex in tears, feeling that something magical from Uncle Pietro had been transferred to her being, something from a previous generation or from the country of Italy, where they had spent three weeks after celebrating the World Series win. As they held each other, the intense warmth left from Uncle Pietro's hand was reaching every fiber of her body. With great energy she turned to the family and announced the good news. "We're having twins...everybody, we're having twins!"

The family closed in around them, each member hugging Sally and then Alex with congratulations. Phillip then bent over Uncle Pietro, joined his right hand on Uncle Pietro's folded hands, and said a prayer as he kissed his cheek. Carol and Grace followed suit.

Then Guy approached to bend over and put his hand out, but slowly Uncle Pietro opened his eyes and lifted his hands to greet Guy's. Pietro looked directly into his eyes to see his youth and strength. He spoke in a whisper as the power in his voice faded.

"Guy, always be a good boy and love your family. Never embarrass them; just make them proud of you. You know, your grandfather was one of the great ones that no one will know about. You will be a great one that everyone will know about. There was no one that ever played the game harder than your namesake, Gaetano Anthony. I know you will play hard like the safety that was murdered. That young man could have been the best ever...you know, but he couldn't outrun his past. Be smart, put your family first, and play to be great!"

Guy slowly let go of his great-uncle's hand, kissed him on the cheek, and turned to find a seat in the living room of the apartment, alone. Suddenly, he felt exhausted, like his whole life had been revealed.

How did Pietro know about Sally's pregnancy? More importantly, did he know about his high-school years? Guy pondered as he felt his heart pounding. He had changed his life after "the promise" and did the right thing. Would it trail him for years in the future?

• • •

As midnight came and left, the fire calmed down to a peaceful glow of embers, creating bottomless blue and regal red colors. Phillip was peaceful, feeling the warmth that still emanated from the remnants of his white oak tree. He thought about how quiet his son Guy had been on the ride back from their visit with Uncle Pietro. It was a transforming event at the end of a magical day. Phillip was proud that his family was able to visit with "the Rock" and learn from such a humble man. Guy must have been dealing with great emotion, feeling so close to his great- uncle and learning about Sally's pregnancy. Guy was not one to volunteer words about his emotions freely.

Phillip was looking forward to Saturday to watch Guy play in his last game of the regular season. If they won, they would play in the ACC championship game and then maybe in a BCS Bowl game in January.

A smile returned to Phillip's face as he tried to pull his gaze away from the fire, to once again pinch himself about the news that he would become a grandfather by the middle of 2013. By next Thanksgiving he might be holding a grandson, a granddaughter, or both as he watched the fire. As great a day as this was, next Thanksgiving would be even better.

CHAPTER 4

AS ALWAYS, DAWN came cautiously with a sheer ray of sunlight that grew through

the window blinds. Phillip fought consciousness as he managed to keep his eyes closed before the morning started. The onset of a morning dream, playing like a newsreel, projected many years of memories with his son, Guy.

The youngest of his three children, Guy was only nine when Joe Gibbs was hired in 2004 to coach Washington for the second time after a twelve-year retirement. Gibbs had won three Super Bowls for Washington during a ten-year period from 1983 to 1992. Washington had only made the playoffs once since Gibbs had retired. As a watchful father, Phillip could tell early on that Guy Finelli was destined to love and play football. He would catch anything thrown to him. using a natural diving skill to snatch the football before it hit the earth. It was perfected when he started in competitive swimming at age seven. The grace of stretching out his body in one motion and landing perfectly in the water with minimal agitation of the surface was the same skill used to catch, intercept, or deflect the football, as well as getting low for a tackle, all with a magical elegance that assured legal play.

Together as father and son, they used any occasion to highlight their football skills. Usually, watching football games together was just an excuse to practice great plays while they were cheering for Washington. On a family weekend trip to Colonial Williamsburg in 1999, Phillip and Guy had stayed in the hotel room on a Sunday afternoon to watch the Washington-New York game at one o'clock while Carol and Grace went to a hands-on seminar on dressmaking during colonial times.

They celebrated continuously that day, watching their favorite team score fifty points against New York. Guy at age five was small enough to run and jump from bed to bed catching the junior football his father would throw to him, as they replayed every catch and the six touchdowns over and over.

It was a great season and the first year the Redskins had made the playoffs since Guy was born. That game they watched with joy in a hotel room became a lasting memory, along with the monster rides at Busch Gardens the next day, of course.

Guy and Phillip watched Washington fall apart the next season, but they found excitement after the 2000 season with a newly born professional football league during the winter called the XFL. It was the brainchild of World Wide Wrestling Federation owner Vince McMahon and NBC. It was a great bonding time to discover something of entertainment involving football together.

All eight teams were owned by the league and given nicknames like the Extreme, Rage, Hitmen, Blast, Enforcers, Maniax, Demons, and Outlaws.

There were two cool things about the new league that Guy especially loved. The first was the opening "scramble" instead of the boring coin toss. A player from each team would stand side by side on the thirty-yard line and on the whistle would run twenty yards to midfield and fight for the football. It was like watching gladiators in the Roman Coliseum. The second was the "no-kick" extra point, which replaced the automatic kick. It was like the touch football league rule of running a play to score the point after a touchdown.

The XFL football was black with red stripes and lettering. Phillip found a youth-sized one at Target before the opening game, so they could play during the time- outs. The games were on Saturday night starting at eight. Guy would usually fall asleep sometime in the second half after catching hundreds of passes running back and forth in the upstairs hallway. Unfortunately, the XFL lasted only one year, but the experiences of those Saturday nights together would be a lifetime of shared bonding.

In the fall of 2001, Guy was in second grade and Grace was in fifth grade at Cresthaven Elementary. It would be their last year of being together in the same school until Grace became a senior, seven years later.

Carol was working downtown near the White House on September 11, 2001, when the first two planes hit the Twin Towers in New York City. Then a third plane hit the Pentagon across the Potomac River from DC, while a rumored fourth plane was heading for the US Capitol or the White House. Mayhem exploded on the downtown streets. Luckily, Carol drove that day and cleared out of the city before the Metro was shut down and thousands of federal employees clogged traffic on the streets. She drove directly to the elementary school, grabbed her two children and made it home safely.

Phillip arrived home soon after and supervised fifteen kids from the neighborhood on their Oakview front lawn; playing whiffle ball and football in between breaks to eat Carol's homemade chili and corn bread, followed by great- smelling, homemade pies. Eating and playing outside were the best diversions to deal with the horror being shown on television that day.

Watching UMD football that fall became a great distraction for Guy and Phillip. It was a magical season with their new coach, Ralph "the Fridge" Freidgen, and an exciting offense. They won the ACC title for the first time since the eighties and went to the Orange Bowl. Carol and Phillip flew down to South Beach in Miami for four days of beautiful beach weather and to see the Orange Bowl.
Guy watched the game at his cousin's house with Grace, hoping to catch his parents on television. Even watching a disappointing loss to Florida, Guy knew he wanted to play college football for UMD.

This feeling was cemented in 2002 when UMD won the NCAA basketball championship in the spring at the Georgia Dome in Atlanta, and on New Year's Eve, the whole family went to the same venue to watch the Maryland Terrapins win the Peach Bowl.

For the next five years, Guy wore the colors of the Maryland state flag exclusively-red, white, black, and gold.

In July of 2002, Phillip started construction of a two-story addition with a new deck on the side of the house. By September, the upstairs was finished, and everyone had new bedrooms except for Guy. His small bedroom was just fine; most of the time he was somewhere else, like outside with the neighborhood kids or watching football with his dad.

Life changed for three weeks in October 2002 when the Washington area was put under siege by "the sniper." The first victim in the DC area was wounded in the Hillandale shopping center, less than a fifteen-minute walk from the Finelli home. Then three more victims were killed in Kensington very close to Uncle Anthony[1]s house. Finally, after a total of ten random murders, the killers were captured. Kids could go to school again and play outside without fear of a loud noise being a gunshot. The three weeks of terror inspired the rock group Train to write a song, "Calling All Angels,11 that was nominated for a Grammy Award in 2003.

Guy and Phillip fell in love with a college player on the NCAA championship team, the Miami Hurricanes, at the end of 2002. He would lurk in the defensive backfield like a panther hiding in the woods, leaping onto his prey without notice. In his senior year

33

of high school as a running back, he had scored forty-four touchdowns. He looked bigger than a linebacker and faster than most receivers. During the 2003 season, he led the NCAA with ten interceptions, three returned for TDs, and led all safeties with seventy-seven solo tackles, most of which made the ESPN highlight film. His name was Sean Taylor.

The day of reckoning for Washington came several months after Coach Joe Gibbs was rehired in January 2004. Phillip was unable to sit because of the nervous energy that kept him pacing in the family room. He tried to keep himself busy by making phone calls while watching the NFL draft on April 24, 2004, on a beautiful Saturday afternoon. The fact that he was not with clients playing golf, working on the yard, or playing quarterback with his son and friends on the front lawn meant that it was a significant event.

Now he was praying that Sean Taylor would drop to Washington's pick at number five in the first round. The first four picks had taken almost an hour, wasting a precious spring day inside for Phillip. Sean Taylor had become a human highlight film every week with his hard-hitting tackling and ball-hawking skills. In Phillip's opinion, the player known as the "Meast," a portmanteau of man and beast, could lead the Redskin defense to greatness as "The Safety."

When the pick was finally announced, Phillip started screaming as he ran to the open front door. He continued his baritone booming of pure joy when he saw his son Guy in the front yard, who was dominating light football play with boys and girls from the neighborhood.

"Guy, they got him-they drafted Sean Taylor! Can you believe we got the Meast?"

Guy ran a fly pattern directly to the family room, still grasping the football with his oversized nine-year-old hands, just in time to watch the NFL commissioner give Sean Taylor his Washington jersey and shake his hand. The six-feet-three, 234-pound "Meast" of a safety sure looked good as he held up a burgundy-and-gold jersey to his wide shoulders. Phillip and Guy were jumping together and yelling for joy while giving each other high fives, and celebrating their favorite football player now on their home team.

Phillip was convinced that Sean Taylor was the first piece of the puzzle to being

• • •

Unlike Thanksgiving Day, sunlight had grown in the morning and now beamed through the windows of the bedroom suite on the second floor of their Parkwood home. As Phillip committed to consciousness, he wondered about the timing of his morning dream, reliving his years with his son Guy. He was delighted to recall the memories as they left feelings of refreshment and fulfillment

Carol and Phillip would travel to Raleigh today to bring their daughter, Grace, back to school at North Carolina State University (NCSU). But just as important in Phillip's mind was the most important football game of the season on Saturday at Carter-Finley Stadium.

The surprising UMD football team was playing against NCSU in that important Saturday game for a chance to win the Atlantic Division of the Atlantic Coast Conference (ACC) and move on to the ACC championship game in Charlotte on following Saturday.

Guy had returned to the UMD campus already and would ride the team bus to Raleigh. He was slowly becoming a media sensation locally even though Washington's rookie sensation, Marcus McNeil III, was dominating most of the sports headlines, especially after beating hated Dallas on Thanksgiving.

UMD was a two-touchdown underdog to NCSU, but Guy was confident of a victory and a chance to finish the regular season 10-2. An Orange Bowl berth would be the prize if they somehow shocked Virginia Tech (VT) in the ACC championship game.

Most of America did not have Guy Finelli on their sights yet, but after his upcoming Saturday afternoon performance, the freshman football player would no longer be as undetectable as a stealth fighter plane playing safety and returning kicks. A blip on the radar in close range would suddenly appear, ready to strike football fans in their hearts throughout the United States.

35

CHAPTER 5

P HILLIP MADE IT to the kitchen to get his coffee and then outside to retrieve
the morning paper. It was a decent morning, so he sat outside on the porch step and started
to unravel the paper while he took a sip of his hazelnut brew. The smell of the paper started
a daydream about his youth. He had been a talented football player, but he was also an
outstanding amateur stud ent of football, baseball, and basketball. Before the age of
Google, Phillip learned to remember the available statistics in the three major sports.
In the sixties, he served the *Washington Daily* almost every morning for the decade. At five
o'clock in the morning, he would pull a freshly printed newspaper out of his stack and put
it up to his nose to catch a whiff of that searing carbon smell from the old-time printing
presses. He would then sit for ten minutes on his pile of seventy- five newspapers and
read the entire sports page, including box scores from any sports reported in the paper-
except for hockey.

On most days he finished his route in thirty-five minutes, except for Thursdays
and Sundays, when the paper was too big to fold and throw from the sidewalk. He would
end up a ten-minute walk from home after the last paper was thrown, so on his walk back,
he would replay a game in his head based on the story and statistics that he had read.

For the exciting parts like a home run, a touchdown drive, or a winning basket, he
would mimic a great broadcaster like Ray Scott in football, Jack Buck in baseball, or Jim
Karvellas in basketball, narrating the game.

Ray Scott had a baritone presence to his voice that was crisp and precise. He would
do all the Packer games during the Lombardi era and the early Super Bowls. Phillip learned
to mimic his omnipresent tone, like the word of God putting his stamp on a play.

Scott would describe a play with minimal use of words, perfect inflections for
effect, and clean pauses as he patiently waited for the play to develop: "Starr under
center...split backfield, Horning and Taylor.. . Dowler split right...McGee flanked
left...calling signals... Starr to *throw...Dowler* at the thirty-two...tackled by Harris
*immediately...*first and *ten Packers!"*

Phillip would fill in the crowd roars after a successful play with sound effects that
sounded like *herrrrrrrrr.*

During the baseball season, Jack Buck was the St. Louis Cardinal announcer. He had a comforting pitch in his voice that made you want to listen to a game regardless of the score or who was playing. Back then, the National League was a foreign nation for those in an American League city like Washington, DC. Phillip would play with the dial on his grandfather's old radio at night to listen to games from Philadelphia to New York to Pittsburgh to Chicago and Cincinnati. But his favorite in baseball was Jack Buck, who had a style that seemed to accentuate the play in the present with a peak into the future. His voice would rise with elegance and perfect emotion on an exciting play.

In the 1968 World Series, he was at his best describing great pitching: "Gibson will be taking the sign from Mccarver. He is ready for the windup...and is throwing the fastball past Horton for another *strikeout...folks,* that is number seventeen, and that will be a new record for a *World Series game!*"

Or the excitement of seeing speed and hitting: "The speedy Lou Brock will bat against the Tigers...the pitch is on the way, and Brock will hit that one into the right-center field gap, and it will roll all the way to the wall... folks, he will be flying by second base and landing his jets for a *stand-up triple...the* Tigers will throw the ball into Freehan, the catcher, to keep Brock from circling the bases on that one."

His most famous call was the Ozzie Smith home run to beat the Dodgers in an '80s playoff game: "Folks, this ball is headed deep down the right field line, and it is going to be...a home run for a Cardinals win...go crazy, folks. Go crazy!"

In 1964, Phillip found NBA basketball just thirty-five miles away in Baltimore by listening to WBAL at night. The great Jim Karvellas, who seemed to be born ready to announce basketball, spoke with clear elocution in announcing the fast pace of an NBA game. He had more of a disc-jockey type of voice than most sports announcers. He described every move on the court as if he were introducing a hit record, with an increasing crescendo.

Each possession that led to scoring was like a mini opera, especially when describing Earl "the Pearl" Monroe: "Earl brings the ball up, right side...at the elbow...now Monroe goes behind the back... spinning into the lane...floating in the air...double pumps between defenders...'the Pearl' lays it up and in!"

He even made a routine pass and shot sound like a top-ten record: "Monroe yo-yoing the dribble at the top of the key...covered by Frazier...now backs inside the circle...drifting to the foul line...now the double- team by Barnett...Earl fires one-handed off the dribble to Loughery...wide open on the left side...from twenty-three...in the air... bull's eye!"

37

The crisp morning air helped Phillip enjoy recalling some favorite scenes during his paper-route days. As he continued to sip his coffee, he remembered how sports in general had been a vital medicine to him ever since he could remember. As a young boy, he had found calm while losing a sense of time or worry, playing and following the world of football or baseball.

Being the youngest boy, Phillip grew up in a household of athletics. His oldest brother, Anthony, was an all- around great athlete who had Phillip pinned to his hip playing sports before he was out of diapers. His first introduction to playing football with teenagers was at four and a half when he became the full-time center during games at the legendary Puller Park. It was only seven months after a life-threatening appendix operation that left Phillip severely underweight. Eating and playing sports became his only two activities. Phillip would stand behind the ball, take both hands to lift and toss it five yards to the quarterback, and then watch the plays develop. He learned to spot the ball after each play and then snap it again on "hike". By the next fall, he was fully healthy, running hook patterns and catching anything that was thrown to him. By the age of seven, he was also rushing the quarterback, and by nine, he was playing receiver and faster than most of the teenagers.

These experiences and stories about the legendary 1929 football season from his father Gaetano Anthony Finelli (Guy I) led him to believe he was a part of a football dynasty that would culminate with him playing for Washington. When a devastating knee injury sidelined him in a cast for six weeks after his last game in high school, his dream of playing football at Princeton University was over. He only hoped that a future son would then be the chosen Finelli to achieve football royalty.

This storybook sense of the Finelli family and Washington being at the center of the football universe were enhanced after Phillip's daughter, Grace, was born during the 1991 season when the Redskins were 10-0. She was four weeks early, so Phillip assumed she wanted to be born before they lost a regular season game. Three months later, baby Grace watched the Redskins win the Super Bowl while bouncing on her daddy's good knee.

Two years later, Phillip's father, Guy I, died after Joe Gibbs first retired and before the worst Redskins season in thirty years. Soon afterward, Phillip's son, Gaetano James Finelli (Guy), was conceived and born in 1994. Finally, in 2004, after ten years of intolerable Redskins football, the "Meast" messiah, Sean Taylor, was drafted, and Joe Gibbs was rehired to save the Redskins.

• • •

Phillip was halfway through his first cup of coffee before he realized that many minutes had passed, and he had not read a word of the *Washington Daily*. Suddenly, he felt a compulsion to quickly flip to the Sports section as though he needed to see a great message. He ignored the headlines showcasing Marcus McNeil III's mastery over Dallas and flipped to the bottom of the page to read the column of his favorite writer, Ron Roswell. His eyes burned from the pronouncement but were quickly soothed by tears of excitement.

His son, Guy, was no longer under the radar-

"Freshmen Finelli Ready to Be the Next Great Safety."

CHAPTER 6

JANUARY 2008 HAD brought little to lessen the effect of Sean Taylor's death in Guy's life. The wound was forgotten for a while in the excitement of Washington's five straight victories to end the regular season, but the first-round defeat in the playoffs exposed an unhealed wound and the reality of the long, cold winter that lay ahead.

Soon after the season was over, Joe Gibbs announced his second and final retirement from coaching, which in effect sealed the lid on the coffin of a Super Bowl victory anytime soon. No one had felt more grief and pressure than Joe Gibbs from losing Sean Taylor. But even though he almost coached a miracle to end the season, he realized at sixty-seven that it was too late to restock the mostly bare shelves of Washington's talent.

The news of his retirement was another blow to Guy that he could hardly digest. It felt as though his hunger for life had been stymied by these events in the middle of a cold winter. It would take several years to thaw those feelings as he was about to face the perils of high school.

The new Xbox 360 at Christmas had been a welcome distraction for Guy, not to be alone with his feelings, and always being able to play games with his friends over the Internet. But most of the time, the emotional hole in his stomach could not be ignored with video distractions or by doing hundreds of push-ups and sit-ups. And even his voracious appetite for food did not fill it. It seemed to be an unending black hole.

• • •

Guy had a sense that he had a love for football in his blood passed down from his grandfather and father. He was catching Nerf footballs as soon as he could stand. At the age of four, he was regularly catching a kid-size football downstairs in the basement from his father, running twenty feet to snag a throw while diving onto the mattress at the end of the room and banging into the thin paneling. When the winter weather broke, he would run hundreds of pass patterns and catch punts off of his father's foot until his knee got sore every day after school. At age five he would play in games with older kids at the park near the swim club. Most games, Phillip would start out quarter backing both sides until bigger kids showed up and turned the game into a quasi-rugby match. Even at a distinct physical disadvantage, Guy showed the ability to catch the ball, avoid tacklers on uns, and grab legs to start a tackle.

His favorite holiday was Thanksgiving, when his half- brother, Alex Santucci, would come out and play with family and friends for the Turkey Bowl. He was eighteen years older than Guy and at age twenty-three was the starting third-baseman for the major-league Kansas City Crowns. Always lining up in the slot position between Alex and his cousin Joe, Guy would be wide open on most plays. Opponents would grudgingly have to cover the little roach of a player with an adult player. Just when the opponent thought he was extinguishing the nasty bug with good coverage, Phillip would call the "slot screen" and have over five-hundred pounds of cousin and brother protecting him running as he scampered for big yardage.

Having a professional athlete in the family was exciting, but to Guy, Alex played in the wrong sport. Guy liked baseball and understood his dad's passion for it, but he did not grow up with it and could not imagine playing it professionally. In 2005, professional baseball returned to Washington after a thirty-four-year absence. Phillip was ecstatic about seeing the Presidents play in their first season.

As a family they traveled to Florida for their first spring training in March and had season tickets during the season. Guy went to a dozen games that first year at RFK Stadium. He enjoyed the time with his dad, roaming the huge concrete walkways with friends and seeing the players up close. But most of the time when they would come early and watch batting practice, he would think of three things in ascending order: the sound of the bats sending baseballs into the evening air, imagining someday that Alex would play for Washington on this emerald- green grass, and mostly how cool it must have been to play football in this stadium.

Guy and Alex would see each other during the holidays, but most of the time, Alex was in Florida or in Kansas City being a baseball player. They tried to stay close, but since they were eighteen years apart and in separate towns, it was difficult. By 2008, with texting and his own cell phone, Guy and Alex had become very close. Alex was making a point of keeping in touch almost daily, especially since Sean Taylor's death. He would check in after school with Guy-"Hey, big guy. What's up?"

Guy would answer, "SSDD."

After several back-and-forth texts with little information, Alex would call and probe a little deeper. He knew that Guy was not sleeping well before the holidays, and the cold of January was freezing his feelings.

"Still having dreams about Sean?"

"Yeah, kinda...sort of seeing a lot of blood."

The police report of the murder scene had reported that Sean Taylor's femoral artery in his groin area was exploded by a single gunshot from the intruders. There was blood everywhere in the bedroom. The doctors could never stop the bleeding internally, and it collected mainly in Taylor's abdominal area. He never regained consciousness.

Guy could never accept that his hero, Sean Taylor, had shed so much blood in his own bedroom defending his girlfriend and daughter.

"I can't believe someone so powerful was destroyed in his own house and bedroom. He never had a chance to defend himself. Why would you rob a house and purposely shoot someone in their own bedroom? Why would someone do that, Alex...why?"

Alex at times found it difficult to show his true feelings over the phone. He wanted to hold his brother and make it all better. All he had was words to soothe his pain. "Being great and powerful on the football field and defending against a gun are two different things. This had nothing to do with him as a football player. It has to do with some awful people that did an awful thing." Alex waited patiently for a response. After a long silence, he asked, "Are you worried that if you become a great football player, you won't be able to defend your family?"

"A great football player...me? I don't see that happening, but bleeding to death in my own house-I will make sure that won't happen."

"You mean you're scared that it could happen?"

"What do you mean?"

"I think you could become a great player, and I think you want that, Guy."

"I did want that, Alex, but now it seems impossible."

"I understand...I lost my adoptive father, Gene, when

I was fifteen. I guess I never thought about giving up baseball...it was all that I had!"

"Well, I'm only thirteen, so maybe I'll feel different in two years, but right now everything seems cold and bloody."

"Let's keep talking...I'm always here for you...and remember, we still have our dad."

"Yeah...luckily, that's true...and he's crazy as ever!"

• • •

The first two weeks of school after the holidays in January 2008 seemed especially torturous. Guy had no interest in his classes or studying for semester finals. Even attaining the eighty-dollar incentive to make the honor roll for the fourteenth consecutive quarter, since it was instituted by Phillip at the start of fifth grade, was in question. Guy was a self-starter when it came to school. He always finished his schoolwork without reminders and attended to chores around the house with a healthy smile. He enjoyed cutting the lawn, vacuuming, taking in the groceries, or anything his mom and dad asked him to do.

Even though Guy liked to stay active, he attended to the world with the calm of a diplomat and the evenness of a juggler. For now, he was able to continue his routine without drawing notice from his parents about his creeping sense of depression, other than the continual look of tiredness of a growing teenager.

On a Saturday night sleepover at his friend Blake Edmund's house during Martin Luther King weekend, Guy was introduced to an alternative lifestyle that would soothe his pain. Blake had been friends with Guy since second grade, but they really connected in sixth grade as they started middle school together. He was a computer game freak who got Guy excited about playing *Halo* and other games for the first time. He was not gifted athletically but was still a bit reckless in his sporting activities; choosing to ski, play tackle football without equipment, and give hard checks in lacrosse and hockey while collecting a dozen broken bones since he was a kid in these endeavors. With the personality of a Jewish comic and the brashness of a Dallas fan, Blake provided an alter ego of sorts for Guy, one that he could experience and enjoy without becoming someone he was not.

Blake had noticed that Guy was not his usual happy self over the past seven weeks. He thought it was silly that it involved Washington losing Joe Gibbs and the death of Sean Taylor, but he would never mention that to Guy. He remembered feeling sad when he was nine and former Cowboys coach Tom Landry died. The feeling was fleeting, but if it was combined with the death of one of his favorite players, he realized it might take a while to get over.

Like most junior-high teenagers, Blake was never one to focus on anything very deeply unless it had a fun ending. Living on the edge in moderation appealed to him.

Being a budding party planner, he organized the sleepover with the idea of providing fun to his sad buddy. With that in mind, he surprised Guy by inviting two of his new friends, Cody and Aaron.

43

Their comrade Mahmoud Abdul-Abar was coming as well, being allowed to stay overnight at a friend's for the first time. Better known to his close friends as "Mach," a nickname stuck to him by Blake because it measured the speed of sound and seemed cool, he was born from Iranian parents who had immigrated to the United States in 1979 during the fall of the shah. They were both engineers and devout Muslims. Guy and Blake had become friends with Mach in second grade when no one would talk to him during recess after 9/11 happened. But Guy took it upon himself to go beyond friendship, teaching him basketball on the playgrounds and football out in the field. Since Guy grew up in a multicultural and multiethnic environment, where Caucasians made up only 8 percent of the school population, it never occurred to him that anybody was different-unless of course they were not Washington fans; then he would notice.

The next fall, the DC sniper was on the prowl for two weeks, isolating Mach again from all the third graders. Guy noticed, spending all of his recess time with Mach. He became the first classmate to be invited to Mach's house after school in fourth grade. Mach's parents were impressed by how well-mannered and calm his new friend appeared. By the time middle school started, Mach became well-accepted by classmates. The trio of friends became solid buddies in middle school.

Blake's two new friends, Cody Watkins and Aaron Strong, went to a different middle school, but he knew them from a lacrosse team and several ski trips. Guy recognized them, having competed against them during summer swim meets and baseball leagues. He knew they played sports with an extreme cockiness that was normal these days in athletics but not a part of Guy's style.

Cody looked straight out of California with his blond surfer appearance. Aaron was African American and seemed to have grown up in the seventies with his hippieish Lenny Kravitz sunglasses and folk guitar. Guy liked their positive personalities and enjoyed the energy they seemed to bring to the overnight. He began to feel an excitement about the evening that had been missing in his life since Thanksgiving.

"Hey, dude...! know you from swimming." Cody was the first to give Guy a man hug. "I think you remember Aaron. Man, he's still pissed you beat him in that fly final in the divisionals last year. He's cool man and pretty laid back."

"Hey Aaron, what's up?" Guy smiled as he looked in Aaron's eyes to see if was still angry at him. Aaron away from sports was as peaceful as a hippie who rarely made eye contact, but this time his eyes lit up at seeing his only swim loss in the previous year.

"Nice to see you, Guy... I'm looking forward to this summer to get back at you!"

"No doubt!" Blake interjected. "Aaron brought his guitar...if that's cool for

44

everybody?"

"Hey, can you play any of the Who or Led Zeppelin? Maybe you could teach me some chords," asked Mach, who had become a classic rock junkie in the past three years.

"You got it, man ... and for real, I'd love to jam with you sometime." Aaron showed some emotion when his music was noticed.

"Yeah... my parents won't let me have a guitar around." "Wow, man ...that's a serious bummer. I got a couple extra guitars. I'll definitely bring one over to Blake's...or really, man, you got to come over sometime!"

"Wow... that would be awesome." Mach could barely tone down his excitement. A future friendship had been cemented.

• • •

Unknown to Guy, Blake had been hanging with Corey and Aaron on a regular basis since fall 2007 learning to smoke weed. Guy was surprised when the black bong appeared and the first toke was lit up. Mach would never smoke because it was counter to the Muslim teachings, but he thought it smelled great and enjoyed the laughing that followed.

Blake had a perfect exhaust system set up in the basement bathroom. He positioned a bong corner just outside the bathroom door with a fan in the door blowing any smoke to the exhaust fan in the bathroom. He had several candles set up to cover up any leftover scent.

"Wow, where did you get that bong?" Mach asked as he held it, feeling the precision of the plastic monolith. "This thing is awesome. It has an exhaust system like my friend's Mustang!"

"I had a friend get it in Baltimore around Fell's Point. There's a great music store up there with vinyl and CDs. You have to ask someone, and they take you in the back. My friend called me...he was hyperventilating about all the choices. I told him to get me a black one at least a foot or two tall!" Cody announced proudly as he took his baby and readied it for action. "They also have great dope up there, if you guys ever want to get in on it. It's a quarter the cost of stuff around here."

"Just fire that thing up, Cody. You won't have to sell anybody on the dope!" Blake answered, showing some impatience.

"Sorry, I can't do it, guys, because of my...you know, but this is cool to be around it...hey, Aaron, let's get some music going."

"No problem, man ...I got this Stones CD that has all of their early stuff. 'Under My Thumb,' 'The Last Time,' 'Nineteenth Nervous Breakdown.' They're all so awesome

45

and easy to play the chords." Aaron felt like he was on stage as he took his first bong hit off the monster contraption.

Guy related to the music talk. "Yeah, my dad loves the early Stones. He used to sing 'Nineteenth Nervous Breakdown' all the time...man, he knew all the words. At first, I thought it was the score of a game, maybe a ball club or something like that, when I was young...or when he was young...that could have happened, maybe...you know?"

The few seconds of silence while trying to figure out Guy's gibberish led to an outbreak of laughter. This was the beginning of the festivities and a state of group stoned-ness.

Guy continued feeling empowered by the attention. "Man...my dad saw the Stones at RFK in '72. He said Stevie Wonder opened for them. It was the summer after baseball left DC... can you believe that shit? Seeing the Stones in '72 and then no baseball for thirty-three years?" Guy was getting emotional thinking about his dad's history.

Aaron jumped in. "Man... talk about highs and lows. Seeing Jagger when he was in his late twenties! That must have been outrageous, man. Back then, most of the rockers never thought they'd live until they were thirty, much less still be playing. Forty years later, they're still playing." Aaron spoke like an easily distracted philosopher. "Hey, don't you have a brother that plays baseball for Kansas City?" he asked as he passed along the bong.

"Yeah, my half-brother, Alex Santucci...he's amazing. I don't get to see him much, but he is the best brother ever."

Guy had no hesitation about expressing love for his half-brother or taking the bong from Aaron. Even though he was an athlete, his emotions told him that something had to change. Guy lit the bowl and took in a swimmer's breath's worth. Like a seasoned pro, he smoothly exhaled. Over the next minute, he started to feel really alive for the first time in months and maybe for the first time ever.

"Hey, dude, have you been practicing or something?" Blake took the bong from Guy and pounded out a hit, smoothly letting out the smoke in Mach's direction. "Hey, Cody, this is the smoothest tool ever...you must have ice in there or something. I mean, that shit is smooth. It's like opening a freezer and inhaling!"

Everybody looked at Blake and started another round of life-extending laughter. He was always the funniest guy that Guy had ever been around. This time it hit Guy perfectly. He felt a stomach cramp that halted his breathing in between laughing, but then he sucked in some air to finish with a thunderous snort that finally became a great laugh. He continued chuckling until his face hurt. His remembered his mother always saying that a good laugh could put months on your life. If that was true, he thought, he must have just earned a decade.

The group then started on the burritos that they had bought at Chipotle. After finishing his first monster burrito, Guy was excited at his decision to have bought a second one until his stomach started to feel bubbly halfway through it. He was glad to feel full.

After a group conversation rating all the girls at school that they thought were hot, Blake brought up Guy's dad again.

"Guy, are you still playing in that basketball league with that psycho coach?"

The bong was being loaded for another round. Guy looked up at Blake and started laughing again. "No, that's over; I think my dad's pretty happy about that being done."

"Hey, dude, you got to tell everyone about your dad going off on the guy by mistake on the phone!"

Guy had told only Blake about an embarrassing situation that his dad had put him in, but Blake thought it was a riot and made him feel good about it and about his dad. He said his dad was really cool even if he went crazy sometimes. "Blake, no one wants to hear about that."

Immediately, Cody and Aaron jumped on the bandwagon. "Come on, man, you got to tell the story... everything stays in the man cave."

"OK, *cool...only* if you promise." All heads were shaking like they had to go pee. "All right...we were driving to my first practice with this team when I was in fifth grade. I only knew two guys who were going to be on the team and none of the coaches or other players. My dad gets the directions from this guy Bob, the head coach. Bob says it is at the corner of Georgia and Spring streets right behind the MNPPC building. Well, my dad has his real estate office up the street and drove a cab for two years in the late seventies while going to graduate school. He knows almost every street in Bethesda and Silver Spring, and he takes directions really, really literal." Guy paused to laugh at the memory. "So, we get out of the car and walk around this dark building looking for this gym. The whole time my dad is bitching. 'Why would someone put a gym in this building?' It was dark, but I was cracking up inside. So then we get back in the car,

47

and he's livid about getting wrong directions from the coach."

The group of five moved to within inches of each other listening to Guy's storytelling. It became a moment of bonding.

"So really...my dad does outrage really well. It must be an Italian thing or something. I mean, it becomes like a mini soap opera. He goes on and on!"

The group exploded with laughter. Blake couldn't take the drama and blurted out," Tell them about the phone."

"All right...shut up...I'm all over it." Guy's eyes were welling up with tears of laughter and emotion as he cherished the moment thinking of his dad. "So he calls the guy on his cell phone from the car and gets his machine and starts to leave a message. He's cool on the message but then hangs up and goes off again about 'What kind of asshole gives wrong directions to a basketball practice for kids?' He is just beside himself and starts driving across the street to look at the diagonal corner for a gym building. After fifteen minutes, he finally finds it just in time for the practice to start and drops me off. So then, while he is still pissed off, he starts apologizing to me about getting pissed off."

Mach became the first to fall backward and hold his stomach. Guy noticed him, pulled him up, and waited for the laughter to subside.

"So, what happened; did he ever talk to the coach about the directions?" Aaron asked with a big smile, enjoying the ambiance of the group.

"Well, kind of...a couple days later, my dad gets a call from the coach...you know Bob, saying I can't be on the team because he doesn't want to coach me. Finally, my dad, who can show amazing patience for a guy that can also go off the deep end, gets the coach to tell him that his whole rant was somehow left on the coach's message machine!"

Blake was already doubled over in laughter because he knew what was coming, but the other three were in disbelief.

"No fucking way, man; that is so embarrassing to get busted like that! Did your dad go off on the coach? How did you get to play on the team?" Cody asked while finishing his last bong hit of the night.

"Well, my dad is pretty quick on his feet and can be incredibly charming. So, he apologized while listening to the guy go on and on for about twenty minutes. Finally, he said to the coach, 'So, Bob... you're going to keep a ten- year-old from playing on a basketball team because I'm such an asshole?' I think that finally got me on the team, and I played for Coach Bob for three years. The funny thing about it was that my dad was right...the coach was an asshole because his son was on the team, and the whole time we played, we set up shots for him. And most of the time, he would give us wrong directions!"

The group reached a laughter crescendo. Guy felt on top of the world as he finished the story. "His kid really was nothing special. I was better, but I knew basketball wasn't my sport. I played to have fun with my friends and go to the practices with my dad."

"Did your dad ever talk to the coach again?" Mach inquired.

"No... he came to the games, and whenever he was pissed about me not playing, he would get my mom to talk to the coach. Now, that was really funny, because she can be a pleasant and adorable hard-ass!"

The rest of the night, they talked like chimpanzees making joyous noises in a zoo, until Guy's brain almost exploded. He had thought a lot about life that night, and nothing about football. For one long evening, it felt liberating to be free of the pain in his life.

CHAPTER 7

IT TOOK A few more sleepovers over the winter before the idea took hold. Blake and Cody first thought up the scheme after they had bought some pot through the record store in Baltimore. They decided to get together for another Friday night bong session to bring it up to the group of five. The idea: maybe they could pool their money and buy four ounces of pot, keeping one for their own party time together and then selling the other three.

After his first bong hit, Cody explained how they could find friends to sell the initial three ounces. He was such a California dreamer. "It's dry out there, man...especially in the winter, nobody has connections, unless you're crazy enough to venture into Langley Park. No disrespect, Aaron, but all these white kids at Northeast are clueless about buying pot. They have money, and they love to smoke herb."

"None taken, Cody... I agree with you; the brothers aren't scared of Langley Park. Hey, herb is like dessert after they snort crack and smoke that shit meth for dinner."

Amazingly, there was no dissent, except that Guy and Mach said they did not want to sell it personally but would put up the money and help with transportation. Blake, Cody, and Aaron backslapped each other over the unity, and that was how the Northeast Consortium (NC) was started.

The NC took the spring and the summer to get organized. Guy approached a man, Rico, who had a landscaping business but had also cleaned the Oakview Pool for cheap every March for the last few years to get it ready to open. Rico had adopted the Oakview Pool because his two sons had been involved in the swim team and pool management.

Rico was an excessively tan, youthful-looking man with great dark hair that fell into place with a stroke of his wide hands. He rarely smiled, seemingly worried about his physically taxing business for a man in his late forties. At times he would flash a golden smile and open his adorable blue eyes wide at the ever-present women at the pool, who loved to watch Rico, shirtless, straining his muscles to make the pool and its grounds beautiful.

Guy came up on his bike and found Rico weed whacking around the baby pool. "Hey, Rico... I got some friends that need a ride to Fells Point in Baltimore and back. Are you going up there anytime soon?" Guy had no clue that Rico was already a minor player in drug and alcohol distribution for the Burtonsville High School area.

"What do you have in mind, Mister Finelli?"

"Just want to go to this record store up there that sells vinyl and CDs. Supposed to be awesome."

"Well, maybe over the weekend, Guy. Maybe your boys can help me in the morning here at the pool, and we'll head up there for some shopping and lunch."

"Absolutely, Rico, you got it! Hey, we'll keep this just between us...all right?"

Rico laughed, realizing that some small-time hippie at a record shop was ripping off young teenagers selling pot. It was small enough not to catch the eye of his Baltimore connection. If these kids were serious, he knew he could save them some money and open a pot of gold for him to exploit. "Yeah, sure, my man ...I'll be looking forward to eating some mussels at Bertha's while you guys shop."

By the beginning of summer 2008, Blake, Cody, and Aaron focused on their known pothead friends at the two middle schools they had attended and kept away from any high- school kids they did not know.

After solving the merchandise pickup from Baltimore, thanks to Rico, Guy and Mach learned all the bus routes in Silver Spring to organize their deliveries. It was only a few hours a week, and they got to hang out together. The idea of carrying illegal contraband-never worried them.

Cody lived alone with his mom in the Colesville area, a short walk through the woods off New Hampshire Avenue. By car, the house was off a gravel road past a development on five acres of mostly woods. He took care of the small lawn and decided to convert the attic in their large shed into the NC "head"-quarters. His mom had grown up in the house and had no interest, time, or energy to walk into the shed, much less notice a hangout in the dusty attic. She worked as a nurse and took second shifts whenever possible to pay the bills. It comforted her that Cory could take care of the house, the yard and seemed to be a responsible son. Her favorite time with him was watching him play soccer and baseball. He was a star at both.

The hangout quickly became party central for the five friends. Access could only come from the woods and usually after dark. A bus stop was only a couple hundred yards from the beginning of the woods. It became the exclusive place to enjoy their product and to review the weekly progress of their business. After many bong hits, grand ideas to build their little business became more popular.

• • •

Guy was in great shape during the summer of 2008. He was in top swimming shape, running five miles a day, and working out at the YMCA in Silver Spring. Rico had showed him a lifting regimen that kept him flexible and increased his strength.

Before ninth-grade tryouts for football at Northeast High School in August, he was starting to feel some excitement about playing football again. He stopped smoking weed in July with his group of five because he was so busy working out and taking care of business.

He showed up for the first practice feeling invincible and confident that he was the best player on the field, even though he was still only five feet five and 13 5 pounds. He was as tough as nails, even as all the jokes were piled on him by the upperclassmen about being a puny boy.

It had been almost a year since he played any organized football in the fall of 2007, but he had kept in football shape with Blake, Cody, and Aaron. Phillip still practiced throwing to him and kicking punts a mile high, Guy would have to catch and return them with his four crazy friends trying to smash him. They would barely get a hand on him most of the time

As he strode out to the practice field, the Northeast coach noticed him. He had seen him play a couple games in the Silver Spring tackle league and was astonished at his speed and quickness for a 'white' kid. The leagues in Silver Spring were 80 percent African American, 10 percent Asian American, and 10 percent white. Most of the white kids played offensive or defensive line. Guy played every position in the backfield on offense and safety on defense, as well as the returner for kickoffs and punts. He was told by the coaches in the league that he was by far the best player, and if he grew to a reasonable size, he could play college football.

After the first practice, it was clear that Guy was the fastest player and had the best hands of any player on his team, even as a freshman. After a week of practice and a scrimmage that showcased Guy scoring on a punt return, a receiving touchdown, and an interception, Coach Gene Kelly made a huge coaching mistake. He decided to challenge Guy by putting him on the junior varsity and having him work his way up to varsity, perhaps by the start of the season. It was a protocol that most coaches would follow with a freshman, but not with such an obviously talented player on a mediocre team.

Guy took the news hard. He only answered "Yes, sir!" after the news from Coach Kelly. His self-confidence had been built on a house of cards since the new year, and it crumbled when Coach Kelly said, "I guess the practices were a little tougher than you thought."

It was a lie that was meant as a challenge. Guy was too young and hurt to see through it. He quietly dressed in tears, turned in his equipment, and never said a word to Coach Kelly. He walked two miles from the school to Cody's shed, crying the whole way, and then smoked weed out of the black monster for the first time during the summer and said good-bye to football in his mind forever.

He finally headed out to New Hampshire Avenue to catch the *CB* bus home. Cody had been in the attic with him and tried to talk to Guy about what had happened, but Guy had little to say. Sitting on the bus, he called his brother, Alex Santucci, in Kansas City, where it was one hundred degrees downtown. Alex sat in his very cool condo three hundred feet up in the air. He had just finished a run in the shade near the Missouri River, but the sweat was pouring out of him as he was getting into the shower. He quickly answered the phone to find out from Guy how football practice went.

"I decided to quit football...Coach wanted me to play JV!"
"What do you mean, a favor?"

"It might be too soon to play this season. You know it's a lot of work, and maybe you need the time for school."

Guy suddenly realized that Alex was right-it was too soon, but not because of schoolwork. Even thinking of the idea of "quitting" and playing football did not go together. He had thought he was past the mental pain of losing Sean Taylor. Loving football when he was doing well was the easy part; accepting the pain of disappointment and still loving football was the hard part.

"I think I made the right decision. Do you think you could call dad for me? He might not recover from this."

"No problem, buddy. He couldn't care less as long as you're happy. He did the same thing."

"Really...what happened?"

"I'll let him tell you when you're ready to hear it."

CHAPTER 8

IN THE FIRST three years of high school, a dark cloud of sad reality seemed to hang over Guy-not that he noticed too often when he spent time in the NC hangout or just with the group of five. Besides toking up in the shed attic, there would be hours of watching movies together at Blake's house, from mobster movies like *Godfather*, *Goodfellas*, and *Scarface* to sports movies like *Any Given Sunday, North Dallas Forty*, and *Major League*. They loved comedies involving John Candy, Adam Sandler, and Jim Carrey, or any movie with a stoner character, like *Fast Times at Ridgemont High, Half-Baked*, or *Smiley Face*.

His athletic world mainly consisted of enjoying isolation by improving his butterfly or freestyle stroke in swimming. After school almost every day, he practiced with the Northeast swim team or in the summer for Oakview. It was a healing sport for him, being unaided in his lane, improving his takeoff and flip-turns, and doing lap after lap without thinking of his unfulfilled dreams of destiny in football.

After dinner, he always committed to his schoolwork, enjoying the isolation of his basement cave. The HDTV was always on with a muted sports contest of some kind. His father would come down every hour or so and sit with him for only a few minutes, not wanting to ruin the den of isolation that Guy created. He enjoyed the quiet of the game on the HDTV while he sat, sometimes with Guy's feet on his lap. Other times he forced physical closeness on his son by diving over the back of the couch to start a short wrestling match or just a quick massage of his ever- growing shoulders.

Guy became most animated when Phillip invaded his physical world. For Guy, it reached his emotional core and kept him in touch with the real world of his family. Otherwise, Phillip felt the emotional distance of his son during the rapid physical growth of his first three high- school years, but he never wavered in staying as close as he could to his heart.

During Guy's tryout for football at Northeast High School in 2008, he became friends with one of the best players on the team, Hank Harrison, who was a junior that played linebacker and tight end. He was already being recruited by area colleges like Towson and ames Madison and had attracted some notice by UMD. After Guy left the team, Hank tracked him down to talk about what had happened. It started a friendship that lasted the next two years of high school. They never hung out together or sent text messages to each other, but every once in a while, Hank would pull Guy aside in the halls and ask him how he was doing. Hank knew that Guy was a great football player but never pushed him to go out for the team.

By the spring of 2009, Hank realized that there was a way to keep Guy interested in football. Seeing that Guy had grown almost seven inches and fifty pounds of mainly muscle, he invited Guy to join him and fellow football friends to work out and play in a seven-on-seven touch- football league between some of the local high schools. They would run drills and then scrimmage without pads.

Hank invited Guy not only because he was the fastest player with the quickest first step he had seen or had the best hands catching the football-no, it was for a selfish reason. Guy had the best throwing arm he had ever seen in high school. Hank needed a QB to make him better in the touch-football league. The Northeast QB was mediocre at best, and besides, he played baseball in the spring.

That spring, Guy experienced the best two months in his life since Sean Taylor died, and he turned an emotional corner. He still had no interest in playing for Coach Kelly, because he thought he was an asshole, and he enjoyed swimming all year round.

Hank and Guy became closer friends but rarely talked in school because they were two years apart. After the spring season was over, Hank saw him to check on his summer plans. "Listen, Guy, I need someone to throw me the ball all summer and work on pass patterns. Will you be around?"

"That would be cool. If you have a car, we could meet in Oakview and work out. I know my father would come out and throw sometimes too, so we could do one-on-one coverage."

"Sounds perfect...but I don't need someone to kiss my ass on coverage and make me look bad. Hey, I'll bet your dad is feeling better about the 'not playing football' thing."

"Yeah, he was really disappointed, but he's cool now about it. He gets all angry sometimes and blows up, but he always apologizes and gets us back on track. He eventually told me that he almost did the same thing in high school, but fortunately his brother Anthony got him back to practice, and the rest is history!" Guy's eyes were moist from the memories.

"Well, at least he's always there for you, and your brother is pretty cool...right? Hey, this will be fun, and it will keep you playing.

"Guy and Hank exchanged a man hug and ended their interaction with a handshake.

The NC crew was coming down the hall and noticed the smooth good-bye. They chimed in with some opinions. "Hey, that Hank is some looker. Have you guys been practicing that in a closet somewhere?" Blake could not control himself with the gay references any chance he could get. It was the norm for teenage boys to distance themselves from being gay by accusing everyone of acting gay when they were not. In the gang of five, everyone but Guy and Mach made gay jokes. Mach had religious reasons to be against homosexuality but never participated in discrimination. Guy knew that his friends were immature and never participated in the jokes.

The rumors about Hank Harrison were subtle and only traveled in some of the boy groups. The girls never considered it because he was "so fine looking!" There are words that kids hear when someone is not "normal" without using the word "gay," like "He seems unusual," or "He's a little different." Guy never gave these conversations much thought, because he had learned from his parents that being gay was as a natural as being straight.

It was confirmed one day when Hank was giving him a ride home. He decided to give Guy a chance to distance himself now that he had heard the rumors about him. "I guess your friends are a little uncomfortable with me being your friend."

Guy never hesitated with his supportive response. "Well, they're pretty immature with people that don't act like them."

"Well, let me know if it's a problem. I don't want our friendship to cause you trouble with your friends."

"Hank...you and I are friends. We play football together, and hopefully we'll keep in touch after high school. Do you think I care what my friends think about someone that is so much cooler than them?"

Hank added a smile to an otherwise serious face. "So you think I'm pretty cool...even if I'm a little different?" Hank's eyes met Guy's as he opened up to the first non-gay person in his life. Their friendship was on the table.

Without hesitation, Guy grabbed Hank's shoulder to make his point. "Maybe the coolest guy I know...and one hell of a ball player!"

Guy felt a chill as he returned the gaze, knowing he had just made a permanent friend. Hank gave Guy a man hug when he left the car; they added the handshake later.

The subject was never brought up again as their friendship continued forever.

CHAPTER 9

AFTER TWO YEARS of playing spring football, Guy decided to move on from the NC world of selling and using marijuana and instead play high-school football during his senior year in the fall 2011. Changes in his family happened as quickly as he was growing, now almost six feet five and 220 pounds. First, his grandmother Rose died in the summer of 2010; then Phillip and Carol purchased her house in Parkwood by the next spring. They quickly remodeled the sixty-year- old rambler by adding an upstairs full of bedrooms, a new kitchen, and a garage on the side. They moved in during late 2011.

His parents gave him the option to finish his senior year at Northeast or transfer to Walter Johnson. It was an easy decision for Guy, because three generations of Finellis had been to WJ, including his parents and brother. Playing football at a new school and being around new friends, meaning less time with his NC buddies, would provide a fresh start.

It was a gorgeous spring day in April 2011 as WJ head coach Furrey Favarro was having a beer after work with his best friend and assistant coach, Joe Finelli. Coach Favarro was in his mid-thirties, married, and expecting his first child. He was educated as a structural engineer and was now working in his own construction business, mainly building custom houses. When he met Joe before a WJ football game during the 2009 season, they knew instantly that they would become best friends. There was something about each other that seemed to be special. It took a couple of beers one night after a practice to cement their instincts after they learned they were football related-by coaching greatness.

Furrey's great-grandfather was Joe Favarro, who had been a football coach at Sommerville High School in New Jersey and coached Joe's grandfather, Guy I, in 1929. They sat in reverence, silenced by the discovery for a few minutes. Then, they ordered two more pitchers of beer to celebrate and map out their coaching future together.

Now it was two years later, and Joe was trying to convince Furrey to see his cousin and grandfather's namesake, Guy Finelli, play in a high school, spring-league touch-football game. This was the off-season, and Furrey had a lot on his plate with his construction business and had little energy to watch a "touch" football game. Joe was emphatic that Guy was for real and was thinking of transferring to WJ. He wanted Furrey to see him with his own eyes. After a few beers, Joe stood up and towered over his friend, describing his cousin's talent with moist eyes. He grabbed Furrey in a massive man hug and said to him, "We will be coaching football together for long time, and I know now how we're going to win our first championship!"

• • •

Furrey's mind began to change quickly when he first stood behind Guy Finelli on the football field. It seemed impossible to believe that this physical specimen with shoulders as wide as goal posts and hands that made the football look like a tennis ball was not on a football team. He wondered if Saint Anthony had finally answered his prayers for a miracle player. Furrey tried to stay calm and appear unexcited as Joe turned to him after every throw, saying, "Can you believe that shit he's doing with the football, Fur-Man? I told you he could wing it. But that's nothing; just watch him run and play safety."

Finally, the team changed to defense, which gave Furrey, a former linebacker, a chance to see if Guy was really a football player. The game was getting a bit physical for a one-hand-touch game. The rival team from Prince George's County, Eleanor Roosevelt (ERHS), had won the football state title in 2010 and liked to play "touch" at "full volume," according to Joe Finelli. "These guys are big-time trash talkers, Fur-Man. I think Guy had enough of that crap today."

Furrey watched Guy intently on defense. ERHS ran an option play to the right side. Guy literally ran through two defenders and grabbed the quarterback's ankle to pull him down in the backfield. The next play, they faked the option with the right-side All-County receiver, on his way to Florida State, running a post pattern. He seemed to be wide open to anyone not watching Guy Finelli, who was lurking on the left side with a perfect angle to intercept the pass. Like a solar eclipse, he passed in front of the receiver, over ten feet in the air, and stole the ball. Furrey Favarro

Coach Furrey was quiet all the way to the car, but once he got behind the wheel, he lit up his face with a big smile and said, "You better get him to transfer to WJ, or I'll knock you out!"

"Don't worry, Fur-Man; I got it covered. Guy owes me big!"

58

· · ·

)nly two incompetent knees and many incompetent teachers in high school had kept Joe
'inelli from becoming a big-time college tight end. In the late eighties, he was six feet four
nd 235 pounds, could run like the wind, and had great hands. Now he was fifty pounds
eavier and all muscle with a sweet personality, if you did not mess with his family.

On the first day of April 2011, his cousin Guy Finelli told him in confidence about
his drug history. He was looking for his help in getting away from the NC and
especially Rico. The first step was to tell Rico, who had made thousands off of the NC
expansion into Northeast.

Guy asked Joe to drive him to meet Rico at the Oakview Pool, where Rico was doing
his thing to get the pool ready by Memorial Day weekend. Guy needed to make it clear
with Rico, man to man, that he was done with the business and the use of drugs.

Joe leaned back against the front of his truck in front of the gate to the pool while Guy
found Rico as he was cutting the lawn. Rico had become very fond of Guy over the years. His
son Red, had swum and played baseball with Guy. Rico and Guy had made money from
the NC and worked together on pool maintenance for the last three years. As a team they
became the go-between with the boys of the NC and the buyers of pot and alcohol.

At times after a couple of beers, Rico would complain about all the money he was
losing from his business and his wife's spending. Guy would listen and see the pressure
Rico was under as his alcohol use rose, as well as a newly found coke habit. Guy had found
out from Rico that Cory wanted to sell cocaine to some unknown clients he had cultivated.
Rico set him up with his connection in Baltimore, which raised the stakes to serious
drug dealing. Guy wanted nothing to do with it and had been complaining about it to
Rico for months. Now he was telling Rico that he was leaving everything and moving to
Kensington to play football.

Rico did not react well to the news. "You're leaving me with all this
mess...everything with the business is crumbling, Guy. I can't compete with the
Mexicans and their pricing anymore. All the landscaping jobs are going to the illegals.
They're lining up at the Home Depot entrance looking for work." He suddenly turned
quiet and got closer to Guy's face. "I need the NC to keep the money flowing." Guy could see
the traces of powder in Rico's nose and could feel his anger. "Your friends can't keep this thing
going. And I don't have time to do it all. We are on the cusp on big money, man, with this
coke thing," he said at almost a whisper. Suddenly, he backed up but then leaned forward and

put his arm on Guy's shoulder. "I can't talk to them like you and I can."

Joe noticed Rico leaning on the taller Guy in the distance, looking like he was pleading for his life. He walked onto the pool lawn and asked Guy if everything was cool. There was no answer from Guy as he tried to calmly keep his eyes on Rico. Joe took a few more steps to get closer and noticed something sticking out of the back of Rico's pants. It was hidden under his sweatshirt but became obvious as Rico leaned over toward Guy. It was the handle of a gun. Joe took several quick strides to get closer and could hear Rico continuing his plea to Guy. His words were crumbling toward incoherence, like a man on a simple raft in thrashing white water trying to get to safety.

Joe could now see the handle of the Glock 19 handgun very clearly. He was an owner of multiple weapons himself and knew that a Glock owner was most likely ex-military, with little fear to use his weapon when he felt danger was imminent. Joe quickly accelerated in on Rico before he could turn around. Even at 285 pounds with surgically repaired knees, Joe strode light as an antelope with several giant steps, diving at Rico from his side. With a magician- quick left hand, he pulled out the gun while they rolled together down a short hill, finally coming to a stop. Joe quickly popped up and, with one motion, heaved the gun like a dart into the middle of the pool while he landed his size 14 shoe on Rico's chest. Dazed but quickly trying to regain his focus, Rico looked up to see the large torso of Joe Finelli leaning over him. "Listen, my man, my cousin Guy is a nice kid who has decided to move on from the business. Leave him alone, or we'll have another talk like this again!"

"All right...all right! Let me up," Rico pleaded. Joe released his WJ-colored sneaker slowly, showing great dexterity as he landed his foot just below Rico's testicular sack. Rico sat up, unaware that his gun was at the bottom of the pool. Still sitting, he tried once more to plead his case to Guy. "Man... Guy, my friend, if that's what you want...it's cool, but I'm not sure I'll make it without you. Everything is a mess!"

Guy put up his hands and turned with his cousin to make their exit. Rico put his head in his hands, shaking it violently while sitting in the newly cut grass. He shouted out, "The guys in Baltimore are not going to be happy, Guy... they had big plans for you."

Joe turned as they were heading out the gate. "Oh, by the way, you may want to check the bottom of the pool for something that dropped out of your pants." Guy smiled at his big cousin Joe, feeling free and impressed at witnessing the takedown. As they got to the car, they hugged violently.

. . .

By noon on April 15, after he mailed his taxes, Rico made sure that the Oakview Pool was ready to open six weeks before the season. The sprouting grass was newly cut. The red-and-white lawn chairs were perfectly aligned in rows set out on top of the suntan hill, the site of the tumble between Rico and Joe two weeks earlier.

The pool water looked deliciously clear as a cocktail on the perfect spring day. The grounds stood quiet except for the backwashing of the water in the pump room. Rico had left instructions on the wall of how to restart the unreliable pump. And as he left the pump room, Rico left a final remark in Greek on the back of the door: "Απρίλ 15, 2011. Ιτ ης Αλλ Φινισηεδ," or "April 15, 2011. It is finished."

Guy's showdown two weeks before was the last time he saw Rico. Now Rico left the pool alone with no witnesses to see his masterpiece. As he drove home, he felt relieved that his obligations were settled. He pulled into his garage and waited for the door opener to finish performing. He pulled out his Glock 19 handgun that he had recovered from the pool, and he shot himself in the chest. After school, his son Red came home and found his father dead, lying back in the front seat of his car. He was shirtless with a bloodied torso, like a fallen Greek God.

CHAPTER 10

Guy SPENT THE following months until August football tryouts getting in football shape.

He spent a great deal of time in his old neighborhood of Oakview practicing with the swim team in the morning and then running plays with friends on the neighboring field. Coach Favarro had given him a set of plays to run as quarterback and the basic calls on defense.

In late July, when the sun was routinely roasting the elementary school field, Guy would be alone running sprints in the afternoon as he waited for his friend Hank Harrison to join him for passing drills. Hank was ready for a breakout sophomore year at Towson University and loved refining his pass patterns with Guy throwing to him.

The field was sheltered from the world's busiest highway, I-495, the Washington Beltway, by just fifty yards of woods and bushes hiding the highway fence. Many white oak trees towered above the field, adding beauty and distraction to the constant sound of thousands of cars. The whirling noise seemed like a crowd reacting to the pair of future stars running the field. Ironically, for Guy, this place next to the busy highway was an oasis from the challenge of an increasingly complex world and allowed him to focus on the future after a deadly spring full of change.

Guy said good-bye to his workout buddy Hank after throwing him passes on eighty-seven patterns for two hours. Hank wore number eighty-seven to honor his football and career idol, Jerry Smith, an All-Pro tight end for Washington from 1965 to 1977. Smith had held the record for career TDs by a tight end at sixty, until it was finally broken in 2003, twenty-six years after the 1978 offensive rule changes. Smith became the first known gay professional athlete to die of AIDS in 1986.

Phillip had made Guy and Hank aware of Smith's greatness as a player and his early death from AIDS several years ago in a conversation about great receivers that he loved in the sixties. Being a statistical freak, Phillip would lay out the argument for Jerry Smith joining fellow receiver teammates Charley Taylor and Bobby Mitchell, along with QB Sonny Jurgensen, in the NFL Hall of Fame.

Unaware of Hank's lifestyle, Phillip showed great emotion when commenting that Smith's career was ignored by the media after he died from AIDS and his lifestyle was revealed. He also mentioned that Vince Lombardi, who coached Washington in 1969 before his death the following year, never tolerated discrimination for color or sexual orientation during his coaching career. Having a brother that was gay, Lombardi realized Smith's orientation and refused to tolerate any kind of prejudice in the locker room.

Hank felt great acceptance in the Finelli family and wanted to help his friend Guy find his way back to high- school football.

Guy was starting to suck down a blue Powerade when Hank grabbed his throwing arm and shoulder. He felt the audacity of those shoulders. It was not something that you would see in a normal athlete. They were wide, limber, and powerful. He could appreciate that in another man without having sexual feelings for his friend. He saw Guy as a younger brother. "You really had it going today, Guy. Everything you threw was on the button."

"Well, it doesn't hurt that you're a big target and never drop anything!"

"Hey, that's my job! Keep up the good work. WJ has struck gold, and the county won't know what hit them." "Well, I still have to make the team, you know." "Yeah...of course...that will be close, I guess, but somehow, I don't think Coach Favarro is going to send you down to JV like Coach...what's-his-name!"

"Thanks, Hank...another eighty-seven tomorrow?"

"Count on it!"

Guy threw a wave toward Hank and headed to the parking lot as he searched for his keys in his gym bag. He was so hot and sweating like a waterfall that even the metal of the car key seemed ready to explode. Finally, he got in the car and pumped on the air conditioner. He closed his eyes and poured cold water over his head. As the radio blared music, he quickly tried to finish the Powerade. Then he felt a jolt from the right side of the car. The blue drink poured over his chest as he turned and saw a gentleman with a suit and tie on in this heat flashing a badge at him as he sat.

"I'm Special Agent Richard Kessinger with the FBI. I hope I'm not interrupting anything, Mr. Finelli. Can I call you Guy for now?"

Guy caught the falling drink without noticing the color descending down his soaked shirt. He screwed the cap back on as he tried to act normal and catch his breath. His mind was moving slowly because of the heat. He had known this day was possible, but the sudden appearance of an FBI special agent in his car was a shock. It was time to act as cool as possible. "What can I do for you, Special Agent Kessinger?"

"I was watching your workout with Mr. Harrison. That was quite impressive. Are you playing this year in the county?"

"Yes, sir... I'm going to Walter Johnson."

"Well, I would love to see you play there...that's funny, because I went to WJ, and so did my supervisor, Regional Director Brooklyn O'Malley. I'm sure he would love to come out as well. He hasn't seen your dad in quite a while. They apparently were very close. I myself knew the older Finelli boy. I'm a little older than your dad, you see. Well, hopefully they can catch up at one of the games...maybe."

Guy was feeling somewhere between throwing up and shitting in his pants as he started to play out his future. He was trying to stay calm, but the cooling-down process was not quite working, because the burning in his stomach was moving up his throat. Finally, he remembered the name-Brooklyn-it was so unusual. His dad called him "Brooks." They were close high-school buddies, played tons of sports together, and went to Bullets games in Baltimore because his dad's cousin was an NBA player, coach, or something. He focused again on the special agent in his car and made no attempt to talk as he waited.

"Let's take a little drive...I have some people that want to talk with you, and this parking lot is just a little hot for my tastes. Are you OK to drive?"

Guy hit the gas pedal without delay as sweat continued to pour down his face. He looked around the parking lot and entrance to the school and pool, and to his relief, he saw no one.

They headed out of Oakview and then north on I-95 to the first exit of Route 212 and into Beltsville. They turned into a parking lot of a warehouse, pulled around back, and got out. The building was wonderfully cool as they went into a room with a table and a wall full of names, pictures, and locations.

Brooklyn O'Malley stood behind the table with several agents. He met Guy with a strong handshake while putting his hand around his broad shoulders. Brooks looked taller than his six-foot, four-inch frame with his wide shoulders and tailored pin-striped suit. With a big smile on his face, he welcomed Guy to sit down.

"Wow...this is quite a pleasure to meet Phillip Finelli's son. Your dad's a special friend. We go way back-too many years for me to admit-and this crazy career has separated us for too long."

Agent O'Malley spoke with a gravelly voice that was the product of throat cancer some twelve years earlier. His voice box had been removed and finally replaced recently with the newest product, which gave him a tough but hearable voice.

After spending his whole academic career at Georgetown University getting his undergraduate and law-school degrees, "Brooks" had disappointed his father, Franklin O'Malley, by not joining his DC law firm. This was a few years after his father had become famous for getting off the only prosecuted person involved in the Watergate cover-up.

It would have been a piece-of-cake career move, but Brooks was always a gritty

64

ballplayer, and he turned to the FBI to get his hands dirty. He played center on the high-school basketball team and middle linebacker on the football team. He played high-school and county sports with Phillip Finelli for many years after being great friends in their teenage years.

In the cocaine eighties, he started fifteen years of undercover work in Baltimore, infiltrating the drug and racketeering world. He was a legend in the FBI. Surviving the street work and all the criminals made him an expert on the drug trade on the East Coast. Brooks learned that nothing was going to change inner-city Baltimore drug use without money raining from the heavens to provide alternatives to the children. His goal from all his years of knowledge was to keep the drug flow out of the rest of the state, especially his hometown area of Montgomery County. It was selfish thinking, but he had earned the right to think that way, according to the FBI elite. They had set him up fifteen years ago to do anything he wanted in the state of Maryland and with the budget to do so.

Guy's head was spinning, he was so unsure of his future. He was still sweating and thirsty. He continued to gulp down the bottle of water sitting in front of him.

"Don't worry, Guy; everything is going to be fine. We just need some information from you, now and maybe in the future. This group here will always watch out for you, especially when you become a big star!"

Guy finally found his voice. "What can I say, Agent O'Malley? I got out of things about six months ago. We were only selling pot until..."

"It's Brooks, please. I like to think we'll be friends in the future, especially when I need tickets...ha-ha!" Brooks O'Malley roared with a laugh that sounded like boulders crashing on the floor. "Here's the deal. Your friends have gotten a little over their heads. They're involved with some bad people. We would like to help them get out of business."

Yes Mr. Brook... anything you need!"

"Remember, Guy...'Brooks'...it will make things easier, because you're going to have to trust me. There is no other choice. Your dad would tell you the same thing." Guy started to feel his eyes moisten, because he knew his dad would be out of his mind if he were in the room right now, but quickly he focused on the smile on Agent O'Malley's face and decided at that instant to trust him like a new religion.

"Remember, if you do the right thing, we will always take care of you. Just play football and become a star. You have made the right choice to come with Agent Kessinger."

For the next two hours, Brooks and Guy got down to business on exchanging information to close down the Northeast Consortium and catch some bad guys. The question would soon follow-would the bad guys ever catch up with Guy?

Brooks assured him that Cody and Aaron were the only two of his friends to be questioned. Blake and Mach would be scared out of the business by some men in suits. The shed attic would be shut down and used as evidence to make Cody and Aaron fully cooperate. An undercover, youthful-looking FBI woman would make a buy at a Friday-night party before the divisional swim meet that would lead to the evidence. Cody, with his surfer looks, would not be able to resist the blazing, redheaded agent who insisted on a private party. Cody would realize that the NC headquarters was the perfect place!

CHAPTER 11

T HE BIG SURPRISE for Brooks O'malley was the $30,000 in cash that Guy turned in to them. This was an unusual but nice problem to encounter while dealing with the drug trade. In all his years in the FBI, no one had ever turned in actual cash. People got involved in selling drugs to make money, either to get rich or to do more drugs.

As Guy explained to him, he had never spent any of the money on himself but just on friends if they needed money. Saving had always been in his DNA; it was the way he first got into the business, by never spending any of his birthday and Christmas money over the years. He had over $1,000 in cash in the middle of eighth grade to start the business in March 2008. Now he had been sitting on it for six months, not sure of how to get rid of it without drawing attention.

With the FBI moving into his world, he got an idea. He brought them the cash and asked if they could anonymously give it to the Oakview Pool, which was always fighting money problems. Agent Kessinger checked the bag and counted the mostly small bills. He shook his head and said, "Are you sure about this before I give it to Agent O'Malley?"

Guy explained, "When I first started on the swim team, my dad spent a good deal of time to first get the pool rebuilt and then raised the money to pay for its upkeep. But recently, the pool is bleeding money again due to the lack of membership and our family has moved from the neighborhood after twenty-seven years. It's questionable if it opens for 2012."

Agent Kessinger took the cash, gave him a receipt, and said, "I'll check into it."

In November 2011, the president of the Oakview Pool opened the annual meeting with some good news about a $30,000 donation that she had just received from an anonymous source. The longest-running out door community pool in Montgomery County would open for another season or more in 2012.

Guy Finelli felt relieved when he heard the news. In a weird way, he had hoped that something positive might come out of the drug business. He knew that if he ever made it big in professional football, he would team up with his brother, Alex, to keep swimming in the lives of kids and their communities

CHAPTER 12

GUY WAS READY to swim one last divisional swim meet for Oakview on the last Saturday in July 2011. The newly installed starting blocks at Tanglewood Swim Club in Silver Spring were like the ones used in his high school meets, up in the air and above the pool. Almost seventeen, Guy Pinelli had broken the thirty- second mark for the fifty-meter butterfly divisional final in 2010, but his times this year had been slower.

He spent the last two weeks concentrating on the butterfly, his favorite stroke, after feeling a great relief from his money donation. He trusted Brooks to take care of him, for some reason. Dad's friends were always a different breed. They seemed to have come from a different era of survival, something he had not encountered until Sean Taylor's death in 2007. Phillip could always connect with an old friend from high school or college, even if they had not talked for years. It had been almost thirty years since Phillip and Brooks had talked. Their careers had taken different roads, life had become complicated and intense, families had been started, health problems had interrupted their worlds-but the soul of the friendship was always there.

After ten years of swimming, this was to be his last competitive swim meet. Oakview swam in the "O" division, the lowest of fifteen in the county but still very competitive. Guy had won his initial heat rather easily, which placed him in the final eight for the butterfly final. He was smooth from start to finish without kicking in his full thrusters. For the final, he was in lane two, which meant he would have to crush the swimmer next to him in lane three to have a chance with the favorites in lanes four and five.

■■■

Guy knew he was at a crossroads in his life. He remembered the promise on that rainy day in late March 2011 to give up smoking weed and drinking. Little did his parents know how deep he had been involved in delivering product and Rico's involvement, or the money that he would donate to save the pool.

As he stood behind the starting blocks waiting for his race, the sun was shining straight at him, causing him to pause and close his eyes for a moment. His emotions swelled up inside as he thought of his family and the Oakview community where he grew up. He wanted to tell his parents how much he loved them, but he always had trouble finding the words.

He remembered that when he started smoking weed, two months after Sean Taylor died, it seemed to relieve his malaise and helped him speak to his friends. The drug business became a game to help out his friends and feel included. When his mother first discovered the smell in the car after he got his license in March 2010, she found a bag in the trunk with pot and alcohol. He convinced his parents that it was not his, which was technically true. Phillip took over and drove him to a place where he could leave it without throwing it out, fearful that more trouble would come to Guy if they threw it out. Guy always thought it was a class act by his dad, even if it was a gullible one.

A year later, Carol found another bag in the trunk that she threw out herself, because Phillip was out playing golf and could not intervene. She was furious with Guy and Phillip after he returned from a great round of breaking eighty. Phillip felt stunned all day, not able to talk to Guy or Carol about what options they had. Carol wanted Guy to be in home detention until the summer. Phillip knew that would never work and would be the beginning of the end of their parenting influence over Guy. He searched for a strategy all day and night on Saturday.

When he woke up on a misty Sunday morning, Phillip suggested they all go to breakfast together. The three of them cautiously talked about safe things before Carol finally brought up what to do with Guy. She wanted a full set of sanctions put on Guy, like she was Hillary Clinton talking about Iran. As parents, they had never "grounded" either Grace or Guy. Phillip believed in interventions that lasted hours instead of days. Up to this point, that strategy had been successful, they thought, but in Guy's case apparently not.

Guy would never forget seeing Phillip taking in the conversation at breakfast contributing very little until he took over. It was like Johnny Unitas running the first two-minute offense.

Phillip knew that emotionally, Guy for some reason was still not feeling the impact of his behavior on himself or his family. At the same time, Carol was arguing on a linear basis about taking away the car, going to the prom, and being with his friends. This helped Phillip think of his parents and especially his grandmother Philomena, the kindest and most spiritual person in his life. He thought of her speaking in broken English and the power of her hands in helping her talk and always in the way she used touch to send the message of love. It deeply affected him to be in her presence at times and helped him in

69

creating his superego, that Freudian concept of a conscience.

Phillip rose from the restaurant table and suggested they go for a ride. In fifteen minutes, they arrived at Gate of Heaven cemetery in front of his parents' plots. Phillip visualized his emotions and started a conversation with Guy and Carol about his feelings. He said, "Trust is the only thing we have with each other as a family. As parents, we have no real power over Guy and his actions. Resentment would be the only by-product of taking privileges away. What we do have...are the values of the family from a hundred and twenty-five years ago, when three of my grandparents immigrated to America." Phillip was hoping that the history of the family would be on his side as he tried to reach Guy emotionally.

Guy remembered how quiet it was in the car as they rode to the cemetery and how nauseated he had felt pulling up to the gravesites as they sat under a huge white oak. Listening to his dad was like taking in the medicine to get better as a kid-at first it did not taste good, but eventually it worked.

Phillip sensed that Carol was not on board while he talked, and so he took a moment and walked her back to the car so that he could be with Phillip alone. She hated the idea but trusted his intervention and prayed it would work from the car.

He then walked to Guy, who was looking at the gravesites of Rose and Guy Anthony Finelli. His namesake had died in 1993, a year before he was born, while his grandmother had died just ten months ago at the age of ninety-five. Guy had been seen as a gift to Rose in 1994 after her husband had died-she truly believed that. She loved him more than anything for all of his fifteen years before her death. Even in her last month of life, suffering in her dementia, she would light up when she saw her "baby."

Guy recalled crying at her funeral for the first time since Sean Taylor died and now was filling up with tears as Phillip talked softly to him again. He was asking him to tell his grandparents that he was a pothead and that he could not change his lifestyle. "Tell them how hard it would be to not smoke pot while you're growing up as a teenager. Tell them you're too emotionally dependent on it and your friends. Now ask them if they understand...if they ever faced hard work like that...had to give up things in their lives."

The next ten minutes seemed like ten hours as Guy fell to his knees, listening to Phillip talk about his grandfather's legacy becoming an All-State football player in his only year of high-school football as a two-way guard at five feet five and 135 pounds in New Jersey. He told Guy how he gave up Princeton to work for his family in 1930 to survive the depression and came to Washington on his own in 1939. He continued talking about how his great-grandmother and grandmother had both worked selflessly for their families their whole lives to give him a chance at a great life. It was a brutal assault by Phillip as a field general, and Guy had no defense for it.

Finally, Phillip walked over, knelt with his son, and asked him what he wanted to do. He said that either way, he asked that he tell his grandparents. Guy remembered wiping his eyes as he stood up to talk. He felt the strength of his dad's touch and his arm on his shoulder. He knew it would be OK and that it had to be done. He struggled with the words, but emotionally, it was a relief. "I promise to change my life, Grandpop and Grandmom." He turned to his dad and hugged his father. "I promise, Dad, no more problems from me; I get it now. You'll be proud of me."

Phillip looked at him with tears flowing down his cheeks. "I love you, son, and I will always be proud of you."

■ ■ ■

Guy heard his name announced as he opened his eyes and stepped up on the starting block. He felt completely at peace as he noticed his parents standing to his right on the side of the pool. Phillip had calmly told him after Guy dominated his heat, "I already see you winning, so just enjoy the swim." It seemed pretty cocky, but Guy agreed with him, and now that his half-brother, Alex, had shown up, it was time for him to turn on the jets and burn some potheads. He looked to his left and saw his four competitors who thought they had a chance against him. Guy had grown to six feet five and 225 pounds as he readied for the football season. In a one-word description, he was a "monster."

A buzz seemed to simmer in the crowd as they started to notice Guy as he lowered his giant hands to get into starting position. A burst of adrenaline jolted his calmness, and he felt ready to fly.

"Burrrrrrrrrrrrrrrrrrrrrrrrrrrrrrrrrrrrrrrrrrrrrup," went the electronic starting noise. Guy exploded into his dive, enjoying the solitude of the cooling water. In butterfly, the race is generally won with the dive and the turn. Sometimes the power of the dive can be disruptive to the emerging and all-important first stroke. If done properly, all the energy of the dive has to be in a smooth displacement of the water so that the body can emerge with power, moving with maximum efficiency in the small space of the air just above and the water just below it.

As Guy started his powerful butterfly stroke and kick, Phillip saw him gliding above the water with an immediate half-length lead over his competitors. After a flawless first lap, he seamlessly glided into the two-hand touch of the turn and launched

71

into the final lap. Guy could not resist his bad habit of glancing now to his right and seeing nothing but calm water for the whole pool, knowing that he was leaving everyone behind him. Phillip fell to his knees as he watched Guy's last ten strokes of perfection putting him into a full length's lead. Phillip's last scream came out without sound as his voice failed him. He lifted both arms in victory as Guy touched in twenty-eight seconds flat!

Carol jumped on Phillip, screaming in victory as she finally tried to help him up, but instead they landed together in a hug. Alex came to the rescue as he helped up the joyous couple from their embarrassment, but he saw that it was worth the tumble. They waited in bubbling silence as Guy rose from the pool into the arms of his excited teammates. The celebration lasted a precious minute or so as a lifetime of swim meets flashed in front of their eyes. For the last time, Guy would remove his cap and shake out his wet hair. As he headed toward his parents, Guy was leaving a local stage for one last celebration with his roots of family and friends. Now it was time for the next stage-to conquer football in the state of Maryland.

• • •

The youthful-looking, redheaded FBI agent, Anna Cobb, was doing her job, being at the divisional finals to watch Cody and Aaron get their asses kicked by Guy in the butterfly. Guy had identified the two suspects to her before the meet while they sat in her car watching everyone enter the swim club. Agent Cobb received last-minute details from Guy that corroborated the site of the NC headquarters. She looked the part for the meet, wearing a Stone Ridge High School T-shirt over a bathing suit.

Cody, Aaron, and Guy had been friends, but they were now rivals since Guy left the business in March. They had ignored Guy for six months and were making fun of him for swimming for Oakview during the summer of 2011.

They were the smallest swim team in the county, but his real friends were there. Every team member headed to the Finelli house for a celebration after the meet. Phillip and Carol were ready with one last swim team cookout at their old house. They enjoyed the neighborhood atmosphere and watched thirty-some kids running around with endless energy.

Agent Cobb sat In the IHOP parking lot off of Tech Road in Silver Spring after the meet, waiting for her targets to show up for their normal celebration with the Tanglewood Swim Team. Technically, their team had won the meet, but Cody and Aaron were pulling out the bong in their car to smoke out their personal defeats in the four strokes, medley, and relays races. Anna waited patiently as she tied up her gorgeous, long red hair into a FBI-looking bun. She could not get Guy Finelli out of her head. She was twenty-four in her first year in the FBI, and he was almost seventeen, but his presence and his quiet certitude made him very attractive to her. Of course, his growing physical stature, as well as watching him burn her "perps" in the meet, did not hurt. She would have to be patient for a few years for her chance, but Anna Cobb had become a big fan. What she did not know was that Guy Finelli, like his brother, father, and grandfather, could not resist redheads. It seemed to be a family trait.

Anna waited until the smoke cleared in their car, because she wanted Cody and Aaron happy and confused before arresting them. They were looking forward to a mountain of pancakes with an IHOP breakfast that would settle a case of regular post-swim-meet hunger, complicated now with a severe onslaught of the complicated now with a severe onslaught of the weekend diet of FBI.

CHAPTER 13

It WAS A relief to finally make it to the first official practice in August 2011 at WJ. Coach

Favarro was exploding with excitement inside, but outside he was trying hard not to give special treatment to his prized recruit, other than granting his request for the number twenty-one jersey. Sean Taylor was on mind as he walked out on practice field for the first time wearing the green and white. He thought about the forty-four touchdowns that Taylor scored as a high-school senior in Florida. He figured that some records were never meant to be broken.

WJ's record the previous year was an improving 5-5 in thetop4A division in the county and the state. WJ was not known as a football school, only having had two winning seasons since Phillip played in 1970.

He stepped out on the baseball field for warm-up drills, because the grass was cooler than the state-of-the- art, artificial-turf football field. WJ may have had lean years of winning football seasons, but nothing kept them from having the best field and stadium in the county. Private donations from the upper-class Bethesda parents paid for the recent renovations. There was never any outward pressure from the parents for a winning team.

That would be beneath them. As long as their uniforms looked stylish and the field was a beautifully artificial football-green color, they could watch the game from club boxes above the students-thrilled to see their boys compete in a man's game.

As he jogged around the outfield, it was hard to miss the big number seven attached to the fence, just under the flag flying above the field with the 1992 high-school state baseball championship banner. His half-brother, Alex Santucci, had become a baseball legend at WJ. Guy hoped that one day he would match Alex's achievement in one season playing football for WJ.

Learning names was never a problem for Guy. He had inherited his father's ability to learn facts and statistics like a tape recorder. The plays that Coach Favarro had sent him were now naturally set in his mind, like doing the backstroke without thinking about it.

Guy towered over his teammates. Only tight end/ defensive end Manuel Ortiz and fullback/linebacker Harold Washington were over six feet two. They were the co-captains, and it was their job to bring Guy on board. "Hey, guys...we don't have much time over the next weeks, so let's, you know, snap to it." Harold looked around pensively. "You feel me on this! Guy here is the real deal. If we don't get all bent out of shape about a new white boy leading us to victory, we can do some real damage this year."

Harold stepped back as Manuel spoke next. "Look, homies...we are going to win this division this year without question and get into the playoffs. But we need to work our asses off in practice. No girlfriends hanging around, no texting, no yapping about your sorry-ass life with her during practice. Guy will be the man! Trust me on this." Manuel was excited, but then he challenged his boys: "Look...if you don't like it, leave now, or I'll throw you out. Let's hear it now...'Big Train Football' on three...one, two, three...*Big Train Football!"*

Guy joined his first huddle and met three of the most important pieces of his expansive offensive line: the Letuli triplets, Mammoth, Obed, and Shyam. They were the sons of the American Samoan congressional representative, Tulo Letuli, who had settled in Bethesda on Johnson Avenue over twenty years ago. He became infatuated with the history of Walter Johnson after meeting Dr. Gene Santucci while walking on the Arylawn fields. Gene was playing catch with his son, Alex, and introduced himself to the five-feet-three, 250-pound Tulo Letuli. They became fast friends that spring and watched many of Alex's baseball games at WJ. Tulo wanted his future children to play baseball but changed his mind when his instant family of three boys were born in 1994 and soon appeared ready for sumo wrestling instead of putting on a glove. Six months later, their friendship ended when Gene left for the heavens, but he never left Tulo's heart.

Tulo was moving slowly up the stands at the first practice as Alex's half-brother, Guy Finelli, entered the huddle. The excitement in the air was as thick as the humidity, which made Tulo feel like being in the South Pacific without the sea breezes. He thought of his friend Gene and realized at this moment how much he missed him.

Tulo focused quickly on his boys and their positions. Mammoth played center, with Obed on his right and Shyam on his left. All three were around five feet five and 240 pounds, give or take a couple of steak dinners. Guy towered over the triplets, more than a foot taller, but he was happy to look down on them, realizing he would have very little trouble seeing over them.

His protective forces were sealed on the outside by the two tackles, Albert and Andrew Christian, better known as the Great Danes. They were identical twins from Denmark and both completely deaf. They were over six feet tall and 220 pounds and still growing. Albert was the athletic gem of two, being good in most American sports, but he enjoyed soccer and kickboxing with his brother Andrew. They both could punch and kick with their feet, which had some advantages in football when the referee was not looking.

Playing American football and keeping up their grades gave them a chance to earn scholarships to Galludet University, located in northeast DC. It was established in 1864 as the only federally chartered college for the deaf and hard of hearing in the United States. They lived in their own world of American Sign Language (ASL), but had no trouble understanding their assignments each play from their lip-reading abilities. Their goal each play was to block as many people as possible for as long as possible. They loved the contact of every play, always hoping for a takedown.

Usually, they could not be bothered by getting to know their teammates, but there was something about Guy that had them interested. It was the way he called the plays. They figured that his father must have told him to stop mumbling if he was going to play quarterback, because he talked slowly and moved his lips nicely. They also figured out he was Italian before they knew his last name, because he talked a lot with his hands.

Two of the last three to show up in the huddle were the outside receivers, Duran Hall and Cary Collins. Duran had a Jamaican father who had sprinted in the Olympics and a Panamanian mother who had named him after the great Panamanian fighter, Roberto Duran. He was learning to become a great football player, especially on defense, which he loved. It was learning to catch the ball that was a problem. He had quickly earned the nickname "Dash" because he seemed to be in two places at one time. Cary was lanky and still growing at six feet two, a great athlete who ran precision routes and had great hands.

They were late to practice because of track practice. Best friends since grade school, they ran most of the sprint events for WJ, including the one hundred, two hundred, and four hundred meters, as well as the hurdle events. They had heard about the white boy coming to play QB with the big arm. What they did not realize was how big he really was until he extended his hand to both of them.

The last of the three to join the huddle was the most versatile athlete besides Guy. Mark Pelligrini was mostly quiet to strangers, but he played football like a hyperactive child bouncing off the walls. This fellow Italian was short at five feet seven but a real fighter. He could play any skill position on offense and loved to hit on defense. Coach Favarro called him his GQ player, for his good looks and for "getting quarterback."

Guy knelt down on one knee in the huddle. He told his team that they would play quite a bit of no-huddle offense, so they had to get into the best shape of their lives. He suggested swimming and running five miles a day, because his idea was to win the state

76

championship. "We are going to have twelve main plays to learn and be able to run in our sleep. The receivers will learn audibles to change patterns, but that won't change the formation or the blocking for the rest of you." Guy felt the attention from his players. "Coach Lombardi would run the power sweep a dozen times a game. He would do eight-hour sessions explaining the play to coaches."

Guy could see most of his teammates wondering, *Who is Coach Lombardi?*

"Anyway, the point is...if we run our plays right, we don't need to have a lot of them." Guy knew that his window of opportunity was closing. "This morning we are going to learn six plays, followed by six this afternoon. Tonight, I will stay and throw patterns to any receiver that wants to stay. That's what we're going to do every day. We have three weeks to get ready"

Guy finished and looked up at his teammates. They seemed on board but quiet. Guy stood up and put his helmet on.

Harold Washington put his hand in the middle of the huddle. "Let's break on three...one, two, three...*Big Train Football!*"

Guy soon fell in love with his three versatile receivers, Duran, Mark, and Cary. He named them Sprint DMC after the groundbreaking rap group Run DMC from the eighties. He came up with a three-man formation mostly on the left side to run a whole set of pass patterns, including screens and reverses. The trio over the next few weeks printed up T-shirts and gave interviews as Sprint DMC to the *Gazette* and the high-school newspaper.

Ultimately, as the season was ready to get started, the *Montgomery County Messenger* (MCM) newspaper picked up on the story, and the buzz about the team became electric in the school. For their only preseason scrimmage, they met a state playoff team from Frederick County. Five hundred fans traveled the thirty miles up I-270 to see WJ score ten touchdowns in a set of fifty plays. On defense they gave up only one play of over ten yards. The only problem was a lack of practice for punting or field-goal kicking. Coach Navarro figured that with this juggernaut of a team, he was not planning on doing much of either.

Usually, students would rather clean up their rooms than return to high school in late August, but the anticipation of the first game was spreading as smooth as a late-night peanut-butter-and-jelly sandwich. By Friday night, September 2, 2011, the first game arrived with tickets scarce against Bethesda rival Walt Whitman HS. The highest-income families in the county had put a lot of money into making Whitman a competing team on the football field. WJ had been an easy win on their schedule for many years. Their coach,

Edward E. Cummings, played up all the hype about WJ to his players during practice. He wanted his Whitman boys to play some smash-mouth football and ground the potential WJ attack.

• • •

Guy Finelli had a lot on his mind as his finished his fourth and last period of the day just before eleven in the morning. He was on a work-study program, which meant he would head to Comcast headquarters off of Tech Road in Silver Spring to do a computer programming internship for three hours a day. Even though it was just the first week, it was still a relief to get out of the hallways of his new school. He was still getting used to the layout of the school, like a freshman. He was also not comfortable with all the attention. It was a stark difference to his almost three years in a fog at Northeast HS.

The twenty-minute ride cleared out his head as he played his latest hip-hip download CD. He always smiled when his music started, because he would imagine his parents trying to be cool with it when they really hated it. He had to give his father credit-he only gave him shit about it when he was uptight about something else. His parents' music was pretty cool, but when he was driving alone, he needed his own groove. He parked on the circle before the security entrance because his permit had not come through yet. It was an easy walk in, so he did not mind it.

Suddenly, three guys wearing hoodies and sunglasses jumped him from behind as he got out of the car. Three others joined them behind the car as they wrestled him down and stole his wallet and keys. Two of the smaller ones kicked him in the stomach fifteen to twenty times. Then the biggest guy pulled out a knife and slid it across his right arm, enough to draw a small river of blood.

He whispered in his ear, "Good luck tonight...from all your buddies that you deserted and ratted out!"

Joe Finelli was working hard to stay calm after answering Guy's call. He bolted from Kensington and found Guy lying beside a car in the grass. Helping him to his feet, Joe saw the blood coming from Guy's arm and wrapped a towel around it. He knew he needed stitches, but Guy refused to go to the urgent-care facility in White Oak. Guy felt his ribs and assumed some severely bruised or broken bones. Luckily, he knew his bones did not break easily and was counting on no internal bleeding. The throbbing pain was another problem. Guy drank some water as they sat in Joe's truck. He could barely talk, but he still refused to the urgent-care facility.

"Let's go the CVS and get some bandages and peroxide. I'll go to the emergency room after the game."

Joe looked at him with a crazy stare. Besides the fact that he was half Italian, he reminded people of Shaquille O'Neal. It was something about the short hair and sarcastic looks. "Game? Football, where people are trying to kill you? Are you nuts? You're not playing any football tonight!"

"It's not up to you, cousin. Do you think I'm going to let those morons ruin my dream?"

Joe was not going to argue with him. Guy had a point, and obviously he would have done the same thing when he was a senior in high school. After laughing to himself, he responded, "All right, you're the boss! At least your mother is going to look at it...she's still a nurse, right?"

"My mother...I don't think so. You're my nurse for now!"

Joe had another idea. "I got a guy in Kensington that should be able to help us...he owes me a favor."

● ● ●

The WJ stadium overlooking Democracy Boulevard and Old Georgetown Road had not seen so many people since 1970, when Phillip Finelli played the unbeaten Northern High School. Back then, Old Georgetown Road was used as a training strip for the informal drag racing on Rockville Pike that happened at night for the fastest cars in the county. The meanest of these racers were known as "greasers" from Northern High. The school had also produced the best football players for a twelve- year period and eight unbeaten seasons from the early sixties to the middle seventies. They unleashed four of the most intimidating fullback/linebacker types that terrorized county opponents, and then college football, and finally the NFL. Eight thousand fans had stuffed the old Spartan stadium that Saturday afternoon to watch a county war that left casualties on both sides and an improbable comeback by WJ in a 20-19 victory. Phillip made the spectacular winning TD reception, holding on to the football seconds after tearing three ligaments and all the cartilage, making his last cut.

Today, a crowd of over ten thousand, including many Bethesda yuppie parents, descended upon the WJ stadium to watch the Bethesda battle. Most of the families delayed their Labor Day beach plans until Saturday morning to watch the biggest football game in decades. Even most of the students from both schools descended on the WJ campus after their social-media outlets exploded their phones, naming "Big Train Field" as the place to be.

79

The six o'clock kickoff had been pushed back to seven thirty to accommodate the traffic disaster. Luckily, it helped Coach Favarro, who had been told by his assistant Joe Finelli that Guy had to see a doctor for a stomach ailment and would be there by seven. He tried to stay calm, fearful that his best player would be "out of sorts" for the game. Cousin Joe kept the real news from him, knowing it would destroy his concentration for game preparation.

Dr. Antonio Sanchez had agreed to see Guy in his Bethesda home after finishing his clinic work for the day. He was the son of a waiter at the Finellis' favorite Bethesda restaurant and a family friend who had worked for Joe during his school years in the landscaping business. Antonio had become a veteran of mending knife wounds during his ten years at the Langley Park Health Clinic. He applied eighteen stitches to the wound and found no broken bones. The bruising covering Guy's knees, stomach, chest, arms, shoulders, and back were consistent with many a gang beating, which focused on arm and stomach bruising. Usually, the next beating would escalate to the face, and then broken legs in the next, and so forth.

"You are a lucky man, Mister Guy Finelli. If you play tonight, you might not be able to protect yourself from further blows, and you'll be out for the season. Not to mention opening up the stitches for some serious bleeding. But I doubt that will happen, since I use only the finest stitching in the fashion industry." Antonio added some levity to ease his patient's pain. "I cannot give you any shots for this...it would be too dangerous to cover this pain. Drink a lot of water, keep the ice on it up until game time, and then take ibuprofen ten minutes before you play. Don't bother warming up. It won't help. You will only be able to move for thirty minutes, maybe an hour or so."

"And then what, Doctor?"

"Without a shot to mask the pain, your muscles will just cramp and eventually stop working."

"I told you it's crazy to play," Joe added in futility.

The patient thanked the doctor quietly and moved gingerly out of the office and into Joe's vehicle for the five-minute ride to the locker room to get dressed for the game. Luckily, Joe knew a back way and drove a four-wheel-drive truck.

Guy knew that the beating was not so much gang related but a personal message that some people from Baltimore had not forgotten about him, especially if he was about to become important. It was meant to look like a carjacking to the public. There was not much he could do other than hope his FBI friend would follow up on it.

Assistant Director Brooklyn O'Malley was the second call he had made after the beating. Brooks appreciated the call but already had a surveillance team following the gang of six after the tap on their phone had produced evidence of an assignment involving "getting the rat." The FBI team had secured the car for evidence from the county police, shortly after the gang abandoned it on Route 108 in Olney on their way back to Baltimore.

The DNA from the scene could seal an indictment against the gang if necessary, but Brooks was looking for their cooperation instead. They would be picked up individually over the next week for their information on the Baltimore connection and their attack on Guy Finelli.

O'Malley was upset that his prized connection was beaten right before his first game. It was a delicate matter to insure Guy's safety versus the greater good of the community, taking down the Baltimore connection. The real story could never become public. For as long as Guy lived in the spotlight, he might be in harm's way, even though he was to become his favorite athlete.

Brooks arrived at the field with a crew of a dozen agents dressed as yuppies with earpieces and firearms under their jackets. He was looking forward to watching, in person, WJ kick the shit out of those pussycats from Whitman. He was very grouchy and was ready to see some hitting. His agents knew that further harm to Finelli would entail reassignments to processing paperwork.

Unfortunately, Brooks knew that the incident was payback, but for the first time in years, he was getting closer to the "the Turk" and his empire in West Baltimore. For some reason, this drug lord was taking an interest in Guy Finelli leaving his network. Brooks would figure it out and eventually stop the Turk from sending their best designer-quality methamphetamines and cocaine to the wealthy population of western Montgomery County.

● ● ●

"The Turk" sat in his West Baltimore bunker and was excited to hear that his order was completed and successful. He wanted to make an example of this young athlete, and besides, he had money on the game with some rich coke client giving him fourteen points and Whitman. It was the first Montgomery County game he had fixed to win a bet. Usually, he was content with private-high- school games in the DC-Baltimore area, but he was now moving business into this lucrative county. His boy

81

Rico and the NC connection had opened some doors from him, but losing Rico had been a problem, and now there was heat on the NC. He assumed that Guy Finelli had something to do with it.

• • •

Coach Favarro received a phone call from Joe. He was hoping to hear an update about the stomach ailment but instead heard about the carjacking details. He almost swallowed his gum when he saw in person the bruises on his best player as he removed his shirt. He decided immediately not to play Guy at that point but held his voice until kickoff. Mark Pelligrini would run the offense and the defense. It should be enough to hold off Whitman -at l e a s t , he hoped.

The overflow crowd descended on the game like it was the first day of Woodstock. Tickets at some point became irrelevant, because people were coming in from everywhere. Security was outnumbered, and the festive atmosphere of mostly white yuppies gave a false sense of euphoria to the crowd.

Guy Pinelli had made it to the sidelines, wearing a hooded parka on a warm, early-September evening. He huddled among the coaches during warm-up and stayed with Coach Pavarro and Cousin Joe as the kickoff approached.

A lot of the fans, especially from Whitman, had no idea what Guy Pinelli looked like except that he was supposed to be tall and big, so it was a shock when the short-statured Mark Pelligrini lined up as QB.

His teammates played like they were in shock as well. Blocking and holding on to the football became a foreign language to them as Whitman's defense caused five turnovers in the first half. On defense, WJ could not hold off Whitman's running game after the offense turned over the football, twice, inside their own ten-yard line. When they stuck Whitman deep in their own territory on two series, Whitman surprised WJ with two bombs of over eighty yards to extend the rout to 27-0.

Then the bummer of a first half was completed with the ultimate football embarrassment of a safety. As WJ tried to run out the clock on a kneel-down play from their own two-yard line, center Mammoth Letuli snapped the ball so hard to Pelligrini that it barely skimmed his hands and sailed through the end zone like a missile seeking a target. The widely built Samoan was used to Guy Pinelli's big hands that could catch anything. He became frustrated by the first half of play when he snapped the ball for a surrender play. He walked off the field at halftime to a quiet crowd and a 29-0 message on the scoreboard.

82

Two minutes before the second-half kickoff, Guy Finelli threw off his hoodie, picked up a football, and stared at Coach Favarro. Finally, Coach looked up at Guy and saw an inferno raging in his eyes. His hands were squeezing the football like a dishrag.

"I guess you're ready to play!" It was not a question by Coach Favarro but just a statement of fact. "Well, look...why don't you return the second-half kickoff for a touchdown first, so we can have a flaming reason to play the rest of the game? And try not to get hit by anyone...I'm sure you've had enough beating for one day!"

"Don't worry, Coach; I'm not planning on getting into any more fights today." Guy turned away as his cousin Joe was recruiting the kick return team for some instructions. "This kid can really boom it...but we're returning it right up the middle. Manuel and Harold, pick off the two quickest guys up the middle, and then double back to reinforce on the left side. I want the Great Danes to run a double-team from left to right from the second level. Triplets, give me straight blocks up the middle ahead of Guy from the third level...and DMC, two of you come from left to right with a double-team behind the Samoans, and then Mark, lead Guy up the hole. No front hits on Guy. Now, let's get back into this game."

Harold pulled them together. "Nothing changed, men. We can score five times, no problem...on three...one, two, three...*Big Train Football!*"

The crowd rose in a big yawn, trying to awake from their bad dream of the first half as they noticed the size of number twenty-one running in slow motion onto the field. They mustered up some polite clapping, unaware that every stride he took was sending daggers of pain up his spine, causing tears to seep out the sides of his eyes as he arrived on the goal line, ready to receive the kick.

Sounds from the crowd went dormant in his ears as he focused on the boot of the football that pierced the windless night above the artificial light of the evening. Guy saw through his glass of tears and eyed the ball into his hands, remembering the thousands of punts off his father's foot that he had secured tightly. He could hear only his words as he strode toward the masses of bodies tangling in front of him: "Head straight up the field, make one cut and then accelerate..."

As Guy briskly crossed the twenty-yard line, the Great Danes were galloping across the field in their own world, ready to punch out several Whitman players. The Samoans were bulldozing the middle of the field ten yards behind them, like snowplows clearing the road. Sprint DMC flashed ahead, yelling instructions to each other as they broke off into a double-team block and pushed blue opponents to the side.

Suddenly, Guy saw a clear passage open up as he crossed the twenty-five. He was feeling above the pain in his body as he plowed his right foot into the turf and shifted into his sprinter's speed to finish the next seventy-five yards. Cousin Joe clicked his always-handy stopwatch as Guy crossed the thirty and then watched in silence as he crossed the forty and then midfield. Like a sudden tidal wave, Joe and the WJ sidelines dashed to follow the superhuman event. Forty, thirty, twenty, ten, goal line; Joe clicked his watch and came to a stop. He bent over, put one hand on his sturdy thigh to catch his breath, turned the watch toward him with the other, and read 6.36 seconds!

As he crossed the goal line and returned to human form, Guy turned to find a referee to hand him the football. Finally, the volume of the crowd hit him like a sonic wave. His body flowed with adrenalin that masked his pain. His stitches, hiding under a wrap covered by his shoulder pads, felt numb. He lowered his head and held up his hand to form a huddle. Guy was about to run his first snap from center for the two-point conversion.

His teammates, following the path of acceleration that he left behind, arrived at the scene knowing that something special had just occurred. They instinctively knew to huddle and nix the congratulations. They listened to the play call but were all hard-pressed to remember their assignments. Eventually, they lined up in formation, listening to Guy as he barked out the play, Blue Twenty-One, a dozen times, trying to defeat the volume of the crowd.

Assignments were remembered as Guy waited patiently for his center, Mammoth, to be ready. Obed, on his right, turned to signal his QB that they were ready to run their first play from scrimmage for him. He gently tapped Mammoth, who looked up at the lineman in front of him that he was going to destroy and then took a quick peek between his legs. Mammoth fired him a perfect snap back to the ten-yard line. Guy took a step left and waited for Harold Washington to come right and lead the caravan of blocking. The carnage of Whitman bodies never came near their QB as Guy walked in for two points untouched.

Coach Favarro held out Guy from the defense for the next two series. The Whitman running game and a key pass here or there kept them grinding out yardage and precious time off the clock. As the game entered the fourth quarter, the three-touchdown deficit looked insurmountable, but Coach Favarro still had a plan to unleash Guy Finelli.

As Whitman moved the ball deep into WJ territory, Coach Favarro looked at his best player. "Get in there and stop this drive, but try not to take a shot to your ribs-protect yourself, for God's sake!" His worry about threatening his player's career penetrated his voice.

Cousin Joe ran with Guy as he jogged onto the field. "You know the quick slant is coming on second down...but let them think it, and watch the in-and-out to the corner."

"I got this, cousin...I mean, Coach." Guy smiled back to Joe before he established his position in the middle of the defense. He had been watching the quarterback and every receiver all day. He remembered every pattern they had run, who was slow, and who was fast. He knew they were trying to get greedy and score in the fourth quarter, instead of letting WJ die a slow death. It was always the coaches' fault in high school, he thought, because their egos were so big, remembering Coach Kelly at Northeast. Guy was ready to take advantage of it.

"The Safety" was on defense for the first time all day. He lined up behind Harold at linebacker on the first play as a Whitman halfback ran for a couple of yards. He stayed inside Pelligrini on second down, near the tight end, leaving the middle open for the slot receiver. Mark made the tackle on the slant in for a six-yard gain.

Third and two on the WJ twenty-three-yard line, Guy lined up inside the slot receiver on the right side and faked a blitz, the QB faked the handoff and looked for the slant again. Mark stepped inside to make a play, but the QB pumped, and the slot headed out toward the corner of the end zone, wide open-except for Finelli, who had faked the blitz, pushed the outside receiver to the ground, and turned his back to the QB, heading for the goal line. He looked up and saw the imperfect spiral heading toward the slot receiver, who was smiling, thinking about how his girlfriend was going to treat him well tonight. Guy cut to his left and leapt into the air to catch the ball "Jerry Smith-style," with his thumbs facing each other. As he landed on his feet at the one-yard line, in one motion he turned, kept in-bounds, and headed up the sidelines with a caravan of the Samoans, joined by Manuel and Harold in front. Whitman wanted no part of the blocking clinic as Guy waltzed untouched again into the end zone. Guy completed his first pass as a QB to Duran Hall for the two- point conversion.

With less than four minutes to play, Whitman's coach Cummings felt confident with a 29-16 lead. But still, Coach Favarro was hesitant to keep playing Guy on defense with the game looking dire. Whitman crossed midfield and faced a third and five to ice the game with less than two minutes to go. Guy headed in and guessed the next play. He stacked Mark to his right and told Duran to blitz from his left corner position and look for the pitch on the option play. The line shifted to the right.

Guy timed the snap and headed from his safety position to the QB to force a quick throw instead. He ran through the QB, hitting him with his left shoulder as he threw to the halfback on a swing pattern, who caught it with a smile on his face, knowing it would ice the game. He turned to head for the first down. Immediately, Duran

Hall rammed his helmet rudely into his stomach. The ball popped into the air like a rocket as Guy Finelli circled back toward the play after disposing of the QB. He grabbed the football on its return flight and turned on his own booster engines to power himself for the fifty-yard ride into the endzone.

The two-point conversion was unsuccessful as Harold Washington dropped a pass as he was walking into the end zone. Guy collapsed as he was hit on his right side after making the throw. He bent over, trying to gasp some air into his lungs as the pain reached an unbearable level. He let out a scream as the air returned to his lungs. The Christian brothers got him to his feet as he tried to control his breathing. He slowly walked to the sidelines, hoping his adrenaline would return to cover his pain.

Whitman ran three unimaginative plays into the WJ defense for no gain as Guy caught his breath on the sidelines. The 29-22 lead with fifteen seconds left seemed insurmountable as they faced a fourth down from their own twenty-three-yard line.

During their final time-out, Guy ran onto the field for the punt return. Cousin Joe called a huddle for the return team and spoke in double-time. "Let's go right-side with this...get their gunners double-teamed...let them nowhere near Guy when he catches the ball...now, push them left...curl back to midfield, and block for a throwback...just don't make it obvious." Joe was out of breath as he tried to finish his instructions. "Cary, you're the biggest target...get way outside on the left...everybody block to the middle...get down the sidelines, Cary... Guy, get to midfield at least...heave it across the field...you won't have any blocking over there, so be careful."

"Thanks for the warning. Don't worry; I got this, Coach." Guy managed a smile as he headed past midfield to return the punt.

The kick was a boomer. Guy headed back to the twenty-five and turned on an angle to catch the punt at full speed as he crossed the thirty. He outran the initial wave of contain to get to the right. At the forty, he saw blue jerseys heading across midfield. He crossed the forty-five with no blockers and a wall of blue ready for a collision. Finelli took one long stride and hurdled the first two defenders. He landed just in front of two more defenders and then skied again into the air, turned to his left, and fired a jump pass as he crossed midfield. The football traveled in a perfect spiral for the 160-foot width of the field.

The lanky Cary Collins turned and caught sight of the football coming in his direction. He was straddling midfield, eyeing a perfect lateral following the fifty-yard marker and into his arms. With Duran Hall and Mark Pelligrini in front of him now, they started down the sidelines with six seconds left on the clock. It seemed to be clear sailing until the twenty-three-yard line, when Cary panicked and saw three defenders coming across the field. He cut back inside at the fifteen, bypassing all but one of the defenders who grabbed him at the ten. The crowd saw the clock hit four zeros as Collins appeared to be the last soldier trying to reach freedom, valiantly making it to the five-yard line. His body seemed to be falling in slow motion as he twisted, keeping himself above the artificial surface of defeat. A roar of thunder from the cheering WJ wall of sound turned into screams of despair.

Suddenly, a monster of green, wearing number twenty-one, was yelling, "Flip it! Flip it!" The ball seemed to be fighting gravity as Collins released it, and the outstretched hands of Guy Finelli scooped the ball three inches from the turf and quickly crossed the goal line to get within one point-29-28. Guy knelt down immediately, hoping to catch his breath. He knew that the two-point conversion would be a piece of cake to complete, if he could stop from passing out. Running was out of the question, but throwing one more pass was possible.

Guy slowly moved to take his position. He leaned over with his hands on his knees and closed his eyes. The pain in his side was overwhelming. His breathing was barely grabbing enough oxygen. To distract himself, he thought of his namesake, Guy I, and his great saving tackle in his first game, and his father Phillip's clutch catch in desperate pain to win a championship. And finally, he thought of Sean Taylor, who was murdered before his greatness was realized by everyone.

He knew that it was his job to create a legacy to honor his heroes, and winning this game would be his start. He looked at the number on his jersey and felt a surge of strength in his legs. He rubbed the stitches on his shoulder and felt the power of his arm. He stood back on the fifteen- yard line and yelled with very little breath, "Extra point number one." In a whisper to his fellow Italian, Mark Pelligrini, on the left wing, he added, "It's coming to you, Paisano!"

He caught the perfect snap from Mammoth and looked on his right at Cary Collins to move the safety, then to Manuel in the middle to draw the linebacker, and finally to Duran Hall on the left to distract the corner. Delay... delay...delay... Pelligrini released out of the backfield, turned, and caught the football for the winning two points and a 30-29 victory.

Guy lifted his left arm into the air and pointed high in the stands, hoping that his final bit of energy would reach his parents. He knew the legacy was still alive.

• • •

In late November 2011, the state championship game was iced by Guy Finelli's forty-fourth scoring TD of the year, setting a Maryland state record for one season and tying Sean Taylor's Florida high-school record. On the last offensive drive with four minutes left in the state title game and WJ comfortably ahead 38-21, Guy refused a chance to score from the one-yard line on a roll out to the right side. Instead, he fired a throwback screen across the field to Cary Collins to finish the scoring. It seemed like a nice payback for a teammate who had saved the season. The 44-21 victory in the championship final finished a 14-0 season.

CHAPTER 14

"Freshmen Finelli Ready to Be the Next Great Safety"

$\mathbf{P}$HILLIP FINELLI! Put down newspaper after reading about his son, Guy Finelli, and his breakout first season at UMD. He thought about the past fifteen months of achievements in sports by his two sons, starting with Guy's high-school championship year, followed by Alex's MVP championship baseball season, and now a chance for Guy to win an ACC division title.

He would join Carol, Alex and Sally Keegan at Carter- Finley Stadium on the state fairgrounds in Raleigh, North Carolina. Tailgating was a Raleigh requirement on this beautiful, late-November Saturday as their daughter, Grace, hosted a parking-lot party wearing her Wolfpack attire with a dozen fellow students. The expansive fairgrounds were a short two miles from the NC State campus, where Grace lived just off campus.

The Wolfpack fans were on their best behavior when their famous Maryland guests arrived for some barbeque and com on the cob. The first couple of baseball, Alex and Sally, drew consistent but mannerly attention during the party. Sally received congratulations on the announcement of her pregnancy, due in late June. The couple had decided to send it out on their Twitter account, which now had over five million followers and was growing exponentially since their wedding day almost three months ago on Labor Day. The deed had been done on their trip to Charlottesville in October to see Guy play against Virginia. In Sally's mind, the celebration of the victory and the conception of their future twins were in line with the growing destiny of this family.

Anna Cobb, Charlotte Roberts (Alex's Step-Sister), and Patty O'Neil (family friend) also made the trip to see Guy Finelli play in Raleigh. All redheads, they had become friends during the fall following his games. Anna, the FBI agent who had played an undercover role in the NC takedown, had a severe crush on Guy as well as a major concern for his welfare after his beating before the first game of his senior high-school season. All the redheads had crushes on Guy and had dated him over the past year at some point. They had no sense of jealously with each other, just an overall concern for Guy's future. They were all older and never thought about settling down with him, but at the same time, they never avoided the opportunity to be with him. This protective trio kept the growing number of College Park groupies away from Guy.

"I hope you three have not been wearing out Guy before this big game!" Sally joked to the trio as they all surrounded the barbeque. They were watching Grace and her boyfriend grill the sausages, pork ribs, and hamburgers.

"I think Anna 1s going to have to answer that question... Patty and I have been on our best behavior since the summer." Charlotte clicked her beer with Patty, followed by a big gulp.

"Actually, girls, I'm just doing my job as a law enforcement officer...to serve and protect!" Anna burst into laughter after trying to keep a straight face.

"Hey, that's a little too much information about my brother. Please, girls, if you can't mind your manners... you know, we are in the South!" Grace retorted, throwing her beautiful, black hair back over her head as she came from behind the cooker to give hugs to all the women. "My goodness...Sally, how can you hang out with such a crowd of unruly girls?"

"Being in academics, I have credentials to supervise these girls...not very well, I might add! I'm going to have two of my own to take care of soon, and I expect babysitting volunteering from all of you...and no boyfriends sneaking over to fool around!" Sally hugged Grace while Charlotte, Patty, and Anna all joined 1n, wanting details of the first trimester.

A tide of red-and-white attire was flowing into their seats from the sunny side of beached UMD fans to the shady side of well-dressed NC State patrons. UMD players wore helmets that also included the black, gold, red, and white of the state flag. Otherwise, UMD were in all-white uniforms with red numbers, and the Wolfpack wore just the opposite. UMD quietly made it to their sidelines as the Wolfpack machine of noise hit high volume and the players swarmed the field with confidence.

The Wolfpack prepared to lay a good licking on these upstarts Terps and this freshman Finelli player with a veteran team of juniors and seniors in the lineup. The coaching staff had emphasized all week that this game could be a post-Thanksgiving turkey shoot because UMD had a bunch of young turkeys running around the field.

They would pay dearly after the game for ignoring the game plan for Guy Finelli. His high-school coach at Northeast had made the same mistake, figuring a true freshman could not make an impact in a varsity game.

The Wolfpack head coach, Riley Roland, had seen the film of sloppy special teams played by other teams that had led to Finelli's six TDs on punt and kickoff returns. He had also witnessed opposing QBs that seemed to simply throw the ball right to him on the five interception returns for TDs. At three in the morning, with just nine hours to game time, Riley woke up from a nightmare and decided to put on a pot of coffee and review more film of Finelli. As he viewed the UMD defense over and over, back and forth, like a Ferris wheel changing directions with every cycle, he worked through most of the pot of coffee. The darkness before a beautiful Raleigh morning did little to hide the play of Guy Finelli on film. Roland had to admit to himself that the other five interceptions by Finelli not for TDs had been nice plays. And he never used the fair catch on punts -*How neat is that,* he thought to himself. And the way he could recover fumbles was uncanny. And the four TDs as a receiver were really precise patterns. "That boy is really an athlete," Coach Roland said out loud, realizing he was becoming a big fan of Guy Finelli.

His heart was pounding now, as he once again had overloaded on caffeine. He froze the film showing Finelli making an interception against an All-ACC receiver, who was over six feet tall. He blew up the image and could not believe what he saw. "Boy...that kid is really, really big."

Roland looked around and hoped no one was up in the house hearing him talk to himself. Then he restarted the film in super-slow motion to see the whole play. He realized he could not get enough of this kid, and for the twentieth time, he watched the young athlete outleap the senior receiver and pull away from him down the sidelines like a cheetah just warming up. He realized, even in super- slow motion, that he was moving quickly. Roland finally stood up, shut off the film, and said in his full voice-what was screaming in his head: "Wow, that boy is really, really fast!"

Guy's opening-game kickoff return for a TD set the table for a UMD rout, followed by the appetizers of a pass interception TD return and a punt TD return to post a 21-0 lead before his team had an offensive play. The offense prepared a main course with two exquisite drives finished with TD runs by Emmitt Excel and topped by a FG to extend the lead to 38-10. Finelli finished by serving a dessert of two interception returns that topped the great meal of football for UMD fans. Luckily, they had left enough appetite after stuffing themselves on Carolina barbeque during the pregame tailgate party. Their young team, led by their talented freshman star, cooked up a feast that would never be forgotten in the state of North Carolina. By the end of the game, the partisan crowd of sixty thousand was overwhelmed by UMD fans cheering as Guy Finelli scored an unheard-of five TDs without scoring on an offensive play.

UMD's performance in the ACC championship game was in stark contrast to the Saturday after Thanksgiving in Raleigh, when they taught the Wolfpack a severe 52-

10 lesson. In Charlotte, the young, upstart UMD squad played well in the ACC championship game, but they could not stop the running game of the Virginia Tech (VT) squad and fell 12-9. And for the first time all season, Guy Finelli was denied an interception or a TD score. After watching the previous week's game, the VT coaching staff knew they had to win with their running game. They won by controlling the football for almost forty of the sixty minutes of play. Finelli was credited with an amazing twenty-one tackles, as he had to play like a linebacker to stop holes in his defensive line to keep them out of the end zone. The VT kicking game was outstanding as well-besides kicking four field goals, all their kickoffs went through the end zones, and their punts were angled perfectly toward the sidelines and patrolled like a Navy Seal team.

There was no shame in UMD's effort that just a missed chance to play on New Year's Day in the Orange Bowl. Each man on the young squad made his goal for the 2013 season-"At least...Miami Beach!"

• • •

The 2012 holiday season brought a great sense of joy and relief to the Finelli family because of the gifts they had received during the year. The marriage of Alex Santucci and Sally Keegan was the highlight, followed by the baseball championship and MVP won by Alex and the Washington Presidents. He was now a folk hero in his hometown, and he and his wife were the most sought- after couple in the DC area and maybe throughout the country.

Sally privately struggled with the newfound fame but embraced her role of love and support of Alex's career. Her future of being an associate professor at Kansas University (KU) was now on hold with the pregnancy and the whirlwind of the previous baseball season.

There was another job she had assumed, besides speaking engagements with the foundation that was started with the Washington Presidents, which was to look after what she broadly called the Finelli women. This group of females included mostly relatives but also friends that all seemed to be involved somehow with the brothers Alex and Guy. Sally found herself caring deeply for all of them. It might have been the hormones from the pregnancy kicking in, but in the past few months, these women had made her feel wanted and needed. The special sorority of women included the high-achieving in-laws, Carol, Grace, and Florence Finelli; her all-caring mother- in-law, Laura Santucci; housemates Dr. Natalie Woodson, reporter Bonnie Bramlett, Patty O'Neil, and Charlotte Roberts; and finally, the FBI agent, Anna Cobb.

The three redheads, Patty, Charlotte, and Anna, had so much in common that they easily became fast friends. Sally was the influential counselor for the trio, steering the boat down the river of emotions when it came to feelings for her brother-in-law, Guy Finelli. His newfound fame had happened mostly under the radar of his brother's performance until the last few months.

In her eyes, this was a good thing, because Guy clearly had some issues following him. She had heard about the beating and knifing in 2011 when she was dating Alex. That was when Anna Cobb first came into the picture. She seemed to be his guardian angel ever since that event and now was becoming the leading redhead in his life. Charlotte had been briefly involved physically with Guy during the summer; then Patty had come onto the scene in the fall after a Halloween party, and now Anna was playing the romantic lead.

Unbelievably, they all seemed committed to keeping the young UMD coeds from derailing Guy's life, along with preventing any future physical attacks. It was not unusual for them to do social events with four or six of them together. Mark Pelligrini, Duran Hall, and Cary Collins rotated as escorts for Charlotte and Patty. The redheaded friends did not at all mind being a part of this good- looking entourage.

• • •

The dream was unusual for Guy. He rarely had dreams, but recently, someone or something seemed to be talking to him right before he woke up. His habit of falling asleep to *SportsCenter* at night had been with him since the HDTV arrived in the basement in the Oakview house five years ago. Sometimes, the sportscasters seemed to be talking to him or about him. He could swear that Sean Taylor and Jerry Smith were being interviewed by that bald UMD alumnus that liked Alex.

He never had the dream when he stayed at Anna Cobb's place because there was no HDTV in her apartment. It seemed un-American to him, but she was worth the sacrifice. Anyway, he was awake now and wanted to get to his dad's house to be the first one there. His College Park apartment with roommates Mark Pelligrini and Cary Collins had been the perfect answer to keep in shape in the off-season.

Alex had purchased a condo for him with twenty-four- hour security at the end of the football season. Guy was overwhelmed with gratitude but not surprised at Alex's oversight. The spring semester and the first month of his summer break had been a great chance to concentrate on his studies, as well as his and Anna's bodies. Besides their great attraction to each other, they shared a passion for fitness. She also taught Guy how to defend himself in a fight, along with kicking and punching if necessary. She lived nearby, so he had been progressively spending more time alone with her at her apartment.

He had grown another inch during the spring and was now bordering on six feet six in his bare feet and was total muscle at 235 pounds. His training regimen included trading a mile of swimming and weight work one day and five miles of running and yoga the next. Anna joined him on most days to give him some competition.

He had grown another inch during the spring and was now bordering on six feet six in his bare feet and was total muscle at 235 pounds. His training regimen included trading a mile of swimming and weight work one day and five miles of running and yoga the next. Anna joined him on most days to give him some competition.

The morning started with a perfect dawn for an ideal day on Friday, June 7, 2013, as Guy drove on 1-495 past his old neighborhood to Kensington, trying to beat the sunrise at 5:42 a.m. He loved this time of the year because it was daylight for almost fifteen hours. He remembered the evenings spent at the pool with his Oakview friends in June, waiting for sunset and the edge of darkness after nine. It was the just the beginning of the night when they would head the few blocks to their yards in the neighborhood to run and play until exhaustion.

He arrived on Everett and Parkwood at 5:15 a.m., a time when Phillip Finelli would be serving the *Washington Daily* from the age of seven until his late high-school years. Guy opened the back door, carrying the newspaper, coffee, and a box of Dunkin' Donuts, and stationed himself at the kitchen counter.

Unexpectedly, Carol was the first one to greet him. Surprised and excited to see her handsome boy, she screamed out, "Gaetano James...what are you doing here so early?" She eyed him and smelled the rich fragrance that she desperately needed. "Do you have coffee already for me?" Then, noticing the dozen doughnuts in their familiar box, she finally deciphered his mission. "Right... your dad's sixtieth birthday...just when I thought you were corning to see me," she said with a big smile. "Oh, he will be so excited to see you." She grabbed her large coffee with two hands. "I'm all set now...so you go to the bedroom and surprise him."

Guy jumped at the chance to complete his mission and went to see his dad, who was surprisingly still asleep in bed. He held a large coffee next to him with the plastic top opened so the aroma would entice him. One eye popped open, then Guy took out a glazed doughnut and situated it on the top of the coffee, along with the rolled- up *Washington Daily,* folded like he did as a boy. The smell of the damp paper, the freshness of the dough, and the impending sugar saturation accomplished the mission; quickly, Phillip managed to rise to a sitting position.

"Wow... this is some birthday present...cream-filled and glazed doughnuts, and coffee in bed! This is going to be hard to beat today." He rumpled his son's hair while they hugged with great devotion. Phillip felt the blessed moment deep inside but could only manage a distraction out of his mouth. "Maybe you do have the early-morning Finelli gene!"

Father and son devoured the dozen doughnuts in ten minutes and rode the sugar high for the next hour discussing the sports section. After reading about the Washington Presidents' rainout last night, they called Alex, hoping to catch him in bed before his morning workout. They were a little too late, as they heard the commotion of Carol and Alex greeting in the family room. Alex had finished his run to greet his dad on his birthday and maybe to steal some breakfast. He would soon be pissed that the doughnuts were gone, especially the cream-filled. "What the hell...you guys are like ravaging wolves," he exclaimed, noticing the white powder all over them like a scene from *Scarface*. "Thanks for saving me one."

"Like we knew you were coming."

"Little brother...I'm always up early."

The wake-up celebration with his two sons to start his sixtieth birthday was more than Phillip could imagine. He was stunned by the sound of sixty. Little could erase the voice in his head that was calculating the years he had left. Was it five, ten, fifteen, twenty? Maybe twenty- five, certainly thirty years tops. His adorable, Asian-looking cardiologist promised she could get him to at least eighty-five with the right medication. She was very bright, confident, and barely weighed triple digits. Phillip reminded himself often to trust her and keep losing the extra weight.

After a period of darkness in the nineties, he had started to realize how much he had to live for. He found a new freedom in his real-estate career and loved being home in the afternoons with the kids. There was so much to do and follow with his children grown and now ready to produce babies. He suddenly thought about Sally's pregnancy and hoped the twins would be Gemini babies like himself.

The sugar from the doughnuts was producing random thoughts in his head. He was looking forward to everyone being together for dinner later in the day.

His cousin Philly in NYC had already texted him, "Happy birthday...I'll see you for dinner!" It would be special to celebrate their birthdays together as double- first cousins, born on the same day only minutes apart but states away. Only Aunt Helen was

95

left of the brother- sister Finellis marrying the sister-brother Angeluccis. He thought of his parents, Guy Anthony Finelli and Rose Angelucci Finelli, both passed, and how excited they would have been to see everyone at his upcoming party.

Phillip felt a rush of emotion thinking of his parents, and then he thought of Uncle Pietro and that he needed to see him. So much to experience...damn those doughnuts. By the end of the day, it would all be too hard to remember. He heard Alex's phone ring, and Alex's face turned serious as he ran his right hand through those blond locks of beautiful hair while he finished the phone call, obviously from Sally, with, "I'll see you at the hospital."

• • •

Sally had awoken before dawn as Alex had quietly left for a morning run. It was getting hard to get out of bed, now that she was in her thirty-seventh week of pregnancy, so she propped herself up and continued with her romance novel, which did little to distract her from discomfort.

She was starting to feel overwhelmed by the w e i g h t of the twins that were lodged on most of her organs. Since Mother's Day, her activities had been limited, not leaving the house except for short walks. They had moved to a small mansion on beautiful Glenbrook Road near downtown Bethesda. Major renovations were just winding up. Otherwise, she had too much to do and no energy to do it. The Pinelli girls had been amazing, keeping watch over her and getting her anything she needed. Charlotte and Patty would be over in the morning to check in on her.

It was time to travel to the bathroom-it had been four hours since her last visit, twice as long as she could last during the day. She felt like a large house as she rolled to the side and planted her feet on the floor. Gravity seemed to make the trip a lot more necessary. Shuffling to the throne, she knew that something was coming quick. She managed to make a pleasant landing just as the relief started. She thought about the day providing some excitement to the boredom of the pregnancy. The birthday dinner at Phillip's house was the one event that she was not planning to miss. Suddenly, there was an unusual feeling between her legs. Something was flushing water other than the toilet beneath her. She looked down below her protruding belly and saw the evidence-her water had broken.

After a call to Dr. Natalie Woodson, Charlotte and Laura brought Sally to Georgetown hospital about seven miles through rush-hour traffic. Laura knew all the back streets from

Johnson Avenue, having to meet her husband, Gene, there over the years. She remembered his years of residency there while the boys were young, as they crossed into DC on Massachusetts Avenue. Dr. Santucci would be in his white lab coat with that great head of hair, when she would bring him dinner for his overnights at the hospital.

For a moment, she wondered if he would be walking the halls when they arrived. Then the honking of the cars snapped her out of the memory, and she sent Charlotte around Ward Circle to Nebraska Avenue.

Alex ran straight home from Phillip's to change and head to the hospital. He covered the two-and-a-half-mile sprint in twelve minutes and felt great. It helped him deal with all the excitement he was feeling from the news. Phillip would follow in the car to his house and bring him to the hospital. When they all arrived, Dr. Natalie met them at the maternity wing and introduced them to Athena Edmunds, who was the head nurse of everything at Georgetown hospital. She had been looking forward to leaving her mainly administrative position for this day to take care of her close friend Carol's stepson and stepdaughter-in-law. Athena had been a longtime Oakview neighbor of the Finellis, living down the street for all those years of child rearing. She was looking forward to catering to the royal couple of DC after getting a call from Carol about the impending twins after last Thanksgiving. Carol wanted to leave nothing to chance and recruited Natalie and Athena to oversee the birth of their grand-twins.

The ob-gyn had filled in Natalie and Athena about Sally's condition as Alex and Phillip arrived. Natalie met them in the parking garage and quietly guided them along the quietest and most direct route to get to Sally. "She is doing quite well because Laura got her here so quickly; we have her on IV medication. Sally will be comfortable soon."

"You convinced her to take the epidural, I hope! Sometimes she believes she is made of steel, just very hardheaded," Alex laughed as Phillip worked hard to keep up with them. "Natalie, we might have to slow down for the birthday boy...he's sixty today!"

"Oh... happy birthday, Mr. Finelli. I can order a birthday cake for the suite. We might be here all day."

"Thank you...please call me Phillip; I feel old enough. And slow down, for Christ's sake!"

They each took an arm and squeezed him gently to feel loved, not hurried. As they entered the delivery suite, Phillip realized that Dr. Woodson had them well taken care of. Alex had ordered the Four Seasons Suite at an extra $20,000, which included the catered food and drinks. Little did Phillip know that Carol and Guy had been on the phone all morning getting the birthday dinner party moved to the hospital suite.

Sally appeared to be ready for the movie role of a mother about to have twins instead of the normal, panicked person fearing the pain and agony of childbirth. She looked beautiful with her designer baby delivery outfit over a maternity gown. She had been walking around every fifteen minutes or so, as the babies were moving quickly to be delivered around dinnertime. She had called Carol and asked that everybody be invited down to the hospital suite so that Phillip's party would not be interrupted.

"Alex... the babies are coming! The doctor says everything is fine. Oh, my God. My parents are flying in from Kansas. Can you believe this is happening?" After diving into Alex's huge chest and arms, she arose and noticed Phillip. "Phillip...you are so dear to come down... I'm ruining your birthday party!"

"Sally, you look fantastic...please, this is the best present I could ever receive. I couldn't be happier!"

Dr. Natalie interrupted the love fest. "I think Miss Energy here should rest some. We can all go into the next room and relax." She happily escorted them into the potential party room next door. It was nice to feel some male hormones next to her skin. Since her divorce, all of her time was given to her surgery practice. She really liked Alex, but something about Phillip gave her a tingle inside as she took a little longer to settle him into couch to watch *SportsCenter.*

The next eight hours became a strange mix of waiting for the babies and the dinner-party guests to arrive. A steady rain outside had already postponed Alex's game tonight for the second day in a row. God was willing to give him a day off for the baby delivery, he guessed. He planned to take off the weekend, but if everything went well, Sally would make him leave for the Saturday-night game and the Sunday doubleheader.

Cousin Philly arrived to compete with Dr. Natalie for Phillip's attention. She quietly left to do some rounds with patients, but she assured him that she would be back for the dinner. Philly had made it to sixty with a youthful style that would impress the New York fashion elite.

"My dear cousin, you look ready to be sixty and a grandfather. Can you stand it? You must be living the right way! Where are Carol and Grace? Are they coming soon?"

Phillip always knew her godchild Grace would replace him for Philly's attention as soon as she arrived. They both had the same personality trait of commanding attention in the most subtle of ways. Together they blended in a sophisticated elegance. "Yes, my dear, in a few hours before the dinner, I suppose. Will you stay with us for a few days? How is your mom...Aunt Helen?"

"I look forward to some time together with you and my dear Grace. My mom is fine and sends her best. Is this all really happening today, on our birthday? This is too good to believe-almost scary!"

The party was grand. Sally was able to attend parts of it, with an IV keeping her hydrated and dripping enough drugs to keep her body happy. After the birthday cake, she quietly retreated to her room with Alex and delivered two beautiful, healthy babies in the next hour, a boy and a girl. Sally was resting in Alex's arms while Nurse Athena took both babies to a team of neonatal doctors to check out the three-week-early duo.

Sally whispered to her husband, "You know what God wants us to name them..."

"I guess I do, my dear...if it's all right with you."

"I would be honored to have those names."

Athena took the babies to the couple, both cleaned up and nestled in blankets. "Do we have names for these beautiful creatures yet?"

Sally sat up strongly and held her daughter as Alex held his son. She looked directly at Athena with her answer. "I think Phillip and Philomena would be great names for our babies."

Athena thought of Phillip and knew he would be pleased. She also knew about the twin cousin that looked just like him. She dreamed about seeing her closet in Manhattan and shopping with her at Saks Fifth Avenue in Chevy Chase on the way home. She came back to reality as she added a baby to each of her strong arms. "I think it would be hard to do any better. Your family will be excited to see them next door. Now, you get some rest. I will take care of Phillip and Philomena for a few hours.[11]

As Athena took the babies through the family room and announced the names, the two cousins sat together on the couch, crying in each other's arms with great happiness. Phillip heard his phone quietly appealing for his attention. Moments later, Philly felt her phone vibrating from her purse. In unison they picked up them phones, looked at each other, and heard the voice saying- Uncle Pietro had just passed away.

Part II

Now Present

The Finelli- Angelluci Family Tree 2013

Geraldo Finelli and Philomena Finelli
(Died 1/19/53)   (Died 1984)
Children
Gaetano (Guy I) Finelli / Pietro Finelli / Helen Finelli
(Died 8/21/93)   (Died 6/72013)

Phillip Angelucci & Rosina Angelucci
(Died 1955)   (Died 1967)
Children
Ernesto Angelucci / Rose Angelucci
(Died 9/4/2012)   (Died 7/7/2010)

Guy I Finelli married Rose Angelucci 1944
Children

Ernesto Angelucci married Helen Finelli 1951
Children

Anthony Finelli   Phillip Finelli   Joseph Angelucci   Philomena (Philly) Angelucci
(Born 1944)   (Born 6/7/53)   (Born 1952 Died 9/4/69)   (Born 6/7/53)

(Anthony, Phillip, Joseph, Philly are known as Double First Cousins. All with the same Grandparents)

Anthony Finelli married Florence Gray 1966
Children

Phillip Finelli married Carol Werner 1986
Children

Child w/ Leah Raines 1976)

Melissa Finelli   Joseph Finelli   *Alex Santucci   Grace Finelli   Gaetano (Guy)Finelli
(Born 1967)   (Cousin Joe-Born 6/4/70)   (Born 8/8/76)   (Born 11/2/91)   (10/04/94)
                                          **Charlotte Roberts
                                          (Born 8/8/83)

*Adopted by Dr. Gene Santucci and Laura Santucci
**Step-Sister to Alex, fathered by Dr. Gene Santucci
(Died 8/15/91)

Alex Santucci married Sally Keegan 2012
Children (Twins -Born 6/72013)
Phillip II Santucci Philomena (Philly II) Santucci

CHAPTER 15

ARE YOU EVER going to go out with us for a brew or something?" Mark Pelligrini resorted to pleading as he saw his roommate Guy Finelli deep in his studies. He was taking four classes during the 2013 summer, because he had decided to graduate in three years. After a stunning freshman football performance for UMD, Guy was aiming to play two more years, win two college championships, and then get ready for the 2015 professional football draft.

His roommates were taking the five-year plan for college studies. They had red-shirted their first year as walk-ons at UMD and still had four years of college eligibility left. Neither Mark Pelligrini nor Cary Collins had notions of leaving school early for the pro football draft, so they were soaking in all the college pleasures in the meantime.

"Mark's right, bro... how much studying can you do at one time? A man needs to take in some delight after eight hours of work, and if my watch is right, you were sitting in that exact spot when I left for work before seven this morning. Who does that?" Cary stood over Guy with his six-foot, four-inch frame and tried to guilt him out of his focused stupor.

"All right...you morons." Guy checked his phone for messages and the time. It said five o'clock, and he had not eaten all day. "I need to get some major food soon. You guys can mainline some brews. I have to stay awake to study this evening, plus..."

"Oh, Jesus...that redhead has you by the balls, man. What's the story?" Mark, eight inches shorter, moved up to hide behind Cary. "She's not even that hot," he added, hoping to elicit an emotional response out of Guy.

Cary turned around to double-high-five with his shorter roommate. Mark, feeling encouraged, went for the killer shot.

"Now, that Patty chick is hot. Why aren't you banging her?"

"Well, maybe they're both coming over tonight!" Guy rose and tackled both of them into the couch. "I can't believe I let either of you guys live here. What was I thinking?" Guy held them both down rather easily, but something was telling him that they were enjoying their captivity, because they had done their job. Guy released his smiling prey and hit the door to get some food, leaving them to catch up with his trail. He made it to his car and waited for the instigators to catch up. It gave him a moment to think about Anna coming over that night. It would be a reward for a week's worth of laborious studying. There was something about having her gun in the room that made the sex exciting. She loved it when he investigated her, playing a detective.

Duran Hall joined them at Ledo's Restaurant, now on Knox Road and US Route 1, in the middle of College Park. For years the flagship location for square pizza had its only restaurant in Adelphi on University Boulevard, about a mile from campus. As a kid, Guy and his family would drive the three miles from Oakview to eat dinner. On one side was a sit-down restaurant, and on the other was a bar that had televisions hanging down to watch sports. Going back to the sixties, it was one of the first sports bars in Maryland. His dad would always get a large sausage- and-green-pepper pizza with anchovies on the side and an antipasto salad. Carol would order a medium cheese pizza with extra sauce, light on the cheese. Grace would put anchovies on the cheese pizza and ask for basil to put on it. That never made any sense to Guy. How could you go light on the cheese and not want sausage and green peppers?

"Coach said I got the scholarship!" Duran announced as he sat down. "I'm in for the fall. We're all going to be back together in the defensive backfield."

"Who said that?" Cary asked with a puzzled look.

"I heard it too, Collins...they think Guy can round us into shape! I'm all for it. Did you hear that Coach Favarro and Cousin Joe are coaching the special teams?"

"No shit...man, we got Big Train Football coming to UMD. I can't believe I'm going to be here, man. The past year at Towson was rough...no women of color up there. It was brutal, man, just stuck-up white chicks."

"Well, Duran, you'll have your choice down here, man. They'll be crawling all over you...being a brother and all that!"

"Pelligrini, how does Finelli put up with you, man?"

"He loves me...right, Finelli?"

"I love all you guys. We're all going to be together in the D-backfield this year and shock the Big Ten in 2014. Collins and Hall, you'll be man-up all the time on the corners. Pelligrini will be cutting the tight ends and slots up for lunch and stuffing the run. And I'll be doin' the rest!" Guy stood up with his slice of pizza and raised it over his head. "Yes, I am 'the Safety'!"

For a moment, there was quiet, as his teammates saw their normally calm and quiet

103

leader make a rare spectacle of himself. Guy cautiously retreated to his seat, holding the pizza. DMC fired balls of napkins at Guy as he tried to hide behind the pizza. The awkward display of Guy's pronouncement had been soothed by his adoring teammates through endless joking and roughhousing. As they settled down to finish the pizza, they were also digesting the testimonial made by the future superhero himself-Guy Finelli was "the Safety."

• • •

His eyes were unfocused from the twelve hours of studying, and he now had the beginnings of a headache. He remembered to take ibuprofen to handle the pain and drank lots of water to rehydrate himself. The pizza and anchovies must have dried him up, he thought. The anchovies were a nasty habit he had learned from Grace, who learned it from Phillip. For him, it was like eating hot sauce on a burrito-once you had it, there was no going back. Even bad pizza tasted good with anchovies. His friends hounded him for having a dozen small metal containers of anchovies from Filippo's Italian Deli stocked at all times. It was a heckling worth taking. Guy smiled as he finished an entire bottle of water.

He noticed it was eight o'clock as he lay back on his pillow and closed his eyes. Anna's shift had just ended, and she would soon appear.

He tried to float into his current favorite fantasy about her striking red hair and hard body but found himself in a daydream remembering his great-uncle Pietro and his visit on June 7, just hours before he died. His dad had wanted to visit, but he ended up driving Alex to the hospital. Guy wanted to see him, so he went by himself to visit without telling anyone. It was on the way home to his College Park condo. He was familiar with the location, having visited him twice a month during the spring semester. It was just the two of them talking football and baseball. Pietro would sometimes go on about his half- brother, Alex Santucci, and his current play, but most of the time it was football, critiquing Guy's play.

Uncle Pietro could tell him every play he had made for UMD in the previous fall. His memory was so sharp, it was haunting. He saw things that Guy had not remembered, especially the bad plays when he missed a tackle or got beaten on a pass.

"Your grandfather never missed a tackle...never! Sometimes he would get bowled over, but he was small, not like you. You are too big to miss a tackle," he would say to Guy. The best part would be replaying his grandfather's plays in games from 1929 like they were just happening. Guy realized that he was probably the last human being alive that saw those games. "He played the game like a pianist. He would follow the music of the game, and his actions would be the right notes. The feel of the game was everything to him, because he had trouble seeing the ball. Of course, things were less complicated back then, and the referee rarely called penalties, so it was harder to rush the line, to get into the backfield."

Sometimes Uncle Pietro would sit back and listen to Guy describe a game, each play in a drive, or an interception that he made. Guy was learning how to talk to adults and describe the philosophy of his play. He would come away from their time together focused on what he needed to do next year.

Guy noticed a slight difference in his great-uncle's voice during their last visit, a deeper tone, when he said, "Good-bye, son." It made him think that something had changed for Uncle Pietro.

Guy shivered for a moment in bed as he remembered the voice. It was a deep baritone, a voice he had only heard on video, viewing his grandfather talking at his fiftieth wedding anniversary party in 1992. Watching the video over the years for Guy was always a haunting experience. Guy I was in control of the crowd of over two hundred as he thanked them all for coming and told quick stories about many of those in front of him. His dark glasses hid his troubled eyes, but his voice carried his strength on the video tape. He saw little Grace, six months old, being carried by Phillip, who looked thin and tired. Carol always young looking with her great smile. His grandmother, Rose, looked adorable and proud, happy at the recognition from her husband.

Within sixteen months, Guy I would be dead from a massive heart attack, just months from his eighty-second birthday. But that deep voice from a powerful, little man seemed to speak to Guy through Uncle Pietro.

■ ■ ■

Anna quietly took off her jacket and the hidden gun holster while quickly and joyously undressing. After shaking her hair, newly cut to settle nicely below her chin, she tilted her head forward to take another look at her dormant catch. She slowly moved her taut body under the covers and slid into a perfect fit, without waking the still- growing teenager. She herself did not look twenty-six and was happy to get away with dating an almost-nineteen- year-old. At five feet six, she was almost a foot shorter than Guy but matched him muscle for muscle. What she added was a powerful-looking backside, developed by her years as a sprinting champion from Ohio, along with strongly built shoulders within her small frame that did nothing to distort her nicely posed breasts that stood at perfect attention. All these features were accented by her naturally freckled skin and vibrant crop of adorable red hair.

She had fallen for him after she saw him during his final swim meet in 2011. Officially, she was on the case for his senior year of high school, following him from afar, making sure he was safe. Brooks O'Malley knew she could blend into the scene if she needed to leave her car. Guy never complained when he noticed her, but he never made contact after he identified Corey and Aaron.

It was not until the summer of 2012 that they actually started talking, after she was officially off the case. There had been no contact from "the Turk" for nine months, so Brooks removed protective surveillance on Guy Finelli. Actually, there had been no official paper trail of Guy Finelli being a part of the investigation of the Baltimore connection. As far as the FBI was concerned, now Assistant Director Brooklyn O'Malley had nothing to do with Guy Finelli.

Unofficially, Brooks encouraged Anna to follow her instincts about Guy Finelli. Brooks took the time to get to know his agents very well. He knew they had very little social life because of their jobs, and he did everything he could to make them feel loved. He took special care of Anna because she was finishing only her second year with the agency. She had no family in the area and very few friends. There was a time when they had a special conversation about Guy.

"Anna, there is nothing wrong with liking him, other than he's a young jock. Most of those guys are social disasters!"

"Well, he's different. I've watched him for a while. He is very mature and deep. He's a quiet leader. None of that fake macho stuff. No pointing to himself, no tattoos, no drinking, no women hanging on him. He has a group of dedicated friends and a close family. And for real...he is a stud-looking hunk of a man!"

"I get it! I just don't want you in the line of fire if they decide to come after him. This could be just the beginning of him being targeted by this organization if his career takes off."

"Well, that's an even better reason to see him...he may need protection. I have no problem with that."

"That would be time off the clock, you know. You would still have a real job outside of being his bodyguard."

"Trust me, it would be more than being a bodyguard...

but I hear you. Actually boss, I think Finelli could be my overtime positions!" She smiled, knowing that she was embarrassing Brooks.

"As long as I don't have to hear about it...you have a deal!"

Guy's dream state had been nicely interrupted by Anna's touch and smell. They spent an hour together, perfectly complementing each other's desires. The energy created by their union could have kept them warm for a hundred years, seemingly an endless resource. Guy turned his legs to the side of the bed, finally escaping their union, and rose to get dressed. Besides the need for clothes, he realized that hunger was once again his dominant need.

Anna leaned on her side, supporting her head with her hand as she took the time to watch him move to his dresser. Feeling voyeuristic, she tried to define what was so different about his athleticism. She had seen him play football, lift weights, go for runs, swim in competition and for leisure, and then, of course, make love to her. She knew lots of athletes and had seen lots of men and women that were physically beautiful and coordinated. What Guy possessed, she finally figured out, was an amazing set of physical skills normally attributed to small athletes that were quick and shifty, strong athletes that were powerful and dominant, sprinters who were graceful and fluid, and lanky athletes who could jump and dominate airspace. She had never witnessed anyone like him, and she knew he was only getting better. Anna assumed there were a hundred sports that Guy would be good at, but the stars were aligning for him to dominate the sport of football.

As she watched him get dressed, she decided to finally make an effort to get out of bed and join him for dinner. She felt a need to find some decent food for Guy, because his diet of pizza and more pizza was not going to feed the furnace of his endless metabolism. She loved to cook, and she ate a perfect diet for an athlete. Teaching Guy the same regimen was a priority for her. He was starting to learn from her about nutrition and diet, but the band of roommates made the progress an uneven journey. With practice starting in a few weeks, his diet would improve drastically. Good nutrition had entered the world of college football.

They walked the sidewalk along the famous US 1 in College Park as an unnoticed couple holding hands. The summer activity of the university was minimal during the evenings. They passed the first iconic entrance that led up the hill to Campus Drive. Acres of green fields, used for softball, football, frisbee or picnics; lined the next quarter mile with fully grown oaks strategically placed. They noticed the dairy building housing the homemade ice cream from the agricultural department of the university. The roots of

107

UMD started in the early nineteenth century as an agricultural school. Above it all on a ridge sat the impressive UMD Chapel, which angelically eyed the passing humans below.

As they discussed having dessert before dinner, they passed Fraternity Row, a long, half circle of a dozen or so Georgian-style structures, housing some of the greatest scenes of partying in the history of mankind. It surrounded an impressive green area that would be the site of six fields of touch-football battles for the fraternity title in the fall.

"My father played on those fields one year while in college here in the early seventies. He had a severe knee injury that turned him into a quarterback because of his limited mobility. In between partying, they would play a schedule of games and playoffs. His fraternity was not even on the Row. It was a pure party house with a lot of guys from Baltimore that sounded hilarious. They would set up beer kegs on the sidelines. Can you imagine? Apparently, quaaludes were big back then, especially at the lacrosse frat parties!"

"They made it to the finals after upsetting Kappa Alpha, the Alabama of frat football! They had ten guys facing KA with thirty guys in new, clean uniforms. Dad intercepted the first two passes for TDs and threw a bunch of TDs to embarrass the defending champs in front of hundreds of drunk coeds!"

"Hell, sounds like a blast; I'm sorry I missed it! At Bowling Green, I barely pulled my head out of a book, graduated early, and then went straight into law school. Maybe we can make up for it this year."

"There'll be plenty of scenes around here during the season, but I avoid most of them. Plus, we're winning the whole thing this year down in New Orleans. That will be a blast down there, especially the celebration."

"Well, at least that's something to look forward to. I'm glad you got this thing mapped out."

"I can see us winning this thing, because our offense 1s coming around. We got Hank Harrison transferring in from Towson after setting the record for TDs and receptions for a tight end. He's something special!"

Anna had witnessed their friendship when Guy was getting ready for his senior year of high school. She saw from afar two talented athletes working in harmony through the sweat and the heat of summer to better their craft. They developed a real bond, something that was noticeable in their body language when they came off the field. Guy had a "one on one" personality, meaning that his first connection with an individual was almost blinding. His persona lit up like a supernova when the right person came in front of him. He was different than his brother, Alex, or his father, Phillip, who could light up a room with their charisma. What she loved about him was his laser- like connection with her when the two of them talked. They could be alone or in a room with others, but when he homed in on her, she was the only person in his universe.

She knew there was also something different about Hank. He was a gorgeous hunk of a man, but she knew that these days, appearance meant nothing about a person's sexuality. He was friendly with women and even had shown up with a date at a party that she attended with Guy. He was charming but seemed to go through many layers of thought before answering a question from her or from his date. When he talked to Guy, the curtain seemed to open, and his confidence returned. Her female antenna had trouble picking up a frequency from him-something that clarified his broadcast, maybe in the range that made her feel like a woman. She usually had no trouble sensing that from a man, but not with Hank. It was easy to notice that Guy had no trouble tuning him in. His airwaves were free and clear. There were no filters on Guy's receptors. He never saw black or white, gay or straight, American or foreign. It was all about the communication that he judged. He looked for friendship, trust, and most of all, the ability to love from a person.

Anna was certain that her young man was straight, but if he found something special in a person, he would not hesitate to befriend him. When Hank had reached out to him in ninth grade during his troubling times, it was a lifesaver that would eventually bring him back to something he loved-football. He was loyal to his friends and would never put up with any bias toward a friend or teammates.

As they walked, she listened to Guy talk about Hank joining his UMD team with such enthusiasm that she realized the connection. Guy had learned a work ethic for football from Hank, while creating a path that would lead him to greatness. But Hank had found more, a real lifeline to the male world, a confidant, a defender of his lifestyle, a friendship without judgment, and a feeling of protection -all of this from "the Safety."

CHAPTER 16

GUY FINISHED A semester's worth of classes during the summer of 2013 with a laser- like focus, in line with his ultimate goal of graduating in December 2014. At the end of July, he finally had time for a couple weeks of vacation with Anna. She brought him to the mountains of West Virginia for some camping, hiking, climbing, hunting, and white- water rafting. These experiences kept him in shape with a regimen of activities that challenged his regular sports skills and prepared him for the rigors of an August of football practice.

In the second week, they joined the family at a trio of houses rented by Phillip, Anthony, and Sally Keegan on the Fenwick Island beach in Delaware. Situated between the high-rises of Ocean City, Maryland, and the yuppie crowds of Bethany Beach, Delaware, Fenwick beaches were the most private and secluded, while still being near all the happenings of the summer season. Sally had the most room available with her grand house, but she had her hands full with the newborn twins. She had her parents in from Kansas and Alex's adopted mother, Laura, from Bethesda, all for grandparenting duties.

Anna and Guy shared a room next to Charlotte and Patty in Sally's house. It was easier for Sally and Alex to be comfortable with the eighteen-year-old and his girlfriend staying together in their house than for Phillip and Carol to host them. When he reached twenty-one, as they had with his sister Grace, his parents would treat him like an adult with inalienable rights. Regardless of his age, it was hard with his size and notoriety to not treat him like an adult. Until he was at least nineteen, his parents would take a "don't ask, don't tell" policy about his relationships.

The trio of redheads (Anna, Charlotte, and Patty) in their bikinis on the beach led to an overload of sun-exposed skin and an onslaught of burgeoning freckles. They loved hanging out together and were comfortable with the look of their athletic bodies, in clothes or mostly out of them. They ran on the beach in the morning, tanned and swam in the ocean during the day, and partied together at night.

Alex Santucci was able to sneak out to Fenwick Island for parts of three days in the middle of the week to join the family. He led the Pinelli boys in conducting surveillance on the trio of redhead bodies, lying in a row on a large beach towel and showing adoration to the sun. The trio added a royal-looking brunet when Sally Keegan, showing off her regained figure from her pregnancy, joined the trio for a game of bocce ball on the beach. The festive atmosphere continued throughout the day and evening, with games of coed volleyball and football, cookouts for dinner, and bonfires on the beach at night.

It was during the bonfires when Phillip and Anthony starting talking about their days of playing football in high school and then the county touch-football leagues. It was that transition from the mainly "running-the-ball first" plays of tackle football to the passing league of touch football that had brought the two of them together to navigate a new phenomenon-the air attack. It would become the prototype for football in the twenty-first century. The wide-open passing offense, with multiple receivers in complex patterns, was developed in the Montgomery County touch leagues in the late sixties-or so the brothers believed and told in their stories.

The moonless dark of the evening led to tales of great performances, revealing true legends-players whose greatness had grown in stature by telling their stories over and over. These players, some great friends, some not, were at the least, kindred spirits to the Finelli brothers. They had outstanding athletic skills in multiple sports that defied description at the time.

As Alex Santucci arrived at the bonfire to join his wife, Sally Keegan, only Laura was inside any of the houses, watching the twins as they slept. Joe Finelli was surrounded by his two teenage children, with his sister Melissa and her three kids on blankets in front of them. Flo, Carol, and Brandy sat with Grace and the three redheads drinking wine near Guy Finelli. Anna nudged Guy and clinked her glass to get the crowd's attention. Guy rose like a slow elevator, extending his now almost six-foot, six-inch frame over the fire. His presence commanded quietness as his soft, deep voice thanked everyone for being there. "This is so great to be here with friends and family that I love, especially my parents. Thanks for everything that you do, Mom and Dad."

Guy was not one to speak up in front of crowds or family. Anna, Charlotte, and Patty all encouraged him to speak his feelings more as a way to show his love. They also knew that the media would kill him if he could not talk in an interview or a press conference. After clinking his oversized can of Arizona Iced Tea with everyone in on the bonfire, Guy smiled at the three redheads and then pointed to his young cousins. "Now, some of you have heard about the old days of football, but in this family, it starts with my grandfather in 1929 and my dad and Uncle Anthony in the sixties and seventies. So, I'm wondering if Dad and Anthony could tell everybody about the story about the heart surgeon that you met at the '69 NIH picnic, who happened to be an All-American quarterback at Columbia in the early sixties and was drafted with Joe Namath by the New York Jets!"

Even the young ones knew Joe Namath, adding gasps of, "What...you guys knew Joe Namath?"

Uncle Anthony leaned forward and placed a hand on his excited grandson. "Not really...we got to know someone just as talented who was an All-American when they both graduated."

"Could he throw like Namath?"

"Well, actually, no one could throw like Joe Namath or Sonny Jurgensen, but after that, he was the best I've ever seen."

"Did you play with him, really? But how did you meet him?"

"Slow down, cowboy... actually, your grandma Flo might remember it better. We were at an NIH picnic; Aunt Melissa was only three, and your dad, Big Joe, wasn't born yet."

"And your grandpop was slim and built like a brick shithouse!" Florence threw both arms around Anthony and embraced him with a big kiss on the cheek. "He loved my fried chicken and ate almost every piece that I brought to the picnic," added Flo as she rubbed his protruding stomach, the result of another great beach cookout.

"Yes, dear...not all of us can still look thirty, you know."

"OK, you two, let's not lose our audience." Guy rose to his feet, trying to help the story along. "How did you know he was a great quarterback?"

"When the football he threw to me over six rows of picnic tables landed like a baby in the crook of my arm, and I could smell the heat from the skin of the football across my T-shirt!"

CHAPTER 17

"The True Legend of Archie Roberts"
(As told by Phillip Finelli)

IN JANUARY 1969, Joe Namath ended the fourth season of his white shoe-wearing,

Fu-Manchu-growing, ground breaking football career by upsetting the Baltimore Colts in Super Bowl III. After that victory, Joe Namath replaced Mickey Mantle for me as the coolest athlete in America. Soon after-football officially replaced baseball as the hippest sport in the country. Most teenage boys, like me, wanted to be like Namath, and soon white cleats were everywhere. Sports in the sixties were an era of boldness, started by Muhammad Ali in boxing. Namath followed in football by guaranteeing victory as a seventeen-point underdog and in victory secured the first Super Bowl win for the upstart AFL.

The next month, professional sports in DC were changed forever when former Green Bay Packer coach, Vince Lombardi, accepted the coaching position for the Washington Redskins. Lombardi is the only coach in NFL history to win three championships in a row, including the first two Super Bowls.

Soon a third event would change Football forever. It happened on the grounds of the greatest medical research facility in the world, the National Institutes of Health (**NIH**). In Bethesda, three individuals came together, me included, for a game of catch. During an eventful picnic, the three individuals met and began to stir up football during the sixties and re-blend them into a recipe that would feed the appetite for more air attacks in football.

The seven-on-seven game of touch football in Montgomery County became their laboratory. The local league was about to leave the confines of running plays, short passes, and good defense; and become the research center for the new all-passing offense, which included bunched receivers, underneath patterns, over-the-top bombs, bubble screens, delays out of the backfield, back- shoulder routes, inside and outside picks, no-huddles, audibles and of course-lots of touchdowns.

It was 1969, the one hundredth year of organized football in America. It would affect the way football would be played for the next fifty years."

• • •

"Anthony lay down on his back, feeling the comforting grass of one of the many well-manicured acres surrounding NIH. He felt like a defeated prize fighter between rounds of boxing, hoping to continue eating the fried chicken that Florence had made for the picnic. But the five juicy pieces he had just devoured put him down for the count. A quick nap on the soft turf might help his stomach cooperate with his intent of eating more of the homemade food that he could smell all around him.

He closed his eyes briefly and remembered being a kid in the early fifties and watching the construction of the massive, fourteen-story, all-brick Clinical Center building, which opened in July 1953. Better known as Building Ten to NIH employees, it was the crown jewel of America's Cancer Research Center with its 520 hospital beds. The beautiful campus was located just across from the old home of Walter Johnson in Bethesda.

Anthony opened his eyes and gazed through a tall maple tree overhead to gauge the sky, as the wind was picking up on this spring weekend. As an amateur meteorologist, the onsets of storms of any kind were especially exciting.

Florence knelt at his side and rubbed her husband's protruding stomach. "You need to work off that meal, dear, if you want to get your waistline back inside your belt. Lying on your back doesn't really help your digestion, you know. Hey, there are some guys over there throwing a football. I think you know some of those docs."

Florence was fully aware that the best way to motivate her husband into activity was to mention the possibility of a ball being thrown. It was an experiment she had designed that worked on Anthony every time.

She had her hands full working at NIH as a secretary, going to night school for an accounting degree, and taking care of a three-year-old daughter. She was at the forefront of a new generation of families with two full-time working parents. At times she felt like her husband was her biggest kid at twenty-five, playing sports all year round in Montgomery County.

Anthony's talent as a home-run hitter was well sought out by county softball teams, and he played almost every night of the week from May to July. But his real love now was football, specifically "passing the football" and discovering new plays on offense.

The county touch leagues had a five-game spring schedule in April before the

114

softball season. He played mainly safety on defense but was enjoying more of the organizing and coaching since his knees had slowed him considerably from his days as a churning halfback in high school. His team this year was playing in the spring to get ready for the top division in the county fall league and had a wealth of talent. Three nights a week, his guys would practice, sometimes with all twenty of his players, including myself, only sixteen-years old at the time. Most of the players had played in high school and some level of college football. A few had been in professional tryout camps, and one had played in the Canadian Football League.

Anthony had been developing his passing offense for the seven-on-seven touch game for the past few seasons after watching the wide-open offense of the Washington Redskins in the sixties led by Sonny Jurgensen throwing to Charley Taylor, Bobby Mitchell and Jerry Smith, and the emergence of the new AFL in the sixties. The upset win by the AFL in the 1969 Super Bowl and Lombardi coming to Washington had tripled the excitement of playing in the touch-football leagues with their wide-open passing game.

Anthony rose to his knees, enough to see the football in the air across the meadow from the picnic. Most of the medical doctors he knew were researchers in the National Cancer Institute (NCI), which was a huge part of NIH. They all loved him because he was a big jock, and they were not. Finally, voices started to yell for him to join them.

"Anthony...we need you over here!" As he trotted over to the gathering, he noticed a guy in green scrubs being coerced into the activity. He had flip-flops on his feet and markings of blood on his green-scrub top. He was clearly a surgeon from the NIH hospital. Anthony had never met any of the surgeons involved in cancer or heart research, but he knew that it was the most prestigious residency in the world in 1969.

As Anthony moved closer, he saw the surge on laughing at all the attention he was receiving, as they flipped him an older, beat-up football. His hands were like a pair of cheetahs, pretty to look at but quick to the target. They were worth their weight in gold and received the ball like it was a long-lost friend. The surgeon looked to be about Anthony's age and height but with a frame carrying the weight of a fit runner at 180 pounds, not a pro football player 20 pounds heavier.

With a broad smile on his face, he noticed Anthony coming within sight about fifty yards away. Dr. Roberts could see his neatly combed black hair, his broad shoulders, and his tree-trunk thighs churning slowly across the field. Suddenly, by instinct, he locked in on his potential football receiver, who had come within range. His juices had been stirred. Feeling more like Archie Roberts, he locked his right-arm cannon on his target. Without warm-up, he fired the beat-up football, whistling against

115

the flourishing wind on a line to his receiver.

Anthony saw the arm cocking and the easy release, thinking that the surgeon was tossing it to someone in the adoring group of research PhDs around him. Silence came over the group as the ball passed them and headed over the rows of picnic tables crowded with hungry families, wondering what damage it might do to someone in its path.

Anthony slowed for a moment and watched the football travel over fellow employees, enjoying their food while chatting away at their tables, completely unaware of the heat-seeking pigskin over their heads.

Against the laws of physics, the football seemed to pick up speed as it homed in on him. He instinctively turned to the side, like a kangaroo opening his pouch to a playful kid, to snag it cleanly. The football left a slight burning smell emanating from his shirt like his Norelco shaver did after finishing on his heavy beard. He savored the smell and the feeling of receiving a perfectly completed football pass. Anthony quickly closed in on the last forty yards to the thrower. He noticed a collective breath of relief from the group around him.

"Hey, nice catch, sport; you looked like you would be a good target. I'm Archie Roberts."

"Anthony Finelli." He quickly recognized the two-sport All-American as quarterback and shortstop from 1962 to 1964 at Columbia University. It was a surprise to see him without his equipment and clearly not at pro football- playing weight, but it did not seem to affect his arm strength. As his excitement was playing out in his mind, Anthony tried to stay calm. "You must be more than a surgeon." From the long handshake, Anthony could feel his fingers, long and manicured; his hands, soft and strong; and his wrists, quick and flexible-a perfect combination of delicate and athletic.

"Yeah... I used to play a little bit in college." Roberts had set seventeen school and fourteen league passing records in his three years as an All-Ivy League quarterback, safety, and punter. He was the sixties version of Sammy Baugh. "Don't have much time for that now, but I sure miss it. I'm guessing you were a ball player?" Archie, ever the doctor, noticed the long scars on both of Anthony's knees. "It looks like they took out your kneecap on the right one. It must have gotten scarred up pretty good underneath." They traded knee and shoulder injury stories for a few minutes, the necessary bonding for football players. "Anthony, I would love to meet your family. Can you join us for a little while?"

Archie and Anthony were only fourteen months apart and seemed to come from the same mold of great athletes with scientific minds. They immediately filled needs for each other-Archie needed the competition of sports as a distraction from the grind of

116

his research residency in heart surgery, and Anthony needed a great multi-athlete who would experiment and appreciate his new ideas in a passing offense.

Archie's boss, Dr. Tariff, approached the two men as they talked, surrounded by their families. He mentioned that some of the research PhDs wanted to play a little game of football on a level area near the National Library of Medicine (NLM), about a ten-minute walk south on the campus. It was the largest medical library in the world since it opened in 1962. It was not on the original ninety- three acres donated by the Wilson family to NIH but on a golf course owned originally by the Woodmont Country Club. In 1948, Woodmont moved to a location in Rockville ten miles north after the government informed them of their need for the land. Since construction was not started until 1956, it was used as a public course known as Glenbrook Golf Course. Anthony had caddied and played the course many times before it closed.

Archie and Anthony talked continuously as they walked to reach the open meadows of fields. Archie explained his journey to NIH. "I was drafted by the New York Jets of the AFL and the world-champion Cleveland Browns of the NFL in 1965 to play professional football, as well as the World Series-champion St. Louis Cardinals to play baseball. The Jets had drafted me in case they couldn't sign Joe Namath, and the Cardinals were loaded with talent, and baseball was a long season.

"So, I knew I wanted to go to medical school, and the owner, Art Modell, offered me a unique contract- he would pay for me and my wife's medical school, plus a salary for four years if I played for Cleveland at least during the exhibition season. Mr. Modell had traded for Frank Ryan in 1962, and he had a PhD in math, so I think he liked the smart QB thing. He also liked the positive press coverage from the unique contract. Anyway, after two seasons in Cleveland, I ended up going to Miami in the '67 expansion draft. Man... that was a real shock to go from one of the best football organizations to the mess of an expansion franchise."

Anthony was mesmerized by the story and watched closely as Archie twirled the old football up in the air again and again, like a juggler warming up with his prized hands.

"Over the next two seasons, I played some as a backup, but Bob Griese (a future Hall-of-Farner) was drafted, and I finished medical school. I knew at that point surgery was my future, not dodging defensive linemen."

As they approached the old first-hole fairway, I caught up with them, breathing hard as an excited sixteen-year- old ready to catch a football. "Hey, Phillip, you made it just in time, this is Archie Roberts. He played QB and Shortstop in college." Normally I was pretty shy, but I was most comfortable playing and talking sports. "Anthony, man is you

117

kidding? Archie Roberts the All-American? It's great to meet you. Can we throw the ball around?"

"You're just in time, my friend. I think I'll need a receiver or two." Archie motioned to me to run a pattern. I instinctively strolled twenty yards to his right as he yelled out, "Post at fifteen!"

I had not been allowed to play football in high school until the fall of 1970 because my father, Guy I, wanted me to focus only school work. It was strange bullshit coming from my father, a former All-State football player, who had the same conflict with his father during high school. Somehow, though I talked him into letting me compete on the track team because he did not think that track was a sport. He saw it as an athletic skill that would help me one day become a better player in me in football, baseball, or basketball because they were real sports. I know... it doesn't make sense does it.

Just having turned sixteen, I was finally eligible to play in the county touch leagues. My brother was just about jumping out of his skin with excitement watching me run the first fifteen yards of the post pattern at medium speed. Then, even without my white cleats, I showed off a trio of outside-inside-outside fakes before accelerating into the deep post. Anthony had never been able to overthrow me on a deep Post, usually having trouble just reaching me in stride, but Archie waited longer than anybody. Anthony watched intently as Archie efficiently cocked his arm and fired the worn-out football like a blasted cannonball into the atmosphere for a landing some sixty-five yards downfield. I saw the launching as I reached top speed and thought I might be outgunned, but I kept my stride as the ball started coming into focus over my left shoulder. Most footballs at this point lose altitude quickly and settle into your hands but this pass was barely losing airspeed and was still spinning against gravity. I remember extending my right stride, hitting the ground hard with my right foot, sailing into the air like my twenty-two-foot-long jump in the state finals, to snag the football over four feet above me. I finished with a perfect landing and a tumble into the fairway grass with the football well secured.

The picnic crowd, led by the usually calm MDs, roared with approval as a friendly game of touch football followed. Archie, Anthony, and I did our best to behave ourselves and let the self-imported researchers win, except for the two times that the MDs scored and celebrated a little too much. Archie hit me on a twenty-yard crossing pattern that appeared like a flash of lightning on the field, leading to a score, and then Archie performed a routine operation with a wide-open swing route to Anthony on the left side of the field, as the whole defense gravitated to fake-screen to me on the right.

Within a few weeks, Archie was taking his cleats to the hospital every day so he could join the practices of our team up the street at the Bethesda YMCA field, where I worked at the front desk, watching Jerry Smith come through in the off-season. As a player coach, Anthony had no problem getting his players to show up for practice, knowing that Dr. Roberts might be on the field. Most of the time, Archie would walk on to the field in his green scrubs and slippers, forgetting to put on his cleats because he was so excited about throwing to the receivers.

When Dr. Archie Roberts* started his post-residence fellowship at NIH in the early seventies, he played for more four years in the Montgomery County touch leagues. The last two years, he commuted on the Eastern Airlines Shuttle from NYC to make the nine o'clock games on Sunday mornings. Most of games were events watched by hundreds, mainly athletes coming from other fields or playing later games. Dozens of ex-college players as well as several professional football players, including an ex-NFL All-Pro receiver and a Canadian League player known as "the Frederick Flash," ended up playing with Archie. When they had all their players on offense, they were unbeatable. I took over as QB in '75 and won two more championships with a similar team.

More importantly, Anthony and Archie became kindred spirits extending their childhood love of sports together for many years."

*Dr. Archie Roberts became a world-renowned cardiothoracic surgeon and performed more than four thousand open-heart surgeries. He taught at medical schools across the county, including Northwestern, Nevada, Florida, Boston, and Temple Universities. He headed cardiac surgery departments at the Heart Institute of Northeast Pennsylvania and Jersey Shore Medical Center. He has written more than one hundred articles and four books on cardiac surgery. In 2001, Dr. Roberts founded the Living Heart Foundation for early intervention of cardiac care, especially for overlooked groups such as college and professional athletes. He has worked with hundreds of ex-NFL players on heart attack and stroke prevention (ref: GoColumbiaLions.com & Living Heart Foundation.org).

CHAPTER 18

THE 2013 SEASON was just around the corner when the news came to Hank Harrison. He had won the starting job as tight end with a spectacular performance during the August practices. Guy and Anna and the DMC boys were meeting Hank and a friend at Ledo's for a celebration. The DMC had a l s o won starting jobs to form an All-WJ defensive backfield. As they headed down US 1, they were in the best of moods.

"This is like being in heaven." Mark Pelligrini was the first to shout out his feelings for the night. "Man, I can't wait for the first game!"

"Hell is the word, not heaven...it's going to be hot as hell on Saturday. But we'll still be the coolest cats on the field." Duran Hall added low fives and a hug to Anna as he danced in front of his friends. "What do you two white boys think? Are you excited, or has the good news not reached those tall brains of yours?"

"Actually, my cornerback brother, I knew I had my job when I walked on the field for the first practice. Coach Brown told me that you had to start because of affirmative action or some shit like that!"

"Cary, for a good-looking dude, you are one dumb son of a bitch! But I still love you, man." Duran hugged his best friend on the team, knowing he always had his back.

"We are going to be the best backfield in the country. Do you guys realize that?" Guy added, trying to get into the spirit of the evening.

Mark jumped in front of all of his friends and screamed, "Oh, he speaks! You are like Moses, man, coming down from the mountain. You know, Mr. Finelli, if you didn't bark out shit on the football field, I wouldn't know if you had a pulse sometimes." Mark had Guy on the ropes but turned to Anna for the knockout joke. "Anna, how are the language classes coming? Is he reaching verbal yet? Does he make noises during...huh...ya know?"

"Only when I need something, Paisano, but you wouldn't know anything about that, right?" Guy grabbed Pelligrini by the shoulders. "My grandfather would have called you a *tradule,* you know, wise guy! But I think asshole would fit you better."

Anna took it all in, knowing that dating an almost- nineteen-year-old meant that he had nineteen-year-old friends. She made the best of it, as she had missed her younger brothers and their hyperactive friends since her college days. Most of the time, she thought of Guy and loved him for being quiet and sincere; and for choosing his words carefully when he did speak. Even as he took her advice about speaking up more in groups, he did so with wise choices and a pattern of success. She knew that his ability to learn a subject and exceed it quickly was like gold, rarely found in a teenager.

As the teammates hopped the curb together for the next block, their phones all vibrated at once with texts from the same source, Coach Brown. Duran was first to the draw, shouting out, "Man, holy shit...something's happened to Hank!" He read the text out loud-"Hank at HC hospital after attack, meet me there!"

"Duran, let's go get the cars. You guys order some pizzas to go. Guy, give me your keys." Cary knew he would get some looks for thinking of his stomach before his teammate's injuries. They all knew the Seinfeld episode when Elaine stopped to buy some Juicy Fruit before heading to see her boyfriend in the hospital. "Hey, we gotta eat sometime today. I'm starved!"

Both former track stars headed back north on US 1, making the mile sprint in less than five minutes. Getting the cars out of the garage and dodging traffic on US 1 took three times as long. Luckily, it gave the pizzas time to finish cooking.

Anna and Guy followed in his car. When Duran handed him the keys, he flipped him a FedEx box. "This was sitting on your seat; it looks unopened. Hey, see you guys at the hospital."

"What is it, Guy? How did it get in your car?"

"Beats me; nobody has key to it."

"I don't like this situation. Open it up. I'm getting O'Malley on the line."

Guy ripped it open, feeling a lot of adrenaline from the news about Hank. It was a cell phone with a note to call a number. He quickly dialed.

It went to a recording after one ring. "This is a message for Guy Finelli. Please pay attention to the following message. Your friend should not be playing football. He will embarrass the team with his lifestyle. It will soon be exposed by a newspaper article. You can help your friend by helping us. The team you play for is a plus-thirty-five against FNU..let them get closer!"

O'Malley was on the phone with Anna within minutes. "Local police are handling the crime scene and the investigation with Hank Harrison. We have to stay in the background on this. You are officially back on the job with security over Guy. Stay with him every moment."

"What do we do about the message?"

"Obviously nothing...is Guy freaked out about it?" "No... he's just pissed about the

121

attack."

"Tell him to talk to Hank about coming out."

"Are you crazy? Nobody does that."

"Guy could make it work with that team. It's going to happen anyway by next week. First it will be a leak about this being a hate crime by a Baltimore sports blogger, and then the *Gay City Paper* will pick it up, and then the *Daily*, and so forth."

"Christ...these guys are animals! I'll talk to Guy." "Oh yeah, Anna..."

"What, Brooks?"

"Carry your gun with you."

The four teammates and Anna were in the emergency room at Holy Cross Hospital within twenty minutes, sneaking in the pizzas. Hank Harrison and his friend Blair Montgomery were in side-by-side beds on IVs. Their faces had been spared, but their ribs and backs would be black and blue by the morning. Blair was not a football player and had taken the worst of the beatings. His personality was not showing any injury.

"Look, Hank, our own fan club. Are these your teammates? Please have a seat, everybody. We would have some wine and cheese, but the nurses aren't cooperating." "Mister Montgomery, I can shuttle your guests out quickly if you don't behave yourself!" Nurse Sheila uttered. "No, my dear, we will behave; I swear!" After she left the room, Blair noticed the pizza boxes. "Well, at least you guys brought dinner. Wow, Leda's pizza... hmmm, yummy." Blair rolled his eyes with disapproval.

Guy stepped up to see his friend Hank, who was trying not to laugh at Blair's antics. Guy recognized the modus operandi of the beatings. Ganged up from behind, six of them, car hijacked. "I'm so sorry, my friend." He took Hank's hand and squeezed it as tears filled his eyes. "These guys won't get away with this; Anna has some friends on it." The look on his face confirmed that Hank was clueless about being a victim in a drug conflict, not a hate crime. He bent over and kissed Hank on the forehead. He pulled back his face inches from Hank and spoke to his eyes. "We need to talk about this when you get out of here, OK?"

"Sure Guy, how about after practice on Monday?"

"No, Hank, it has to be first thing tomorrow. We'll pick you and Blair up for brunch about ten?"

"If we can walk..."

"How about if Anna and I bring some bagels and lox to your place in the morning."

"Sounds good."

"And two French lattes?" "Even better."

CHAPTER 19

THE NEWS ON Hank Harrison and his friend Blair Montgomery was better than expected. After eight hours in the emergency room, including interviews with the police, they were released. Anna and Guy drove them to Blair's place in downtown Silver Spring for some rest. They were on the tenth floor of a condo building on Wayne Avenue with good security.

Blair was twenty-five with a mechanical engineering degree. He worked at the Discovery Network headquarters a block away, an anchor in the rebuilding of downtown Silver Spring over a dozen years ago. He had moved to the DC area after graduation for a great job but more importantly to feel the freedom to pursue his gay lifestyle. Growing up in North Carolina, he was spared from most of the heartache about his nature, because all of his friends thought he was a tech-nerd instead of gay. His parents were clueless but fairly liberal, with careers in academia at Duke University. They were disappointed that he chose NCSU and engineering, even though it was only twenty minutes away. It was an obvious choice for him, because figuring out how machines worked was the only thing that interested him besides other men. It helped having some space from his parents, being an only child, and having some urban night life in Raleigh to explore his feelings.

He met Hank at a club in DC during the spring and was shocked that he noticed him. They had become close during the summer, feeling comfortable spending time in the privacy of his condo. Blair was extremely bright and understood social situations. He was happy to be in Hank's life and was willing to be in the background for his career if necessary. Being in the spotlight and becoming a social pioneer were not in his plans.

Hank grew up with his mother and her parents, never knowing his father, who had left the area long before he knew that he had a son. He was very close with his grandparents, who were baby boomers with well- paid federal positions. Both were very athletic, playing on various county teams. They always brought Hank to games with them. They were aware of his orientation in high school well before his mom was; she had only learned about it within the last few months. His mom was always too into some drama about her own life to notice, and she did freak out a bit, but after a few days, she came around to support her son's lifestyle now that he was twenty-one. All three had met Blair and had supported getting Hank his own apartment in College Park now that he was going to UMD. They were happy to know that it was in the same building as his friend Guy Finelli.

Hank had called his grandparents from the hospital to make sure they knew he was fine. He reported only about the carjacking and that he had a few scratches. He said that Guy and Anna were helping him get home, and he would see them on Sunday.

The next morning, Anna and Guy hit a deli for the food but could not ignore the Dunkin' Donuts on US 1 for some donuts and coffee. "Hey, I have to keep my carbs up for the season, or I'll lose too much weight!"

"It must be nice to have that excuse to eat that crap. Someday it will catch up to you," Anna laughed at him, noticing the stares from the high-school girls behind the counter, scanning his tall, iron-man body. From his swimmer's shoulders to his thunder thighs, he was quite a sight, wearing a cutoff shirt and shorts.

"This is not going to be easy, getting them to understand their situation without knowing about your situation." Anna said with exasperation as they entered the car for the ride to Silver Spring.

"They're both pretty smart and unemotional. I think they'll see it's the only solution to the problem."

"Well, only a guy would say that, but it might be true in this situation. You have to do most of the talking!"

"I got it!"

It was decided after the meeting that reporter Ron Roswell would be contacted to write the story for the *Washington Daily.* He would hold the story until Monday evening so that Coach Brown could meet with the football team after practice on Monday. A press conference would be called Tuesday afternoon, followed by an interview with Bonnie Bramlett from ESPN.

Brooks O'Malley wanted to undercut the leverage that the Baltimore cartel thought they had over Guy. Besides, he thought, it was time for the gay athlete to compete openly. He was excited to oversee some social engineering. "Anna, this is the best thing that could ever happen to sports; plus, it's a great cover for what's happening to Guy.

I think this will end the terrorism of him."

"I hope you're right. This is going to set off a shit storm of publicity for these guys. I'm not excited about being a part of it."

124

"You're right...we can give you some cover with some additional agents dressed up as security. You can't be at the press conference or interview, but Guy has to be there for everything."

"He is all over it and will rally the team around it. He doesn't show it much, but I think he is pretty pissed about them messing with his friend."

Coach Gerry Brown was struggling to stay cool in his chair as he sat listening to Guy Finelli. He was trying to comprehend that he would be the first to coach an openly gay player in college or professional sports.

He had played with the great tight end Jerry Smith in 1969 and suspected that he had a gay lifestyle, but as a strong safety, he had to cover him every day in practice. He could attest to what the team knew, that Jerry Smith was the toughest football player he ever played against. That was all that mattered to anyone on the team, and it helped that Coach Lombardi had his back. It was hard to believe that it would take until September 2013 for a gay player to be known during his career.

As his sophomore superstar, Guy Finelli explained the story, leaving out the part about his drug-connection past and being threatened to throw a football game. "Coach, this is a hate crime-pure and simple. Somebody connected to Towson... maybe a booster, betting money on the season, was getting back at Hank for transferring and wanted to get nasty about his lifestyle choice. Somebody lost some money because he left...who knows? I got a message that it would be leaked after the game Saturday, so we don't have a choice."

"Hank, do you think you can handle all the shit you're going to get from opponents on the field and fans off the field?"

"Coach, I think this can bring the team together. Guy is behind me with his support; that's all that matters to me." "You are a brave man, Hank Harrison. We have to take this one day at a time. After Tuesday we'll have to focus on football. Wow, they could make a movie out of this shit! How are the ribs?"

"Saturday they'll be fine, no worse than playing a game."

The newly refurbished, modern locker room for UMD was full of old-fashioned ideas from the young men surrounding Coach Brown. It would soon become a setting found more in the psychology labs on campus, because a new experiment was about to come alive. Views about human sexuality from college-age football players were focused on one thing-intercourse with a female. Some were in love, some were collecting offspring

125

like tattoos, and some were even married with kids, but most were single, with or without a girlfriend, looking for intercourse with a female. Getting them to accept another viewpoint on sexuality was going to be as hard as finding a cure for cancer.

Hank Harrison's teammates did not know him very well as a person, but as a player, most thought that he could be the best addition to the offense. They had only witnessed his relentless work on the practice field for the past month. The real test would be when they went to war with him in a game. Only his friend, Guy Finelli, could vouch for him from the past. He was the first to talk, and he explained the attack on Hank and the threatening phone message.

Hank then stood up to announce that he was gay, and that under the circumstances, it was important to go public. The uncomfortable shuffling of cleats was the only sound vibrating from the new rug in the locker room. Then Hank did something brave-he gave them permission to hate him. "If I were sitting where you are, I would be pissed. Like-what is this faggot, wasting my time about being queer for assholes? Just shut your cock- sucking mouth, and keep your homo-loving hands away from me!"

The relief of collective laughter swept the room. From the back of the room came, "You're speaking the truth, bro, right on!"

Hank suddenly felt that he was fighting for his career and maybe his life for the first time. He knew that surviving the beatings and the name-calling over the years had strengthened him for this moment. "I am an ass-fucking, cock-sucking, AIDS-carrying faggot...that's right!" He paused to get their attention as the room got uncomfortably quiet.

Hank was trembling as he moved to his right to look at Pete White, a huge offensive tackle that he lined up with on the practice field. "Just like you're a hillbilly, cousin-fucking hick from West Virginia!" There was another pause as the silence was broken with scattered laughter. Hank was in a trance of anger, releasing the hate dumped on him over the years. On his left, he eyed his quarterback, Russell Reiner, from Long Island, who was a favorite of the women on campus. "Russell, you are too ugly to fuck with that kinky hair and those money-sucking lips. You're a liberal-sniffing, Holocaust-blaming, Jewish piece of shit!"

The team roared with relief, and the laughter followed Hank as he walked through his teammates toward the back of the room, crowded with African Americans. He felt like a gladiator without armor, waiting for the final judgment from the crowd. Hank extended his arms to his sides as he made his final plea for inclusion. "I could call you all a bunch of down-low-loving, crack-pipe-smoking, lazy-ass, black motherfuckers, but that would be as wrong as calling me a fucking, cock-sucking faggot! In reality, you're all my brothers, because your families have taken this shit for centuries, and you should know better." Hank fell to one knee as the pain in his ribs took his breath away. He put his hand over his eyes to keep from crying.

Star running back Emmitt Excel knelt down in front of Hank, lifted him slowly, and then hugged him without breaking his ribs. "You're my teammate, man, and that's all that counts!" A roar of approval came from the room as Emmitt led Hank back to his seat.

Coach Brown took the floor and asked his players to bow their heads for a prayer. He was a man with great spiritual conviction but rarely spoke about it to his players. "Lord, look over this healing that has taken place in this room, and bless it with all of your spirit. Let the bond of these words spoken in this room never be uttered to those that would misunderstand their power and healing. Pray for us in our journey for fairness and peace. Amen."

● ● ●

UMD Football Player Becomes 1st Openly Gay Athlete Harrison Announces Lifestyle after Carjacking Attack
By Ron Roswell

At an 11:00 a.m. news conference this morning, Hank Harrison, the starting tight end for UMD, will announce that he is gay. After suffering a physical attack on Saturday along with his friend, he received a message that his lifestyle would be announced after this Saturday's game against Florida National.

After talking with his friend and teammate Guy Finelli and UMD coach Gerry Brown, they decided to go public. The team was told after Monday's practice.

Coach Brown hopes to get back to "just football" after the Tuesday press conference. "Hank is very courageous coming forward at this time. I expect the team to rally around him. We are relieved that he is recovering from his injuries. This kind of hate crime needs to end."

Preseason ACC Player of the Year candidate Guy Finelli went to high school with Harrison. "Hank has been my friend since my unsuccessful freshman football tryout in high school. He helped me rediscover my love for playing football. I support him one hundred percent for making this decision. Our team is lucky to have such a great player."

I grew up watching a great Washington tight end, number eighty-seven, Jerry

127

Smith. Harrison wears the same number and hopes to emulate his career as a tight end. Let's hope that years from now, this generation can talk about Hank Harrison in the same vein. My wish is that the fact that they both lived as gay men will become just another truth in the story of their lives.

• • •

The 11:00 a.m. press conference was held on the UMD practice field with all eighty-five scholarship players, coaches, and staff members in attendance. Players surrounded Hank and Coach Brown in their practice gear without pads, and each held their helmets, backs facing forward, with the name "Hank" scribbled with a sharpie.

Coach Brown spoke first. "We hope today is the last and only day that we as a team need to let everyone know that we have Hank Harrison's back. Hank was the victim of an assault and was forced to reveal a private part of his life. He has courageously faced his teammates like no player in history has before, and his teammates are one hundred percent supportive. After today our only goal will be to win the Atlantic Division and compete for the ACC championship and a BCS Bowl bid. Hank Harrison, Guy Finelli, and Emmitt Excel will now answer any questions about this subject for the only time. Thank you."

Kelly Browner from the Big Atlantic Sports Network (BASC) eased into the first question. She was torn between her admiration for Hank and her need to ask a tough question. "Hank, do you think this will be a distraction to the team?"

"Today it is, but we hope to get into practice for Florida National and have a great season."

She quickly turned to Guy; having followed his brother for a season, she knew he would be less ready for a media onslaught. "Guy, why do you think you were contacted about outing Hank after the game?"

"I've known Hank for five years, and they knew we were good friends. Hank got offers from over fifty schools when he announced his wish to transfer to a BCS school. Somebody tried to make UMD look bad, but it has made us stronger."

Clark Battle with the *Nation's Times* felt no need to coddle the area star. "Have you guys ever dated?"

With the straightest of faces, Guy answered, "Not at this time. We are both in relationships."

Emmitt grabbed the microphone. "I think I can speak for everybody on this team, especially the brothers." He turned to his fellow African-American players surrounding him and high-fived them. "Hank is the toughest guy I've ever met and maybe the best player on this offense. For him to do today what no male athlete has done in the history of approval from "the brothers" as Hank's teammates put to sleep any question about unity on this team. America, makes me wish I was gay! I'm just proud to be his teammate and a friend." A roar of approval from "the brothers" as Hank's teammates put to sleep any question about unity on this team.

In the hullabaloo, Clark slowly melted into his chair, realizing that he had lost the battle. But he would retreat to try to win the war at a later time. Something seemed fishy to him about the liberals getting their way for gay acceptance so easily in the world of college football.

Always fearful of the "liberal media," Clark Battle had found his conservative voice working for the *Nation's Times*. Rarely in the sports world, in his opinion, did the LGBT community get their claws into manly sports so easily. He was not going to let it happen without some digging. Why would Guy Pinelli be involved in this scenario? He suspected that Ron Roswell, Bonnie Bramlett, and Larry Leonard were in the Finellis' back pocket based on the rosy coverage Alex Santucci had received last season. A feeling inside was telling him that Guy Finelli had dodged a bullet.

CHAPTER 20

T HE FLORIDA NATIONAL game sold out by Thursday after the Tuesday press
conference. Hundreds of media from news organizations all over the world descended
on Byrd Stadium. Protesters from Christian groups and many more supporters from the
LGBTQ (Q for questioning) community lined the entrances, passing out literature
to fans as they entered the stadium.

What went unnoticed for most was the Vegas betting line on the game, which had
grown to forty-two points because of all the publicity. This meant that tons of bettors
were on the UMD bandwagon, making the Baltimore cartel money in a great position to have
their bet go unnoticed. If UMD won by less than forty-two points, they were set to collect
at least $250,000 dollars.

Guy Finelli was in his own world on the sidelines, waiting for the anthem to finish
and the game to start. He had seen the current Vegas line in the morning paper but had
put the point-spread threat out of his head. There was extra security at the game,
including four FBI sharpshooters patrolling several rooftops around the stadium, which
sat in a bowl below ground level. Brooks O'Malley had a team of agents in the stands
quietly looking for weapons or unruly groups. The Harrison-Montgomery attack had
turned up several leads to a van that was seen in the Catonsville area just outside
Baltimore. The phone line with the message had gone silent, and no DNA had turned
up from the crime scene, but Brooks knew it was the same gang of six.

Anna was sitting with the Finellis and Hank's grandparents on the shady side of the
original bowl of the stadium, built in time for the 1950 football season for $1 million. She
was armed and nervous, waiting for the game to get started. She positioned herself on the
seat next to the aisle for a quick exit if necessary, and for the many breaks she would
take during the game to relieve her of anxiety and to tour the multitude.

The festive crowd could not purchase alcohol but were not alcohol-free. The student
section was especially well lubricated for the game, harvesting a partying mood that
would aid in support of their team. They were looking forward to a UMD blowout to open
the season, followed by an evening full of fiestas.

The 145th year of college football was ready to begin in perfect fall weather, seemingly made for the sport.

Guy Finelli quietly took his spot on the field to receive the kickoff. His senses were fully prepared as always for the experience on the field.

"Watch the football into your hands," he reminded himself, feeling his dad's strength and presence. His senses and instincts took over his body:

Loud roaring from the crowd isolating his thoughts. The football is boomed toward the end zone.

He backs up from the goal line, secures the ball, feels his stride on the perfect, manmade field turf.

"Guy, follow me to the right!" a teammate screams.

A crashing sound of collisions to his side, as he follows the white of friendly jerseys. Cousin Joe screaming, "Sidelines, sidelines!"

No hesitation, pushing off his right foot, feeling free as foreign hands fall off his thighs.

Wind in his face, blue jerseys before him hurdled near midfield.

Rangy-looking kicker coming into view ahead; should be freedom to his left, cuts quickly.

Left ear drum is silenced with a thump; his shoulder is jolted by a defender, who is holding on with gloves and searching for his waist.

Another pair of gloves grabs his hips and finally secures his thrusting thighs from behind.

Guy's brain automatically commands to prepare for a fall.

His free right shoulder tucks inside, securing the new pigskin as he slams the turf, five-hundred pounds of men echoing his crash.

Instinctively he rolls, seeing blue, hearing "We got you, Finelli, you faggot lover!"

Finelli gets to his feet, surrounded by a gang of six opponents, reminding him of past events, the gang spewing sorry statements of hate.

Feeling adrenaline of no comparison, he sticks the ball in their faces.

Teammates are flying to the scene as Guy hones in on the stupidest-looking kid in a blue jersey who is screaming, "cocksucker, faggot lover..."

He finally understands the intensity of Sean Taylor!

Behind his grill, Guy loads up and lets it fly...a load of fluid jets out of his mouth.

It perfectly finds a seam through his opponent's facemask and lands directly in his left eye socket.

The wounded, worthless noisemaker grabs for Guy's helmet.

All that officials see of his humiliation is his obvious foul, and they penalize him.

Each side grabs their hero and retreats.

Noise roars at concert levels as Guy sees the red and white of humanity in the stands.

Replay after replay surges the noise.

Their hero retreats to the sidelines to watch the offense score quickly from the thirty-yard line.

Tribal, triumphant thumps on his pads and cries of support pass through him from a parade of teammates.

Then a cleansing bear hug from his cousin, Joe, seals his surge of acceptance.

A glowing smile suggests that he knows the game l swon.

A score, a kickoff, he dons his headdress once again to defend his territory.

Sounds of the crowd's eruption follow him onto his field.

A field that he now owns.

UMD rolled over FNU 56-7. Guy Finelli had only one touchdown in the game, but it made all the highlights because no one had ever seen it before. With five minutes to go in the fourth quarter, Guy was playing his last series on defense. FNU had been stopped on the UMD twenty-three-yard line, facing fourth and seven for a first down, losing 49-7. Their coach sent in the field-goal unit to try a very doable forty-yard field goal that would cut the lead to thirty-nine points. It seemed a little weird to the play-by-play team to kick a field goal losing by forty-two, but the broadcast team expressed the normal reasons why a coach would do such a thing. Guy knew otherwise. The drug money had hedged their bet with someone on the FNU coaching staff. At first the offense stayed on the field, and then the kicking team was sent in, and then a time-out was called. Lots of arguing among the coaches followed, with a decision to keep the kicker on the field.

Guy huddled with his teammates. "I'm going to block his kick. Everybody up front, go in low to take down the linemen; corners, stay outside in case they release a receiver."

There was no "What are talking about?" or "We're up by forty-two; who cares?" from the huddle. After a year of playing with Guy Finelli, who did not say too much, his teammates had learned not to question him when he gave directions. They knew that he was something special and that he had his reasons to block this kick.

Guy's strategy was predicated on FNU using their regular snap count. He knew there was no reason to draw the defense offside; somebody on FNU wanted to get under a forty-two-point loss. The special team coach, Fred Marston, looked unprepared and was shouting out instructions. Guy knew it wasn't him. But the offensive coordinator, Rick Angelis, was quietly barking in coach Marston's ear. Head Coach Nolan Barnes was uninvolved, twenty yards down the sidelines, waiting for the day to be over.

Guy, who was coming from the defensive left side at an angle to the middle of the field about ten feet in front of the kicker, timed his start on "Ready." He was at full speed on "Set" and started his hurdle on "Hike."

He was on his way down, twenty-two feet later, as the football was struck perfectly, heading up and end over end to perfectly meet Guy's hands.

Then it happened-the ball disappeared. Like a thief dashing across the screen, he was gone with the football in an instant. The camera was eyeing the uprights, hoping to catch the ball headed through, but instead Guy Finelli caught the ball in the air, landed without falling, and headed downfield via the sidelines. He sprinted seventy yards in front of the FNU coaching staff for a touchdown. Beating the Vegas spread was secured.

• • •

A modestly furnished basement room in the middle of a set of abandoned row houses in West Baltimore went quiet, as a certain payday faded when a flash of greatness came across the screen. An older gentleman, casually dressed like a grandfather to help with the grandkids, known as "the Turk," rose and spoke to his dozen soldiers sitting around the turned-off television. "Mr. Finelli, this 'safety,' I believe, does not understand the situation. I thought you boys took care of this for me. Well, I am disappointed. We take tomorrow to rest and pray. Then we talk about this problem on Monday. I hate to see talent wasted against making money, but he is a strong opponent that does not understand the power of money. We have to move against him strategically and wait for our chance. He acts like a chess player on offense not caring for the protection of his king...or queen, for that matter!" He stopped his walk around the room and turned to his soldiers with one final question. "I thought this 'safety' was a defense player?"

CHAPTER 21

Clark BATTLE WAS asked to appear on the *"Group of Four"*, to express his opinion about the outing of Hank Harrison. The *"Group"* included three conservative media personalities and one lame-stream progressive, tired of arguing but still willing to collect a paycheck. They hashed out subjects at the five o'clock hour in a generally entertaining, mostly friendly discussion, if you enjoyed their irreverent approach to the "liberal elite."

Today they were discussing the possible downfall of sports in America now that a gay football player had openly announced his lifestyle. Each member made some opening comments, including the only female member, a mother, who expressed concern about her ten-year-old possibly having to play soccer with an openly gay schoolmate. Even the progressive member wondered if this could become a political liability for the Democrats in the midterm elections in 2014.

Chance Angel, the smart aleck, unofficial host was in charge of bringing the guest journalist into the discussion. A surprise accusation fell into the laps of the "gang" that would dominate the next forty-eight news cycles. They quickly became part of a real news event.

Clark Battle was a veteran professional-sports journalist with no time for making fun of the liberal elite. He was chasing a story. "I believe Guy Finelli is involved in some kind of cover-up. My sources tell me that he was involved in drugs as a teenager and may have been assaulted before his senior year of high school by a drug gang. This situation with Hank Harrison might be payback for the death of a drug member in his network."

Chance removed his glasses and let them lie on his chest, attached to a leather cord full of beads around his neck.

"Mr. Battle...that is quite a mouthful for a potential All-American football player." He looked truly shaken by the accusation. "What is it...or let me say...what do you have as evidence that Mr. Finelli is involved?"

"Well, I find it interesting that he was contacted by the people that supposedly assaulted his friend with a message. Why would he be contacted if he wasn't involved? The LGBT community has stepped forward to label this a hate crime, when we have no evidence of it."

"Are you saying that Hank Harrison announcing he was gay was a staged event by the LGBT community for publicity?"

"That is exactly what I am saying!"

• • •

Brooks O'Malley was pacing behind his desk, trying to keep his voice clear. Anxiety at times would close down his rebuilt voice box. He chugged some water and took several deep, yoga-type breaths.

"Anna, we need to go quiet on any comment on this story about Hank and Guy. We have received some information to get closer to the Turk and his organization. This would be a disaster if it got into the open."

"I get it, sir, but Guy is the wide-open target, not Hank. Shit, Hank's relieved just to play football. Nobody cares about his lifestyle, not in this neck of the woods. Did you see his performance Saturday? Ten catches, one hundred forty-two yards, and two TDs. He was awesome!"

"I saw the game...hell, even Guy's boring seventeen tackles and no interceptions were perfect, until he pulled that stunt at the end of the game."

"Stunt! That was the greatest play I've ever witnessed. Besides, he wasn't going to let the Turk win. Guy's stubborn that way."

"I'm not talking about his performance...shit, *nobody* could make that play...but I'm saying we're getting closer to the Turk, so who cares if he wins the stupid bet? It drew attention to the betting situation. People in Vegas will notice that kind of crap. I just want to get his empire. If he gets pissed off, then he'll shut down."

"You're right; I get it...but Guy's only eighteen, going on nineteen. Shit...what can I say? He's a young stud."

"Did you ever think that The Turk was counting on him to try to beat the point spread?"

"Not yet, he's too macho to think like that. He wants to beat Guy, mano a mano, not trick him."

"I disagree! The Turk is a guy who probably likes to play chess, and he may have found a challenger in Guy. He may have just realized it and might take some

135

time for his next move. Either way, we are all over Guy with protection, but the targets maybe those around him. We'll just have to wait for the next pawn to fall. You stay safe, my dear."

"I never liked chess...too slow. Don't worry about me, boss; I'll be fine. I think this could be an interesting season of football. I guess you could say I'm protecting the king."

"Just remember, you're still the most important piece." "Let me guess...that makes me the queen!"

• • •

A month later, Anna was enjoying her first trip to Tallahassee. Luckily, the FBI was able to secure a private room in the best Italian restaurant in town, Z. *Bardhi's*. She wanted to host as mall party for Guy's nineteenth birthday on Friday night before the big game on Saturday, October 5, against Florida Capital University (FCU). Anna had a feeling that this weekend would be magical, with a big upset win over FCU. She booked a room at the *Hotel Duval* on North Monroe to celebrate, just in case.

Coach Brown had given his superstar sophomore permission to celebrate his birthday on Friday night with his family and stay the weekend at the *Hotel Duval*. UMD had quietly landed in college football's top twenty by winning their first five contests in convincing fashion.

Guy Finelli had exceeded the hype, leading the defense to outscore their opponents themselves. They had given up five field goals and four TDs in five games, for a total of forty-three points. The UMD defense had scored six TDs- four on interceptions (three by Guy) and two on fumble returns-and one safety, for forty-four points. That was not counting Guy's two TDs on punt returns.

His best friend on offense, Hank Harrison, was leading the team in all categories of receptions, including TDs. It was one category that Hank kept track of, because as a tight end, scoring in the red zone (inside the twenty- yard-line) helped his team the most. His hero, Jerry Smith, had scored sixty TDs (a tight end record for twenty-seven years) and lost a net of one fumble in his fourteen-year career. Hank liked to remind himself of those two facts before every game.

The team was built on running the football, with Emmitt Excel averaging 175 yards per game and Russell Reiner's short precision passing at a 75 percent completion rate. Along with a stifling defense, the offense was controlling the ball over thirty-five minutes a game.

136

None of those statistics meant anything to those in the media. They had not played from behind and had not faced the talented Capital Indians of Florida. UMD was a three-touchdown underdog to the number-one team in the country. The eighty thousand fans in Tallahassee would present a brutal atmosphere of noise, tomahawk chops, and slinging arrows of verbal brutality.

In the restaurant, Guy was only worried about the menu in front of him and what to order. He was totally confident about the game but not confident about going to an Italian restaurant not named the *Pines of Rome* and without the "roast veal." He decided to go with the "linguine with clams." He figured that being so close to the Gulf would give the dish a chance to be fresh and maybe as tasty as his dad's.

Phillip and Carol had driven down from Maryland, picking up Grace in Raleigh on the way. Alex had flown down with the redheads, Charlotte, Patty, and Anna, along with Anthony and Florence Finelli, for the night and the game tomorrow. The Washington Presidents' baseball team owner, Frederick Meyers, had generously provided his private plane to keep his best player's travel out of media glare and ensure his return for the Presidents game Saturday night. Alex's team had already clinched their second straight NL East Division title and were looking forward to the playoffs starting next week. He was a cinch to win the NL MVP with another potential triple-crown performance and a fifty-homer season. Sally Keegan had stayed home with the twins, trying to catch up on some sleep with the playoffs coming up.

Cousin Joe Finelli and his friend Furrey Favarro, both now assistant coaches for UMD, rounded out the dozen at the back-room table. Joe was the first to present a toast with the red wine. "My dear cousin is finally almost *not* a teenager! Only one year to being twenty. These kids, they seem to age slowly...now, I'm sure Anna is happy that Guy is at least starting his twentieth year of life." Joe winked at her, knowing firsthand that being with an older woman has its advantages. His wife, Brandy, was seven years his senior, and it had worked out just fine. "Let's toast"-he looked behind him to the dinner crowd to see how loud he could get-"to the best player in college football!" Joe chugged down his glass, double-high-fived Coach Favarro, and went around the table to bear-hug his smiling cousin. "This boy is going to steal Capital's warhorse tomorrow... wahoo!" Heads turned in the other room as Joe returned to his seat, tomahawking to the crowd. Most of them politely clapped, having no idea who the wild men were huddling in that back room.

After dinner, a chocolate cake with red-and-white icing, nineteen black candles, and one gold one for good luck was brought out. His mother, Carol, came up behind Guy to give him a big hug and a kiss. It was hard for her to see her baby so grown up. She placed a small gift and three birthday cards sealed up next to his plate. "I know this one is from Wendy, your godmother, but this other one doesn't have an address. Maybe Stanley sent you something from Arizona."

"Sorry, Mom, I have to open this first. I'm very curious!"

"It's your birthday, son. You're in charge."

Guy ripped open the card, put the enclosed note in his pocket, read the card, and closed it quickly. "Boy, that Stanley is something, to remember my birthday."[11] He lunged for the small box from his mom and dad and quickly opened it. She gave him another kiss on his cheek, enjoying the excuse to cuddle him like a baby. "Mom, Dad...this is perfect!" He pulled the new wallet from the box and noticed the two hundred-dollar bills inside. Cash was nice to have, but his brother had given him a credit card in high school that covered all his expenses. It had made him feel secure during a very dark time. Even though he was involved in selling pot at the time, he had made a point of using the card judiciously. As he thought about his drug-selling history, he knew he needed to read the note in his pocket. He gave Anna a quick look and stood up.

"Hey, let's cut this cake." He stepped back and allowed Carol and Anna to hand out cake from his seat. Reaching in his pocket while accepting the first slice, he opened the note and read it to himself.

"So glad I could help you celebrate your birthday weekend! A victory tomorrow will be your special gift. Amazing how the experts do not believe in your team, but I have great faith in your ability to lead them. You are a formidable challenger. Someday you will have a gift for my birthday, perhaps after the new year. Remember, the night hides a world but reveals a universe. Enjoy the evening with your family."

Guy crumpled the note and slid it back into his pocket. He took a bite of the cake.

Anna finished handing out the cake and nestled up to Guy. "Is everything OK, my dear?"

"He's got me in his web, Anna. You might not want to get too close; you may never get out!"

Anna knew that the Turk had revealed another message. *He is so creepy,* she thought, but then she forced herself to turn on her charm with Guy. She knew he needed to feel out of harm's way, and therefore his security was in her hands, which were searching for the small of his back. She arched her back and pressed her chest deep into Guy's soul, connecting as one body. "My dear, you are my king, and I am your queen. We will figure out our next move in the morning. You have your family here, and this is not going to ruin this evening."

The dinner party moved to the Diamond Suite of the *Hotel Duval* in Tallahassee. The wine had flowed freely during dinner, affecting Charlotte and Patty the most. Guy was not a wine drinker like his dad and brother; plus, he was only nineteen. Pot would still be his drug of choice if he were still involved in using drugs. He had another two years before the deal with his parents would expire, but with drug testing in his sport, it was not worth the gamble.

Anna had retreated to the bedroom to talk with Brooks about the latest gambit by the Turk. She did not want to ruin the party but thought about rescuing Guy from her fellow redheads as soon as possible. Florence was in charge of opening new bottles of her favorite wine, flown down with her on the plane.

In the living-room part of the suite, Cousin Joe had the music flowing from his smartphone and was engaging his mom and Carol in dancing. Anthony joined in on the fun by grabbing Charlotte off the coach for a twirl. Finally, Grace joined in when "19th Nervous Breakdown" came on. Phillip had to join the soul train as well after hearing his favorite opening guitar riff of all time.

Alex was on the balcony calling Sally, making sure she had survived the day and hoping she was able to get the twins to sleep. Sally assured him that she missed him and had accomplished said mission. She encouraged him to get back to the party that she could hear in the background, "Those Finellis are sure good at the 'instant party' thing. Wish I was there, dear; go enjoy yourself."

Patty was not feeling any pain and was looking forward to a good night's sleep. She nestled in next to Guy's chest, feeling his giant wingspan across the couch as he drummed his feet to the music. The song selection made him happy to see his dad in such a festive mood. Patty was comfortable around Guy; she loved everything about him, except that he was nineteen. They had been together once after Anthony Halloween party last year, which left many of the attendees waking up with massive hangovers. She had been one of those, and the alcohol had given her permission to be aggressive toward Guy after the party. When she woke up in his apartment the next morning, she was horrified at her lack of control and left as Guy slept. Now she was having similar feelings, but having drunk only wine, she was confident about sleeping alone tonight.

Anna and Alex arrived behind the couch at the same time. Anna commented, "Thank goodness my spot with Guy is interchangeable with another redhead!"

"Well, she does look a little bit like you, and it is his birthday."

139

"Somehow, I think he knows the difference; he's good at defending offensive passes!" With that, Anna grabbed Alex's power-hitting shoulders and joined in on the last verse of the Stones' masterpiece.

The "instant party" had fizzled before Guy's normal eleven o'clock curfew, but Anna had no trouble keeping him awake for some final birthday celebrations. They were both turned on by the evening of family, great food, and dancing to sixties music.

Anna wanted to be in control as she looked down at Guy, moving her hands on his armor-like chest muscles and thickly padded swimming shoulders. She closed her eyes and let her head fall back, feeling his pulse throughout her body. The jerking and thrusting led to a perfect feeling of serenity and a stationary pose.

She slowly moved her hands from her thighs up her torso, while letting her forefingers feel the moisture hiding under her breasts. She assessed the curved beauties by touch, feeling the perfect balance of soft and firm.

Finally, she reached her face, noticing "As Tears Go By," then moved slowly to lie next to him, knowing that for the rest of the night, he was "Under My Thumb." Like her fellow redhead, she felt the same need to sleep, but contrary to her friend's night, she found perfect "Satisfaction."

CHAPTER 22

G UY FINELL! COULD feel the fans of Florida Capital football shake the stadium

field as he warmed up in the end zone, catching field goals from his kicker. Playing at noon on the first Saturday in October in the Sunshine State gave him a sense of what Sean Taylor had grown up feeling, as he learned to love this game on the eternal green fields of Florida. He too had faced this in-state rival crowd a dozen years ago as he led his team to a championship game. Like Sean Taylor, Guy would learn today how an unknown sideline referee could change the course of a college football game.

Moving toward midfield during warm-ups, he watched second-year FCU QB Phillip Morris warm up, throwing bombs on a bell curve down the sidelines to an endless number of extra-tall receivers. Guy had studied Morris's tendencies and knew that he loved to throw down the seams of the field between the hash marks (HM) and the numbers. Most teams had given up on that idea against UMD after watching film from Guy's freshman year. He would consistently disrupt or intercept passes thrown between the HM and the numbers. This year, teams were keeping any long passes down the sidelines, hoping that Finelli would be late getting there. It had cut down on interceptions, but most long pass attempts were still unsuccessful.

FCU was a cocky team and had easily handled UMD in College Park early in the 2012 season. It had been Guy's first ACC game, and he made sure that it did not happen the rest of the regular season. With only one loss and FCU's two unexpected league losses, UMD had advanced to the ACC championship game that season, only to lose to VT.

Finelli's interceptions and defensive TDs were down so far in the first five games of the current season, but he was averaging seventeen tackles and three pass breakups a game, besides leading the country in punt and kickoff return yardage. Coach Brown had not chosen to use him on offense so far, but he had a package up his sleeve if UMD fell behind against FCU. Finelli and his Sprint DMC defensive backfield teammates would join Hank Harrison for at least three plays after a punt return. Hank and Guy would line up as double tight ends with Mark Pelligrini as a single back and Cary Collins and Duran Hall as the wideouts. It would be labeled by BASN reporter Kelly Browner as the "Turtle

Shuffle."

• • •

"This creep is in on this game, Brooks. He's acting like it's a birthday gift for Guy."

"We have no unusual information on the betting line. It is holding at twenty-one points. He's making a play for an unusual bet, maybe offshore with an Arab sheik; who knows? He's trying to make up for that half-million swing on the last bet we know about."

"There's minimum security around Hank and Guy. I hope everything is cool down here."

"I think the Hank thing is old news. I would expect good ole Southern hospitality down there."

■ ■ ■

Two early UMD turnovers led to an early 14-0 FCU lead. UMD's defense finally held, and Guy returned a punt to midfield. The "Turtle Shuffle" was melting into the offensive huddle without FCU recognition. QB Russell Reiner led them out of the huddle. Guy Finelli came from the left tight-end spot and sat in a tailback spot, ten yards deep. Pelligrini left the backfield and lined up outside right. Reiner called "blue 21" and went in motion to the left. Two counts later, the ball was snapped to Guy, who followed a crushing double-team block from Hank and Mark and ran up the numbers on the right side for twenty-three yards.

Without a huddle, they lined up on FCU twenty-seven. In the same formation, Guy received the ball and rolled left. He stopped, turned his shoulders, and threw a strike to Cary Collins, coming left to right on a diagonal to the FCU two-yard line.

Guy ran up quickly to the line of scrimmage and set up behind center in the T-formation. He called "black twenty-one," waited two counts, called "hike," and bulldozed into the end zone.

The FCU crowd sat silent and restless for the rest of the quarter as they watched a Finelli interception and a caused fumble from a jarring Finelli tackle set up two short UMD TD drives before halftime. Phillip thought he had gone to heaven as he watched his son lead the young, underdog UMD squad to a 21-14 halftime lead. Anna continued to keep an eye on Guy's welfare as he filed by thousands of angry fans on his way into the locker room.

The second half was a pure slugfest, as the UMD ground game controlled the line of scrimmage and managed two short field goals from long drives. The FCU crowd was lulled to a quiet, complaining mumble, as Emmitt Excel darted and danced on outside sweeps and screen passes; and then pounded the tired defense with runs between the tackles.

FCU QB Phillip Morris was inconsistent all day, but he managed a perfect strike down the sidelines over Duran Hall for a long score in the fourth quarter. It was the type of throw that had landed Morris on an August cover of *Sports Illustrated,* announcing him as the top Heisman candidate.

With two minutes to go 1n the game, UMD was clinging to a 27-21 lead. FCU managed to move into the redzone with fifteen seconds left. Morris tried his favorite seam pattern to his giant TE, but Guy made superficial contact over the TE's back to knock the ball away. The sideline referee kept his flag in his pocket as the crowd protested.

With seven seconds left, Phillip Morris tried a corner throw to his lanky wide receiver, but Cary Collins played perfect position to knock down the pass.

The stopped clock showed one tick left in the game as a little-known sideline referee, Roy Clark, stood in the end zone as an enormous amount of sweat poured down his back. He was close to securing that fifty-grand bonus in the Cayman Island account that a young man named Mahmood Abdul-Abar had set up for him with an initial $20,000 balance. He knew the bonus would arrive in his account if the UMD lead prevailed for one more play. His credit-card debt would be gone and he could end his drinking and the fighting with his wife. It was all possible if he could secure the victory.

Morris took the snap and rolled to the right to set up for a diagonal throw to the left corner of the end zone, but Duran Hall had blanket coverage. With his protection breaking down, Morris abandoned the right-side pocket and reversed his field toward the left side. Suddenly, he cut straight to the middle, seeing an open field. He galloped like a stallion, all six feet, six inches of him, crossing the twenty-five, the twenty, the fifteen; then Morris suddenly stopped and spotted his giant tight end pushing off Guy Finelli as he came across the back of the end zone to provide a big target just over the goal line. Referee Clark was reaching for his flag to call the legitimate push-off, hoping he would be able to leave town with his life, as Morris set his feet and rifled a pass to hit his TE square in the numbers.

Guy Finelli had no choice but to spin away from the push-off and take a couple of strides toward the target. He then timed a dive as the football sailed past the ten-yard line. Soaring into a parallel flight, Guy looked effortless heading for the TE's shoulders, not to shake this block of granite from the ball with a hit but to extend his right arm lightly around his massive shoulders and successfully deflect the ball away with his left forefinger.

The people in the crowd were mostly numb as they tried to understand the superhuman defensive play they had just witnessed. They sat down with an extra push of gravity as though they had just received some really bad news over the phone. A few were still standing, expecting to see the winning extra-point try. Others that were far away were screaming for a flag, until they saw a replay showing the perfect ballet of "The Safety." As the crowd left the stadium, there was an unusual quiet besides the shuffling of shoes. "That Guy Finelli" seemed to start most conversations at the postgame tailgate parties.

Roy Clark felt relieved as he held on to his flag, seeing no flying handkerchiefs on the field after the exceptional defensive play. He finally released his tight grip and looked for an exit from the field. Florida state troopers quickly surrounded him and the other six referees as they left the field to a quiet murmur of disbelief. Roy Clark tried to contain the cheering going on in his head at the thought of celebrating with a bottle of Chevas Regal scotch tonight when he got home to Georgia, a four-hour drive. With no one to talk to about his payday, the bottle would once again become his best friend.

UMD celebrated in the end zone for ten minutes, drinking in the sight of a quiet FCU crowd leaving the stadium. It was their last ACC game in Florida before moving to the Big Ten for the 2014 season.

Guy Finelli and Hank Harrison were surrounded by the whole team as Coach Gerry Brown summed up the victory before they left the field.

"We came on this field as a team. Take a moment and smell how it feels to win on this perfect grass in October, and close your eyes to see the field in Atlanta for the ACC championship in December feeling the same way. You see it?" The players answered the coach three times with screams of joy. "OK then..let's leave the field as a team... and protect our own."

Like a military unit, UMD paraded through the field exit surrounded by minor insults and plastic cups thrown their way. With perfect discipline, they made it to the locker room and then to their charter flight home with partying on their minds. UMD was 6-0 and would soon be on its way to the ACC championship game with an undefeated 12-0 record.

The media reaction was mixed throughout the country on the final play. The Northeast from DC to Boston thought it was a great play; the Southeast from Charlottesville to Miami thought it was "highway robbery for FCU to lose to an inferior team." But they all agreed on the fact that Guy Finelli could be the best player in the country.

In Tallahassee for one last night at the *Hotel Duval,* first, there was room service for Guy to eat up a storm. Anna's eyes were once again in disbelief at the tonnage of food that Guy was inhaling. She shook her head, remembering that he was still very much a growing boy. He had lost eight pounds of fluids and weight on the field. After this feast, he would be back at his playing weight of 237.

After some time to enjoy early-evening football and digestion, they made it down to the indoor pool and jacuzzi. Having the place to themselves, they warmed up in the jacuzzi for ten minutes, followed by some laps in the pool. Anna was able to do fifteen minutes of laps before resting at the end of the pool to watch Guy move the water with his body. He continued for another thirty minutes in an effortless freestyle. Finally, on his last two laps, he exploded with his butterfly at full speed. Anna felt the need to cheer his last few strokes as he emerged, looking like her king.

She heard his phone buzzing and looked at the unknown number. It quickly went to voice mail. Guy grabbed a towel and retrieved his phone message. He recognized the voice as his former friend, Mahmood Abdul-Abar, better known as Mach. They had not talked but only texted since Guy had left for his senior year at WJ. Mach was a computer engineering student at the University of Maryland-Baltimore County (UMBC)- he had always been great with computers. He sounded desperate. "Call me at this number from another phone."

Guy and Anna quietly found a cubicle without being recognized. Mach answered quickly. "My friend...it is you; I know it. Don't say anything; just listen. I'm scared. I can't keep working for him. He is threatening to tell my parents if I try to leave him. Please meet with me tomorrow night. Come into my parents' driveway, and I will follow you in my car to the Indian restaurant at the Hillandale Shopping Center-you know, our old neighborhood. Come just after dark. Thank you, my friend."

The phone clicked, and Guy looked like he had seen a ghost. "My God, Mach is in their web. I have to meet him tomorrow night."

"I'm coming with you." "No, it should be just me."

"Bullshit, I'll be there...besides, after tonight, you'll owe me a nice dinner out!"

After Anna had settled the issue, she was determined to enjoy the rest of their Saturday night together. With Guy's notoriety rising, having him all to herself would be getting tougher. Guy starting singing, "Under my thumb... the girl who once had me down," as they moved like a stealth couple down the hall and into the elevator. On the ride up, Guy pulled Anna to his chest to continue his serenade. "The girl who once pushed me around...it's down to me...yeah!" The polite older couple in the elevator, visiting family in town, laughed to each other, failing to recognize the vibrant young couple. They arrived back to the Diamond Suite just in time to enjoy dessert.

• • •

Anna was uneasy about meeting Guy's former NC drug friend, even though Guy assured her that Mach never did drugs. According to Guy, Mach had developed a sweet tooth for nice cars from his early money that kept him connected to the NC even after he was warned by Agent Richard Kessinger several times to move on to another trade. He was watched for a year, according to Brooks O'Malley, enough to get some leads. Mach had been providing help to the Turk with cell phones, wireless connections, and most importantly, offshore bank accounts. He was responsible for setting up illegal and legal offshore betting systems for the Turk that would separate him from the other mobsters. Between his grueling schoolwork and serving the Turk, the pressure was enormous. Ironically, staying with his parents was the saving grace, because he had the whole basement to himself. They never entered his domain, and he was not expected to be with them except for Friday-night dinner and prayer.

Anna and Guy pulled into a parking space in front of the *Jewel of India*, an upscale restaurant next to a *Domino's Pizza* and across from *Value Village*. There was a combination of twenty or so stores that kept the parking lot packed. Mach pulled up in an $80,000 black 2014 Porsche Cayman S, which he had paid for in cash last month. He looked extremely thin as he jumped out of the car and hugged Guy in front of the restaurant. He seemed unconcerned but happy to meet Anna as they sat down near a window with a great view of his car and the *Safeway,* looking south across the busy parking lot.

Mach was full of news about some shared friends and was excited to watch Guy's ascension to football greatness. When Anna excused herself for the ladies' room in a rehearsed exit to give them time alone, Mach started to talk to Guy about his trouble. Guy immediately told him that he should wait for Anna to return, because she was an FBI agent. They had discussed their strategy with Brooks, and all had agreed to convince

Mach to talk to both of them.

"Mach... this is your only way out. Anna can care for you."

"I do not think so, my good friend. I had my chance after you left in 2011. Agent Kessinger told me it was time, but I wanted the money, the freedom. I became popular when I got my first car. My parents think I work so hard fixing computers. They are so proud of me. I have a girlfriend from Baltimore that my parents think is a nice girl, but she runs money for him. They are related somehow. She is Iraqi, like him."

"We can help her too, Mach," Anna added as she returned to her seat.

"They will kill her if you contact her; please, this is scary enough!"

Guy tried to calm Mach, knowing he was feeling boxed in. "What can I do for you, Mach? Tell me something that will help you."

"He is planning a big bet for the championship game, if you get there...otherwise, this last game made him plenty to stay under the radar until then. He may leave me alone if the big game goes his way. I pray to Allah!"

Guy looked intently at Mach as he played with his food. Anna grabbed Guy's hand under the table and intertwined her fingers with his.

"Maybe by next summer we can all meet for dinner. Her name is Parand. You may not like her though." "You're crazy, man; of course, I would. I'm sure she is hot!"

"Well, she is very beautiful, with lovely, dark skin, but you may not think she is attractive, because she has one problem."

"Let me guess-she is overweight or something silly like that. I'm much more grown up now, much more accepting of the way girls look than I was in high school."

Mach took a good look at Anna and her physical beauty. "Oh yes, I can see that Anna is a project for you. I do not think you have changed a bit, my friend!"

"So, what is her problem? Do I have to hold your upside down or something?"

"No, she 1s not overweight. She 1s quite extraordinary...she is just not..." Mach hesitated, enjoying the playful time with his friend and feeling his acceptance for a moment, knowing it would not have a chance to last past this evening. "You know, Guy... just not a redhead!"

CHAPTER 23

CLARK BATTLE HAD followed the UMD football team story all season. Now they were in Atlanta for the 2013 ACC championship game. The undefeated UMD squad was once again facing the Virginia Tech (VT) squad that they had lost to in 2012. Clark was doing some last questions with both coaching staffs after the final Friday walk-through practice for a huge story that was coming out in the *Nation's Times* on Saturday morning. The hope was that its release online on game day would lead to great coverage on the pregame shows.

His main source was Parand Shamar, who was being used by her boss, the Turk, to spread rumors about Guy Finelli. She was also in love with Guy's friend, Mach, which was causing her great tension, because the information was groundbreaking. She told about Guy's high-school drug dealing and use with a group of friends called the Northeast Consortium (NC). Clark was given information about Rico Gilliespie's suicide as proof of Guy's involvement. Rico's wife had confirmed that Guy met with her husband a week before his suicide to discuss their involvement in using and dealing drugs. She received a healthy payoff from the Turk to cooperate.

The accusations made about the LGBT involvement In Hank Harrison's outing and beating had also been supplied earlier in the season by Parand. All the media had been critical of Battle's accusations because the story was based on an unconfirmed source. But in the right-wing media, he had become a hero, arguing that a gay player and his friend were getting "hands off" treatment by the left- leaning media.

Besides the drug use and dealing accusations, Clark Battle had more damaging information about Guy Finelli's beating before his first WJ game. He questioned the "car accident" explanation, reporting that "According to police sources, Finelli was attacked by six men before his car was stolen." Clark reported that the FBI had cleaned up the case to cover up details.

The most provable allegation accused Guy of affiliation with the MS-13 gang because he was stitched up by Dr. Antonio Sanchez, who was known to treat residents of the Langley Park area, including MS-13 members, in a community medical center. Current UMD assistant coaches Fury Favarro and Joe Finelli were also accused of hiding

Guy's injuries so that he could play in the opening game.

This brilliant misdirection of misinformation by the Turk gave reporters some bits of the truth to explore. It was another gambit to put pressure on Guy to cooperate with the Turk in the future and to put the blame for the drug activity on the Langley Park-based MS-13 drug gang. The strategy was meant to narrow Guy's options and ensure his inevitable cooperation in what the Turk hoped would be the BCS championship game. He was very happy to find a willing reporter looking for fame.

On Saturday morning, the *Nation's Times* had the front-page headlines:

"UMD's Finelli Accused of Drug Dealing in High School
Star Safety Covered Up a Beating by Drug Gang"

The "fair and balanced" news and sports channels ran the headlines all day and had a morning interview with Clark Battle running almost hourly on different shows. The left-wing media ignored the drug aspect of the story, other than reporting that Guy Finelli knew Rico Gillespie, but they did focus on reports of Guy Finelli suffering rib injuries from a car crash before the first WJ season. Quickly, though, ESPN got hold of the comeback highlights in the 30-29 high-school victory, which became a better story to watch, because everybody currently loved "The Safety."

• • •

What do you think about the story, sir?"

"It's good and bad, but I think it all goes away if UMD wins, to be honest."

"Well, that's encouraging. I feel bad for Mach and Farand. They're nice kids caught up in this creep's sick empire."

"Settle down, Anna. They had chances to get out. They still could get out, but it's getting harder. We'll reach out to them after the season is over; otherwise, our surveillance on them is paying off."

"We have no communication so far from the creep about the betting. Is he sitting this game out?"

"Unlikely-he's addicted to making his chess moves. He won't miss this one. The Vegas money has swung to UMD by four and a half, which is a little unusual. I'm guessing he has laid out a good deal of money on UMD and giving the points." Kiddingly, O'Malley remarked, "Tell your boy not to win by more than a field goal."

Guy was in his usual spot, the end zone, snagging practice kickoffs before game time.

After his final catch, he ran toward the right corner of the end zone and looked up to the seats about twenty rows deep, where he had sat with his family on New Year's Eve 2002, over a decade ago. It was the most exciting night in his eight-year-old life up to that point and full of highlights in a UMD 3 0-3 win over Tennessee. All he could remember that night, before he fell asleep, was replaying the touchdowns in that same end zone and seeing himself on that same field someday playing for UMD under the Georgia Dome. His flashback sent a chill that raised the hair on his neck. He took off his helmet and rubbed his neatly cropped hair and then his neck, hoping to feel the good luck of that family memory leaving his body. He reattached his head armor, which he never removed during the game, and trotted to huddle with his teammates before the opening kickoff.

Coach Brown's game plan was simple: score first and play good field position to make VT earn their scores. VT was a team built to play like UMD, except for better mobility at their QB position. Guy and his DMC group knew they were in for a lot of tackling today. It would be a black-and-blue game without the dirt on their jerseys. Both sides still had final exams to finish for the fall semester, but they would get very little studying done today.

Guy tried to focus on the red and white of the UMD fans in the crowd and not the "puke colors" he hated as VT fan attire. He always wondered why an engineering school would choose Chicago maroon and burnt orange together as a pair of colors, but then he thought, nothing really goes with orange...does it?

The random thinking helped him relax as the kickoff came floating out of the dome lighting. A wave of maroon came from his left, led by a flying lightweight of a player coming at his midsection, which Guy swatted away with a stiff-arm. A full head-on collision with two linebackers in front of him at the twenty was coming, just as two cornerbacks were coming from his left for his legs. The collision of five was nasty, but Guy hesitated and spun out of it as the cornerbacks missed him and blocked the linebackers for him.

He headed back toward the middle of the field as mayhem ruled the coverage and blocking. Sidestepping the crossing waves of linemen from both teams at the thirty, he hurdled the last pile of bodies at the forty and found the stoic VT kicker ready to make a stand at midfield. Guy did a Bobby Mitchell shake and bake leaving him frozen like he was in the falling ash of Pompeii. Surprisingly, the same flying, lightweight defender had recovered and was sprinting into his view from the side, looking like he had just come off the sidelines. Guy tried to strong-arm him, but he was too small to disengage. Finally, the defender jumped on his back around the thirty and rode Guy for twenty yards until he wrestled him down inside the ten-yard line. Guy landed softly on his back, directly on the lightweight's chest, extinguishing the air in his lungs. "The Safety" had dropped his full weight on the maroon and orange.

Guy led his defense all game as they established good field position with exceptional tackling and coverage as they entered the fourth quarter with a slim 13-12 lead over VT. The UMD offense had little success in scoring on their own, mustering only one short touchdown drive after the opening kickoff return and two field goals from defensive turnovers. Coach Brown was hesitant to use his "Turtle Shuffle" to ignite the offense, because they were being dominant on defense while using every ounce of energy on making tackle after tackle.

Shortly into the fourth quarter, the offense gained control of the line of scrimmage. Emmitt Excel ran the ball twelve times, and QB Russell Reiner hit Hank Harrison on four key first-down passes as UMD marched on a sixteen- play, ten-minute drive to the VT two-yard line. On fourth and goal, Coach Brown had to follow his game plan and not his instincts to kick a nineteen-yard field goal for a 16-12 lead.

Those bettors giving the Vegas line of UMD minus four and a half points, were not happy. "The Turk" had invested less than a hundred grand on that line without any" certainty," as he put it, but he still had confidence that his favorite player might make a difference in the score.

With less than two minutes left, VT finally opened up their offense and let their QB throw the ball downfield. With some well-maneuvered scrambles and two completions for over thirty yards, VT drove down to the UMD twenty-yard line with twenty-three seconds left in the game.

Guy knew what play VT would run. Guy's corners, Duran and Cary, had been playing soft corners on every other play on this drive. Guy knew that the VT coaches had picked it up, so he made the call on the next play, enticing the QB to throw the down and out for half the yardage and out-of-bounds to stop the clock. As VT got set in formation, Cary Collins was backed off the receiver to Guy's right, and Duran was tightening up on the receiver to his left. Pelligrini faked the blitz up the middle and bailed out just before the snap to back up Duran. Guy took two steps to his right as the ball was snapped and then put his head down in a full sprint for two counts toward his right, and smelled the ball coming. As he hit top speed on the count of three, he stood tall, located the ball, and snatched the pigskin as it was just about to fly over his head and out of his reach. He kept his feet and headed downfield. Towels were whipping from his teammates on the sidelines as he flew past midfield. The Georgia Dome

151

reverberated sound that seemed to be coming in waves all around him. Totally alone as he passed the thirty, he slowed as he saw the score of 16-12 and the clock winding down to under ten seconds. Suddenly, he stopped on the five-yard line as the meaning of the score became clear. He sidestepped one defender from behind as the clock hit five seconds. A posse of three more defenders caught him, followed by three of his teammates as Guy refused to be tackled. Punches and elbows were exchanged, and he finally went out-of-bounds as the clock hit zero. Guy Finelli emerged from the scrum of players on the ground, holding the ball up high, running to his teammates, crashing into a mass of red-and-white jerseys, all celebrating like conference champions.

Anna was flushed with joy, her face burning red to blend with her hair. Charlotte and Patty hugged her in a triangle of emotion. Carol had her arm around Phillip, who sat with his head in his hands, crying tears of relief, remembering years of practice, months of uncertainty, days of promises, and the thrill of this moment. Fans escaped the chains of mediocrity in the bedlam of ecstasy around them, while Phillip confronted the breakout of greatness by his two sons.

A trip to New Orleans for the college championship loomed after the New Year. With almost a month to finish the semester and enjoy the holidays, they would return to practice to prepare for the biggest game of their lives, now a reality for the young men from UMD.

After the first round of hugging was finished, Anna found a way down the steps to the field, hoping to see and touch her young king. As she waited her turn, Anna looked at all the UMD football fans and the disappointed VT fans. She knew almost all of them admired the selfless play by "the Safety" as he ran out the game clock to secure the victory Safety" as he ran out the game clock to secure the victory his motivation was not selfless, but a bold move that put the Turk on notice that his kingdom was now "in check!"

CHAPTER 24

SHE TRIED TO act normal, but the excitement of the last few weeks was too good to be

true. Her family wanted her home for the holidays in Ohio, but for now, being with Guy was her family. As they drove north on Route 97 in central Maryland, the sunlight was falling quickly through the horizon on Christmas Eve.

There was not much time now before arriving at Cousin Melissa's mansion on the hill for the Finellis' Christmas Eve gathering. It was her first time, and she was feeling everything so intensely. She took Guy's hand as he drove and blurted it out: "I'm pregnant!" Guy stayed steady on the road but slowed down at the next intersection to pull over.

"It was my birthday weekend, wasn't it? It felt like a bull's-eye! This is awesome. We'll have a baby by July?" Guy did the quick math in his head as he reached across the car to hug Anna.

"You mean you're not upset?"

"God, no. This is boss...it's the best...I can't wait to be a father! My parents are going to shit, though, but whatever. I have to try to tell Alex and Sally first tonight to soften the blow to my parents."

"Tonight...you think that's a good idea?"

"Absolutely; he's my financial support until my first contract. They'll take care of us. My parents will want to, but Alex has the cash and would be upset if I didn't tell him first. Then we can tell my parents next, and then everybody else later, after the food. By the way, I am starved. Melissa puts out a gourmet spread, including my grandmother's crab melts for appetizers and the gnocchi with meatballs, along with a ton of other food. I've been waiting all year for this."

"You boys are all about sports, sex, and food!"

"I'm not sure about the order, but what is your point?" "I'm not complaining, just observing."

"This is going to be awesome-a kid-my parents will be the best grandparents."

"And you will be the best father!"

They arrived to the perfect Christmas Eve scene: a crowded and festive house, dressed up to match the holidays and fashioned perfectly for the times. Guy was too young to remember his grandmother Rose hosting the Christmas Eve celebration. Guy I and Rose had been the perfect hosts for the sacred family event since the kitchen was moved to the remodeled basement in the late fifties. Guy I would distribute the champagne and the conversation while Rose managed to cook a feast of fish, meats, and pasta. It was her homemade gnocchi, meatballs, bakala, and crab melts that made the event an evening that stopped time in its tracks.

After Rose's stroke in 1998, the tradition had been hosted by Anthony Finelli for several years, even though Rose continued to do most of the cooking before Cousin Melissa took over a dozen years ago.

Melissa was the perfect host. Looking like the COO of Facebook, she could lean into many roles, including being a successful executive, a great athlete, a mother of three, a wife, and of course a fabulous cook. It helped having housemaids continue to make the kitchen area look like a studio cooking show.

Alex and Sally had come early to the grand house on the hill overlooking Route 97, with the twins trying to match nap times. As Melissa greeted Alex and Sally, DC's famous couple, at the door, she congratulated him on his MVP season, landing one game short of back-to-back World Series wins. She grabbed six-month-old Philomena from the baby carriage and marveled at her size and beauty. It filled her mothering instinct to hold her as she noticed her Christmas outfit of red and green. Her little head was covered with blond curls matching her dad's, while little Phillip had the jet-black look of his mother's hair. They quickly entered the grand foyer with an ascending stairway. Alex and Sally fondly remembered having the house to themselves during the 2012 baseball season, when they fled the media in Bethesda on the way to a series in Philadelphia.

Guy pulled up to the house, seeing his parents already getting out of their car in the large driveway. They stopped and waited as Guy and Anna caught up to them. Carol quickly took Anna aside. "I hope you're hungry. You look fabulous. How do you keep such color in this cold weather?"

Phillip took Guy in his arms, still able to hold him like a growing boy with his long arms and six-foot, two-inch frame. "This is a great day for celebration, my son; it has been quite a couple of years for all of us. Now, let's get inside and get to those crab melts before Alex eats them all!"

The two couples moved inside and found Alex still in the foyer, a target for all the incoming relatives. Sally was coming down the stairway after successfully putting the twins down for a five o'clock nap. She quickly joined in with Anna and Carol as she gave Phillip and Guy big kisses. She looked radiant as usual, holding her husband's arm for closeness. It comforted her to feel his strength; it made her feel sexy and in love.

Alex hugged his younger brother, feeling the stature of a still-growing boy. Guy had been in an eight-hour-a-day regimen of running, swimming, lifting, and stretching for three weeks since his last game. His red sweater hardly could contain his arms and shoulders. The collar of his new shirt, containing their father's wedding tie, seemed to barely outline his neck. As Alex released his brother's body, his heart felt a bond of greatness, and he exhaled deeply, relieved to be playing a noncontact sport.

Carol and Phillip joined the greetings as Guy guided them all into the house office off of the foyer and closed the double doors. He took Anna's hand and faced his favorite people. "I know this is crazy, but Anna and I are pregnant. She just told me on the way up Route Ninety-Seven. I hope you can be as happy as we are. Anna is shocked that I'm telling you all so quickly, but we need your support."

Carol extended her arms to Anna as Sally joined her quickly. "How far are you along? You look fantastic!"

"About eleven weeks...it was the birthday weekend!"

"Let's blame Alex for the hotel suite!" Sally chimed in quickly, holding Anna's hand with grace and support.

Grace walked into to find her family. "What's going on? I've been looking for Mom; I've got her gin and tonic."

"Thanks, dear...I may need another soon. Anna's pregnant!" Carol laughed as she took a big gulp from her favorite drink.

"Guy, you dog...wow, this family is exploding!" Grace leaned in to hug Anna. "Don't worry, Anna; Guy will be making plenty of money soon."

Phillip and Alex cornered Guy as he looked the happiest, they had ever seen him. "Whatever you need, brother, we will provide for you. Now you have to win the college championship so the baby isn't disappointed!"

"Son, you're a grown man now...too young to be a father but old enough to be responsible. You have family to help out. Focus on caring for Anna and your career. This will all hit you when you're twenty-five."

"Thanks, Dad; thanks, Alex..." Guy wanted to say more, but his mind had no words to express his truth. His feelings were full of gratitude for the acceptance of the two most important males to him in the world. In this fleeting moment, it became

155

clear to him that he was happy. Alex would help financially, and Phillip would give him time and emotional support. He would just have to try his best as a father and a ballplayer.

The three stood for several seconds while the sounds of the party echoed off the grand staircase behind them. Guy decided to finally speak the next truth, now coming from his stomach. "I'm really starved-let's see what Cousin Melissa has on the menu tonight after the crab melts!"

CHAPTER 25

NEW ORLEANS WAS the perfect site to hold the college championship. Almost a decade after Katrina, the partying had never been drowned out by the storm. If you were a college student, you did not need an excuse to party, but going to the "Big Easy" to watch your school in the college championship game was a great one. It was close enough to the DC area for students to drive down, with or without a ticket. Going to the game was not as important as being there. You could always find a place to watch the game. UMD was not expected to travel well, meaning they would not come to see their team, but this was different. Most UMD fans knew that this was a once-in-a-lifetime dream, and they were not going to miss it.

The drinking and drug use were in full force with UMD fans that had arrived on the Monday before New Year's Eve, which would give them a full week of partying. The UMD football team landed on New Year's Day and showed up to their hotel to thousands of fans, who were mostly drunk and using lines of cocaine as chasers to keep their buzz on an even keel. Coach Brown did his best to move his team past the loud crowds, but most of players stayed for autographs and to get a feel of the festive atmosphere. The game was on Monday night, six days later, a challenge for any coach.

The Turk's crew from Baltimore had secretly stationed a distribution network out of a local hotel. The word had been spread to the UMD students where to get product. The Turk had made a deal with his New Orleans cocaine distributor to sell in the area for the small sum of 30 percent of the profits. Besides cocaine and pot, he also had loaded up his dealers with Adderall and Ecstasy to keep the party going all week.

The Turk was now officially obsessed with Guy Finelli and his playing style. His admiration had reached a very high level after witnessing his non-scoring move at the end of the last game, even if it had cost him a good deal of money. He called off his news leaks to Clark Battle and secret messages to Guy. The Turk saw him as a bold, strategic thinker after Guy had sent a strong message to him as his opponent. It was clarification of his status as an equal competitor to this great athlete. A statement showing that he, the Turk, was on the mind of this great All-American known as "The Safety." The thought brought a smile to the Turk.

The business of betting, though, could not be an emotional decision, the Turk told himself. He was still convinced that taking the two-time defending champion, Alabama Central (ACU), and giving fourteen points was the steal of a lifetime. This UMD team just did not have the "Arabian Horses" that he remembered as a boy to compete on the offensive and defensive lines.

Because he now respected his adversary, the Turk would play the bet without interference. It would be his intelligence against athleticism-a challenge he had won all of his life. He believed that it was time to show "The Safety" that he could dominate him without interference when necessary. The Turk would let him play his game with the rational that Guy would soon make money, and then understand the real value of controlling his market in the future.

For this week, the Turk would see himself as another great multimillion-dollar businessman in the American market, making his money selling drugs to UMD students who wanted to party and carefully investing his $500,000 bet legally in Vegas right before the game. He was proud of himself, just starting to feel like a solid, upstanding citizen.

• • •

Brooks O'Malley was excited as he met with Anna in the Maryland governor's suite before the game. "We have clean silence from Baltimore since the last game about any involvement in the championship game. Lots of Vegas betting on ACU, and drugs flowing in from Baltimore for the week, but overall a cease-fire. Go enjoy the game."

"I think I'd rather stay up here for now. I won't be able to sit. This is too nerve-racking, and I can't drink!"

"Great, it will be nice to have company up here in the suite with all the clueless staff around. I'm glad somebody will be cheering with me."

"What if they lose, Brooks?" Anna looked fearful. "If your boy has anything to do with it, they won't."

"He thinks they're going to kill them. Is he crazy? These ACU guys look enormous!"

"Well, let's hope he knows something that we don't know."

Guy Finelli had not talked to anybody in the media since the Hank Harrison news conference before the season started. Unlike his brother, Alex Santucci, he found the media to be clueless, and unlike his father, Phillip Finelli, he did not read the papers. After the Clark Battle story, it was even easier to keep quiet. Luckily, his coach, Gerry Brown, agreed and shielded him from the media all year. For the past month, he had allowed QB Russell Reiner, RB Emmit Excell, and TE Hank Harrison to speak to the media for the team.

Besides his intense workouts, Guy had been meeting with Joe Finelli and Fury Favarro to go over ACU offensive film and specifically their senior QB, Mike Mcclendon. Guy thought he was overrated and easy to read. They picked up several key "tells" from their formations to know when they were throwing down the middle of the field. Cousin Joe was worried about tackling their horses in the backfield. Guy assured him that ACU's offensive line was slow, and his backfield was up for the challenge.

Cousin Joe also set up two punt-return formations that could break for TDs. On both, Guy would have to catch the ball on the run from the opposite side to hide their blocking. Guy practiced for three weeks, catching a thousand punts on the run. Coach Fury told him that his great-grandfather had coached "Freckles" Ferraro in that technique in the late '20s, and the great Sammy Baugh had returned punts like that in the '30s. He said that when the pigskin got slimmer and harder, the punts went higher, with more spin, and became harder to catch on the run.

What Coach Fury did not know was that Guy had learned the same technique from his father when he was seven. It was second nature to him by the time he was ten. No coach had ever brought it up and planned for it, until this big game. He was ready to score some TDs.

The UMD players had successfully navigated the crazy week of partying in New Orleans without breaking any of the tested rules. Guy was resting most of the week, which rallied the defense to focus solely on the game. Reiner and Excel on offense had kept vigilant tabs on the players, especially the linemen, to stay out of trouble. Fortunately, the strip clubs kept the big boys happy even without alcohol. By game time, every pundit in the country was counting on a big ACU win. The Vegas line had stretched to seventeen points.

The explosions of fireworks before the game left a cloud over the first quarter, and both teams played like they were in a fog, rarely throwing the ball, content with pounding the line with running backs of different sizes, who were taking horrendous hits from both sides. By the time the air cleared, there was no score to start the second quarter. Then, a third ACU running back was knocked out by the UMD defense. This time, cornerback Cary Collins had come on a corner blitz to blindside the shifty ACU running back, changing directions to find a cutback lane on a right-side stretch play. The lanky Collins enveloped the shortage back and knocked the air out of him.

UMD was finally winning the field-position game and would receive their third punt around the UMD forty-yard line. Coach Joe Finelli called his special punt-return play from left to right. On the first two punts, ACU had punted away from Guy Finelli to pin UMD inside the ten-yard line. This time, coaches Joe and Fury were counting on that. On cue, the punt headed in a beautiful, tight spiral, turning over in the direction of the right side of the field and wanting to land around the thirty-yard line. If left to its own desires, the football would have gladly bounced end over end toward the goal line. Guy was running a perfect route from the left side, feeling time slow down as he saw the ball spinning against a sea of red and white, perfectly aiming for his arms. Only the sound of his breath was audible as he united with the ball, feeling time quickly shifting back to regular motion with the football secured. He switched his full attention to the wall of crimson uniforms coming vertically down the field. The opponents had been watching the ball, not focusing on Guy speeding to catch it. The wall of blockers for UMD had retreated to the thirty-yard line and, like a picket fence, quickly closed off the first ACU defenders. Three yards from the sidelines, Guy made an impossible right-angle cut and turned up-field. For twenty yards, UMD held their fence in hand-to-hand combat against ACU defenders. As Guy hurdled a last defender at midfield, it suddenly looked like low tide at Cape Canaveral-fifty yards of no one until the ocean. With the UMD sidelines on his right screaming directions to finish his gallop, his extra-large cousin escorted him until the twenty-yard line, pumping both fists, hailing the first score of the game.

The 7-0 lead carried into the fourth quarter as the ACU running game was brought to a halt. The UMD offense was efficiently running time off the clock and maintaining good field position. TE Hank Harrison was in the battle of his life, absorbing blows to his body and his manhood throughout the game. He refused to lose his concentration or his temper as he plowed vicious blocks throughout the game.

On the sidelines, he told QB Russell Reiner and Coach Brown that his side was ready for any sweep or cutback run, and he would be open for any hook pattern after clearing the linebacker. "These farm boys are wearing down. They're not used to the work on the fields like we are. They can't handle the counterpunching we're giving them. We got them now by the throat." Hank's blue eyes looked like a sunlit, open sky, beautiful and overwhelming.

Russell Reiner was caught in the trance and believed in Hank's vision. "You're the man, Hank. We'll follow you down the field." He turned to Coach Brown. "You heard him, Coach; now just call the right plays, and we'll score for you!"

160

Feeling some pressure to move the offense, ACU QB Mike Mcclendon read the call from the sidelines and came to line of scrimmage set to throw his first deep turn- in pattern of the night. Guy could tell because of the formation and because Mcclendon would wipe his crotch and then wipe his stomach and lick his fingers as he got into the shotgun formation. Guy thought it was cool but disgusting. It was on film 90 percent of the time they ran this play. Guy went into deep coverage and called off the blitz to disguise the coming interception. On cue, the speedy receiver went downfield eighteen yards and cut ninety degrees across the field where the tight end and slot receiver had cleared the middle of the field.

Guy Finelli crossed in front of TE Amos Enos to hide himself from McClendon's vision and cut in front of him as the ball was let go. The wide receiver never saw Finelli and bounced off of him, falling backward in complete despair without the football. Guy secured the football and ran straight down the middle of the field. His defensive linemen quickly blocked the slower ACU linemen, leaving only Mcclendon to stop "The Safety" coming at him. Finelli churned his thighs into McClendon's crotch, knocking him backward holding his wounds. McClendon's head banged against the padded turf, leaving him a headache to go along with his heartache. He was carted off the field along with his wide receiver as UMD led 14-0.

The ACU backup QB found no success in his final three tries at throwing the football. In between, the UMD offense scored ten points on two dominant drives, following Hank's advice. RB Emmit Excel scored on a thirty-five run, and Hank's longest reception of the night put them in field-goal range in the final two minutes.

The score reached 31-0 as the final TD came on Guy Finelli's twenty-first tackle, when the enormous ACU All- American tight end, Amos Enos, caught a short pass over the middle and tried to run over Finelli. Guy stood his ground, picked him up with perfect tackle technique, and laid him on his back. The ball flew into the air just before his landing and was picked off by Duran Hall and run back for a TD. "Famous" Amos was the sixth ACU player knocked out of the game.

161

CHAPTER 26

BY FIVE IN the morning, Guy and Hank were finishing off a bottle of brandy that Hank had bought at a Bourbon Street bar. Guy was still sipping from his only glass of brandy, as Hank worked on the rest of the bottle. Guy was figuring out how he would drag such a drunken character back to the hotel. His DMC buddies had stopped answering his texts hours ago, and Anna was already asleep in her room.

Hank was Guy's roommate on game trips. As much as everyone had voiced support for him at the beginning of the year, Guy realized that no one would volunteer to room with him, so he went to Coach Brown before the first road game to ask to be his roommate.

Hank was celebrating his complete performance against ACU. It was not because of his reception total of five catches for sixty yards or the one TD reception-he was most proud of his blocking. His ability to handle the ACU defensive ends and outside linebackers was key to UMD's ability to run the football and wind down the game clock. It was the part of his game that he found most rewarding, since he was an undersized TE like his hero, Jerry Smith. "They can't say I can't block anymore...can they, my friend?" Hank slurred as he tried to finish the last sip of his brandy.

"I took care of my job tonight, a real macho son of a bitch...not bad for a fucking faggot!"

Guy took his time avoiding the spitting coming out of Hank's mouth. "How do you drink this sweet, nasty shit? Is that a gay drink or something?" Guy tried to look his friend in the eye after his joke but realized Hank was way past eye-to-eye contact. "Listen, let's call it a night and get you back to the hotel. Can you walk at all? Maybe I can call a cab."

"I can always walk when I'm drunk...so just show me the way."

Guy found a cab on the street quickly and settled Hank in first. He was hoping the driver was clueless about who they were, with Hank's head nestling in his shoulder.

Hank whispered to Guy on the way back to the hotel. "We did it, Guy. We made it happen together. You are my best friend, Guy... thanks for caring about me. You're like the brother I never had. I really love you like a brother." With that, Hank closed his eyes. "I'm so glad it's over. Now I can finally sleep!"

• • •

Flying on his jet back from Vegas, the Turk had been up all night, pondering the results from his bets on the college championship game. He had hedged his doomed ACU bet with a close win on the over/under bet. He had been certain that it would be a low-scoring ACU win by two touchdowns, but the late-game scoring barrage by UMD had almost made him a double loser. Overall, it was an even outcome, but he thought that was not the point. His mind moved to paranoia as he interpreted Guy Finelli's play as another chess move against him. In his mind, he thought he had tried to play fair with his worthy opponent, and yet "The Safety" still tried to show him up by trying to exceed the over/under bet. "How did he know my bet? His friends Mach and Parand were in on it. They found out on the computer what my bets were. Why did he try to beat me unfairly with his touchdown plays at the end? I played him fair...like a worthy opponent!"

His audience of protectors was all asleep, not hearing his frustrated words. "You fools...wake up! We will crush his Iranian friend and his girl. This special one, they call him, has disrespected me for the last time. I must move on his queen, so I can bring his kingdom to his knees." Most eyes looked puzzled as the Turk waved them away; wondering if this was a bad dream or a call to arms.

• • •

Guy was very happy to return to school during the semester break. Besides a celebration rally at Cole Field House and attending several basketball games in January, he was able to avoid the adoring crowds. There was something almost dangerous about being sought out by so many people he did not know, when he was not playing. He saw his brother, Alex, handle fans with an easy dexterity, moving through autographs and silly conversations like a politician. Guy saw that as a baseball thing. It was a more laid-back atmosphere; people were more patient. The football fan was more aggressive, even on a college campus.

He and Anna did spend a week in Cape Canaveral with Phillip, Alex, and Sally, playing with the twins all day at the pool and being on the beach.

He was planning out his spring semester and realized that by taking eighteen credits, he could easily graduate next December. He was planning on playing one more season for UMD and then would enter the 2015 professional draft in May without having to worry about classes. He wanted to be like Sean Taylor and goin the first five picks.

• • •

When he started the spring semester, at first it was hard to get into a rhythm with going to class, studying, and finding time to be with Anna. Being a celebrity every time he stepped outside his condo was exhausting. He had always been taught good manners, but now he wore his headphones most of the time and looked forward, not seeing or hearing most of the well-wishers. Unlike his brother, he rarely and now almost never gave out autographs. He disliked the idea of putting himself on some kind of distinguished level, someone that should be sought out because of playing a game.

Guy knew he would not play football forever. He wanted an education that would get him into a safer business at some point, maybe engineering or architecture, or even the arts, like acting or directing films. At times he felt like a director on the football field. Each play was a scene from a movie that he could see developing ahead of time.

He loved his sense of vision. As a youngster he had seen it only working on the football field, but more recently, after long talks with his father, it was expanding into the fields of love, friendship, and the greater good of society.

Phillip was finishing his second sports novel and was looking forward to starting his third novel in the fall. After the championship game, Guy's father talked to him about his next book. They were both at Cape Canaveral, alone on the beach, tossing the football and swimming in the ocean. As they dried off and sat in the beach chairs, watching the sun drop quickly in the January sky, Phillip talked about his next idea for a novel. "It will be scary to write, because it will be a novel with me as the central character, much closer to reality, unlike the first two books."

"Wow... that sounds awesome. I'm jealous it won't include me!" Guy laughed, shooting Phillip his million- dollar smile." Won't it be easier to write if you don't have to make stuff up?"

"Sometimes it's easier to hide behind fantasy and fiction, and it can be more entertaining for people to read. I don't think I will care as much if people read this book.

I'll be writing more for me than for an audience. I think I wrote the first two books for confidence and practice."

"I promise that when I finish school, I will learn how to read for fun without getting a headache. Then I can really take my time and enjoy your books. I do love to listen to you reading to me."

Phillip felt a wave of emotion, like nourishment after a long journey. It was the memories of reading to Guy before bed, hoping to interest him in reading like his sister Grace, starting with kids' books and then moving to sports books and his own books. Guy had always politely listened but never responded. It was something he had always wanted to hear from his sweet boy. "Anytime you're willing to listen, you are my favorite practice audience."

"I'm always ready to listen to you, Dad."

CHAPTER 27

EVENTUALLY, AFTER SPRING break, normalcy returned to the campus as March

Madness took over. Students were disappointed that UMD did not make the tournament for the fourth straight year, but they cared more about making money on their March Madness brackets.

Guy still went to class in a hoodie and sunglasses. He begged Coach Brown to let him miss most of the spring practices to focus on schoolwork and avoid more attention. He attended all the defensive meetings at night away from the media.

Late on a beautiful Thursday night, he was walking toward his condo with his backfield crew after a spring football meeting on campus when he saw his friend Mach in the back of the engineering building, standing near a car and waving to him. He sent his crew ahead and got into the car with Mach. Sitting together in the front seat of his Porsche, he was able to finally see Mach's face, which looked ghostly, and his frame, which was getting very thin.

Mach would not look at Guy; he just stared nervously at his chewed-up fingernails. "I don't think I can go on much longer. He is ruining my life and putting Parand in much danger." Mach went on to describe how life had become miserable since the championship game. Somehow, he said, the Turk had blamed Guy for disrespecting him and costing him a lot of money, according to something that Parand had overheard. Mach had never been closed enough to the Turk's inner circle to know these things. His problem was the new project that the Turk was now expanding. The Turk had recruited a small army of young criminals, mostly Asian, to steal credit-card information. Mach was being paid great money to train these individuals to hack into accounts. Parand had been moved to the same project, and now both were having trouble keeping up with their schoolwork. The pressure was enormous, and his privacy was virtually gone. Coming to the College Park campus for a supposed special lecture was a way for him to contact Guy.

Guy was floored after hearing about the new illegal venture. "This guy is really creative. Well, don't do anything stupid, Mach. Let me talk to Anna. She'll think of something."

"Please, my friend, don't forget me!"

• • •

"This could be the break we were looking for. All of our information and leads have reached a dead end. This guy is becoming a Walmart of illegal activities, and we can't get next to him." Brooks stood up from behind his desk and came to stand in front of Anna, leaning back on his desk. "I don't think you can get involved with this." He looked at her belly, six months pregnant.

Anna stood up and walked behind her chair. She was the fittest pregnant woman in the FBI. Her hair was getting longer, now down to her shoulders. Her chest was expanding nicely, along with other body parts. She was looking the most feminine in her life, wearing a pretty maternity dress that Sally had bought for her. "Well, if we're going to go with the stupid plan that Guy sold to you, I have to be involved. I think the plan is ludicrous and dangerous."

Brooks smiled at her frustration. He noticed that the extra weight from the pregnancy made her look healthier and downright beautiful.

"Actually, it might be the only way to get them out of Turk's network. It would put some heat on him as well." Brooklyn O'Malley was excited to have a play against the drug lord, who was now apparently expanding his empire into credit-card fraud. The silence on any leads to him had been killing Brooks. This was a chance to learn about his new project and maybe a connection into his drug empire, which was expanding across the state into wealthy Howard and Montgomery Counties. He corralled Anna, who was pacing back and forth, into a chair next to him. He leaned in toward her and smelled her beauty. "Anna, you need to sit down with Guy and come up with something that makes this plan workable. When can we get to Mach and Farand?"

"Well, tomorrow they are going to Columbia Mall to do some training for this credit-card thing. He is worried that it might be a setup, but he has to play along." She noticed Brooks's intensity and tried to calm herself. He was a bit old for her to say the least, but his looks were still interesting. His hair was full and mainly dark; his body was trim and strong. Other than the voice thing, he was a handsome gentleman for sixty-two. She was confident, of course, that he had no interest in her or her in him, but the pregnancy was pushing her hormones to recognize anything sexual.

"I'll have as many units as needed on call in the morning, including SWAT teams. Whatever it is, it has to look real." He pulled back from Anna and thought for a moment. "Let's call that reporter...that Battle guy, and leak something ahead of time on this as it's

167

going down. That will really piss off the Turk."

• • •

The shoe store that the Turk owned in Columbia Mall was advertised as an importer of the best shoes from Europe and the Middle East. In reality, he had a Chinese factory make knockoffs of exotically named shoe brands, not in existence. It was also a front for a warehouse that stored many illegal things and served as a training center for his new adventure.

This space had become the only place where Mach and Parand could meet without suspicion. The endless training sessions, mainly with Asians who spoke little English, were exhausting.

The operation started Saturday morning at seven forty-five with a call to the police from Parand, saying she was being held hostage along with a dozen people in the Columbia Mall. She also called Clark Battle shortly after to report that her coworker, Mahmood Abdul-Abar, wanted Guy Finelli to come to the store. She went on to mention that he had placed a knapsack in front of the store with explosives and had a remote device on him, and he was holding everyone at gunpoint in a circle on the floor.

Clark Battle was stunned by the call as he noticed the 911 call coming across the wire in the newsroom. He asked, "Is this involved with the Baltimore connection?"

"No, no, something else...please hurry! He is very angry and is talking against the government."

"What is it? Is it terrorism...an act of terrorism?" "Maybe...! do not know...he's so angry. I have to go."

Guy was waiting for the call in Anna's car, hiding away in the Merriweather Post outdoor-concert parking lot surrounded by woods, only a mile from the mall.

"It took some time to get your number, but Coach Brown was very cooperative. Your friend Mahmood Abdul- Abar needs you to go to Columbia Mall. The police will meet you at the Macy's entrance."

"Who is this?" Guy said playfully.

"Oh, I'm sorry...I'm a little frazzled. This is Clark Battle from the *Nation's Times*. Please turn on the news if you don't believe me."

"Aren't you the wiseass that asked me if I was dating Hank Harrison at that news conference? And you wrote all that bullshit about me and drugs."

"Well...yes, but this is terrorism or possible terrorism, with your friend Mahmood!"

"Oh, you mean Mach...! don't think he could be a terrorist. He's way too smart for that. I think he's pulling your leg."

Anna was pulling her hair, ready to clock Guy in the stomach as she listened to him ridiculing the reporter. Finally, Guy got with the program.

"So, I need to see Mach in person because he is upset about something? That's cool. He was pretty upset on Thursday night about school and work. He was worried about failing and disgracing his family. You know they're from Iran, fled during the fall of the shah in' 79."

"You talked to him Thursday night?"

"Yeah... he came to see me on campus, and we talked awhile. I told him to stay cool and call me if he needed to talk. So, I guess he did...well, good talking to you. I got to go if I want to get up there. It takes about twenty minutes."

Anna stared at Guy as he finished the call in a combination of anger and astonishment at his talent. "Are you high or something? That was awesome but scary! I think Mr. Battle took the bait."

"I think he got excited about the word *terrorist,* and now he can't think straight. My father always said, 'You can score on defense, if you know their next play.' Fortunately for us, Clark Battle's play calling is a little too predictable."

Anna took the next fifteen minutes to go over the game plan with Guy. She received a text from Brooks that the FBI had arrived at the scene before the local police and were in control of the situation. FBI SWAT teams were in place, and a bomb squad was on its way. It seemed that everything was setting up perfectly. "Listen, don't say or do anything stupid, OK? Just fall back if a weapon shows up. We don't know if the creep has this place staked out or not. He may have security in the warehouse part of the store. In fact, I'm certain of it."

"Once Baltimore hears about the store on the news, he will have soldiers there to protect his stash. That's why we need to do this quick."

"But slow enough to make it look real."

"Got it, boss...now drive this thing over there like a cop!"

"OK, but one more thing." She grabbed his shirt and gave him a full, thirty-second kiss, knocking him back against his passenger-side door. Quickly, she moved back to her seat and snapped on her seat belt. As she floored the gas pedal on the four-hundred-horsepower, black FBI Dodge Charger, it left a large mark on a remote corner of the music-loving, pot-smoking parking lot. Guy grabbed his seat belt to buckle it and held on for the ride of his life.

Columbia Mall was clear of cars and people at eight thirty on a Saturday morning. Security had been doubled since a random shooting in late January 2014, when nineteen-year-old Darien Aguilar had shot two employers at Zumiez, an apparel store for skaters and snowboarders, and then himself, after wounding five others. Aguilar had been a high-school classmate of Guy and Mach.

Part of the background that would be leaked to Clark Battle would link Mach and Aguilar as friends interested in terrorism. Of course, Guy knew that neither he nor his friend Mach had any connection to the murderer.

The FBI security let the fast-moving Dodge Charger past the barriers to park next to the Macy's entrance. A SWAT team led Guy through the endless displays at Macy's into the main part of the mall. Anna followed at a slower pace and met up with Guy and Brooks O'Malley, overseeing the operation about a hundred feet from the shoe store.

"We have established contact with Mach on his phone," Brooks reported in his serious voice. "Get on the phone, Guy, and talk him down to come out."

Guy took the phone and had a conversation with Mach. He realized quickly that something was wrong. What he could not see was that both Mach and Parand had guns to their heads. Two soldiers, who slept at the store in a hidden basement room, had been woken up by noise in the storage room. On a below ground camera, they had watched a half-dozen FBI SWAT team members, looking like cops, sweep the room before Parand and Mach entered. When the truckload of students arrived through the back door at seven forty-five, Mach pulled out a gun and made the class and Parand sit on the floor in a circle. After watching some phone calls by Parand, the pair of soldiers called their leader and then quietly rose from the basement entrance, hidden in a closet, and burst onto the scene to take Mach and Parand at gunpoint.

They forced Mach to demand that Guy come into the storage room behind the store, trying to sell his role as hostage taker. Brooks O'Malley signaled for Guy to end the call, but Guy was cool. "Mach, I will be there in five minutes; everything will be fine."

Mach was shaking all over as he replied, "Thank you, my friend."

"There is no chance you are going in there!" both Anna and Brooks chimed in, like a duet. "This could become a disaster for all of us," Brooks added.

Guy thought for a moment and then looked at his phone. "Well, I have four minutes to get in there. So, let's go."

Brooks thought about ordering his team to take Guy down physically, but that could get ugly. "Wait...all right, but this is really stupid."

"Brooks, you can't let him goin there!"

"Well, Anna, we don't have a choice right now that works. They're not going to hurt him. The Turk is a creep, but he is not that stupid."

"Calm down, you two; just relax. I have my phone if I need you." Guy left quickly and entered the storeto head to the back warehouse.

Brooks motioned his SWAT team to stand down and let him through. He turned to see Anna with her hands on her hips and her eyes at full attention. She started to scream but muted her anger to an incredulous, low tone. "'I have my phone if I need you!' 'They're not going to hurt him!' Are you kidding me? You two are acting like high-noon sheriffs. Why don't we just shoot up some pure heroin and see if we live?" Anna turned away from Brooks, finding a chair to calm down. "Guy Finelli thinks he's a superhero, I guess!"

Guy entered the big storage room and followed the instructions of the two soldiers. "Why don't you let everyone go and hold on to me? I promise the FBI will go away and leave the warehouse alone. Call the Turk for me"

After some mumbling, the Turk was on the phone. "Mr. Guy, we finally talk; what can I do for you?"

"Mach has a bomb in front of the store and the detonator physically attached to him. We have to let him go, or you will have a mess on your hands. I'm sure you are smart enough to understand."

"I see... how do I know that the FBI will leave my operation alone, Mr. Guy?"

"Because they have no interest in it, all they care about Is stopping the drugs into Montgomery County."

"Ah yes...the precious rich ones...well, I believe you, Mr. Guy, but I don't think you can convince them to leave this operation alone, so please leave before something happens."

Guy was standing away from both soldiers and talking loudly to the Turk. He realized that they had lowered their guns slightly, trying to listen to the conversation. As he took another step away from them, they shouted to him to stop. In one motion, Guy took a last step away and quickly turned toward them, hurling the borrowed phone like a missile. It hit the first soldier in the right arm, knocking away his gun and glancing off to smash the second soldier in the face as he fired his gun into the air. As he finished his follow-through, Guy in one step was instantly airborne into a perfect dive toward them, punching the first soldier out cold with his right hand and wrestling the second into a choke hold

171

with his left. He rose to his feet with his foot on the soldier's throat, instructing everyone to leave, while grabbing his phone to call Anna.

"Hey, everything's cool in here and under control." His breathing was amazingly calm. "Everybody is coming out, and I got two soldiers in custody."

Anna looked relieved after the sound of a gunshot and hugged Brooks as they watched the Asians escaping out of the store and into the safe arms of the SWAT team. She put down the phone as she saw Mach and Parand walk out slowly, to be handcuffed and taken into custody, according to the plan. "Send in Team B, code green," she shouted to the SWAT team to secure the soldiers and search the room. Her heart was racing with a thousand emotions as she sat down and let her hair cover her face and hands.

Brooks knelt in front of her and patted her knees. "Are you OK?"

She looked up with a smile and tears in her eyes as she imagined Guy's heroics in the warehouse. "My God, we've created a monster!"

Brooks laughed as he witnessed Anna's conflicted emotions.

"No my dear, not a monster...just 'The Safety'!"

CHAPTER 28

T HANK YOU, MY friend; we are both very happy. Now that the exams are over, we are headed to New Mexico to work with the FBI for the summer. Our families can visit us there as well. They are happy that we are protected by the FBI for national security reasons. Mr. O'Malley has put them at ease with his story of how we got caught up in the Baltimore network. It is patriotic work we do now. Being Arabic speaking has made us valuable assets for our country. Hopefully, we can finish college with protection. We feel safe now."

Guy smiled, pausing to take in Mach's happiness. He was walking to the condo from campus, feeling the warm May sun on his face. He had just completed his last final exam, finishing an eighteen-credit semester. Life felt good, and now he was free from schoolwork until August. Listening to Mach on the phone, he wondered about hanging out in New Mexico. It sounded like the culture and scenery blended to make a peaceful place for exploration of the mind and body, especially if you liked smoking pot and eating mushrooms. He laughed as he caught his mind drifting while Mach finished some details of his time with the FBI since the Columbia Mall rescue.

"Mach, take care of yourself, best of luck, and call me when you can. My best to Parand."

"Gaetano, thank you once again for saving our lives. And I think...you will need good luck once the baby arrives, as a father-that will be a new position for you. You will need to practice, I'm sure."

Guy laughed as he said good-bye. He had never thought about practicing to be a father, but Mach seemed to be right about many things. Lots of ballplayers he knew had kids. Most, he figured, had never thought about practicing to be a dad.

Mach was the only friend who ever called him by his real name when he meant something important. Guy enjoyed it because it made him feel Italian and reminded him of his grandfather. "Wow, what would he think of me having a baby at nineteen?" Guy pondered out loud. "Probably not too happy about it." He chuckled. "I guess I'd better do the 'practice' thing to become a good father." Once again, he remembered his friend and quietly wished him a safe and happy summer with a two-finger hand-tap on his heart as he put away his phone.

The emotion of finishing the semester and saying good-bye to his friend hit him with a wave of excitement as he left the campus and was alone on the paved trail through some woods to cross US 1. He yelled out loud to the audience of trees with his arms extended, "Mahmood Abdul-Abar, you are a wise friend!"

• • •

Memorial Day weekend was coming up in a few days. It meant the beginning of summer for his friends and family. His old neighborhood of Oakview was usually the place to be on Saturday afternoon, when the pool opened. This year, he was taking Anna to a quiet spot in Buckingham County, Virginia, for two hundred acres of beautiful rolling hills with open fields, creeks, and woods to explore, in addition to a grand, four-bedroom farmhouse, some forty minutes south of Charlottesville on State Road 20.

The farm was literally in the middle of nowhere, where the mostly clay soil made farming crops difficult. Only the quaint towns of Scottsville, on the scenic James River to the north, and Farmville, a college town of Longwood University to the south, both some twenty minutes away, brought some civilization to the area. The farm had been owned by Carol's parents, who bought it for cheap and in disarray in the late sixties.

She had spent large parts of summers and weekends during her childhood years swimming, fishing, fixing the fences with her dad, riding the tractor, bush-hogging, and mowing fields, while showing off for her friends that visited. Besides working many hours clearing underbrush from the trails and helping her engineering father dam a creek to build a sizable pond, she spent most of her free hours with her favorite passion of reading, at times floating on a homemade raft in the half-girl-made, well- stocked-of-fish pond.

Carol's mother's family had come from the Charlottesville area. It was the special history of the area that Carol loved so dearly and that made her feel like a Southern lady. Her maternal grandmother, Annie, who proudly referred to the creator of Monticello as "Mr. Jefferson," had spent many years working on a farm in Albemarle County and then for the federal government aiding area farmers.

Annie spent most of her life as a single mom of two children after disposing of her abusive, alcoholic husband. After the children reached adulthood, she lived in a small apartment on top of a barn on a farm owned by a family friend, paying thirty dollars a month. The nonworking farm had a stable of horses in that barn that reminded her of the smells of nature. Guy and Grace had spent precious time with their great-grandmother Annie to witness her quiet strength and steadiness. It was in great contrast to the high-volume Italian side of their family.

Guy had not visited his grandparents' farm since middle school. Alex had invested in the farm through his stepmother, Carol, to update the house and the smaller cottage on the farm. They hired a full-time caretaker to live in the cottage and maintain the property. Carol and Phillip were excited when Guy asked them for the keys to spend the weekend there alone with Anna. They hoped that this special heirloom from Carol's family would become a retreat for family members.

Anna Cobb was given permission by her boss to take the weekend holiday to be with Guy, and she used the FBI Charger to head out on Friday morning to Central Virginia. Finishing her thirty-fifth week of the pregnancy, Anna was very comfortable with the feel of her body. She had gained only twelve pounds and was able to hide her protruding tummy with her loose clothing.

They stopped in Scottsville for lunch at *Amici's Italian Bistro*, a trendy restaurant with some outside tables that mirrored the descending road to the river. In the last decade, young yuppies had brought life to this sleepy town, discovering a much smaller, cheaper alternative to Charlottesville. Several fine chefs had followed to provide fine cuisine.

The last twenty minutes to the farm off State Road 20 to County Road 602 was a fun test of Anna's driving skills handling the monster power of the Charger. It was full of isolated acres of land that included random groups of horses, cows, and goats. The final turnoff from pavement led them to a half-mile gravel road to the main house. After passing the old, unoccupied Hearthwell family house and farm on the right, they approached and opened the gate to the farm. The road narrowed as they noticed a herd of 15 7 goats, led by their shepherd, a seventy-two- year-old known only as Giovanni. He led a Franciscan-type lifestyle, tending to nature with his herd. He named and remembered each goat as they kept several fields trimmed and maintained. He lived throughout the year in a large tent with a kerosene heater when needed. The caretaker made sure that plenty of food was available for him during the coldest months, even though he lived on picked fruit and caught fish most of the year.

Farther down the road, past the acres of fruit trees, bales of hay were sitting, rolled into large wheels, parked in the middle of undulating fields.

Anna left along trail of clouded dust behind her, all the way back to the county road. She finally slowed down after reaching the front lawn of the main house. The updated structure looked ready to attend to the happy couple as they left to check the insides. Guy was thrilled to see the 130-year-old house looking so vibrant from the outside.

The front yard was level enough for a football game and mowed for running or tumbling. The caretaker, Morris Peters, met them on the front porch, excited to meet the star football player and his pregnant girlfriend.

A big UVA fan, he remembered Guy Finelli taking over the game for UMD at Charlottesville in 2012 during his freshman year for a big win. He was not used to seeing someone so young look like a big, grown man.

They walked through the first floor of the house and ended up in the newly added kitchen. A set of French doors led onto the expansive deck addition on the back of the house. The house stood on the tallest land on the property, and the view from the deck looked west over acres of Virginia countryside toward the Shenandoah Valley.

The first two days presented perfect weather for long walks, swimming in the pond, and picnics in the fields. Spending time with Giovanni and the goats took up three hours on Saturday afternoon. They learned several names of the most unique goats that kept him company.

Anna took a nap on the deck for a couple hours while Guy toured more of the property with Morris in his jeep. He learned a bit more of the history of the area all the way back to the Civil War.

Guy fell asleep early Saturday night as Anna stayed up reading. She was enjoying the moonlight over the wide- open landscape. Finally, she moved to the bedroom to go to sleep. Guy turned over, away from her, to continue his dream. He was watching a moonlit field with two players running against each other and then stopping to talk. He walked and then ran as fast as he could to get closer. He could see the mop-haired man standing with his hands on his hips and laughing as he turned to look at Guy. Across from him was a younger black man making fun of him, calling him an old man. They both stopped to look at Guy as he approached, "Hey, Sean, finally someone to throw us the ball. Now I get to embarrass your bad ass!"

"Please, Mr. Smith...you're dealing with the Meast from the U. That Finelli kid is not a quarterback anyway, but I guess you got used to Kilmer throwing to you instead of Jurgensen!"

"Unfortunately, you're right about that, Sean Taylor. Billy was a great football player, but not a great QB. I can still see that ball hit the crossbar in Super Bowl VII in '73. I think Charley Taylor and I would have caught another one hundred balls each if Sonny had

176

stayed healthy, and maybe a couple of Super Bowls."

"Hell yeah...and put your ass where you deserve, the Hall of Fame. I mean, that shit is a crime...not putting you in. Bunch of homophobes."

"Appreciate the support, my football brother. What happened to you is the crime. You would have been the best, even better than Kenny Houston or my man Paul Krause, because you could really fly!"

"I'm with you on that, my man. Hey, let's give this kid a chance to throw some; he may need the practice."

Guy could see Sean Taylor and Jerry Smith calling for him. They were both good-looking athletes in their prime, as they were in the farm fields among the bales of hay. Sean and Jerry shouted together, "Hey, Guy, you're one of us...when you're ready...only when you're ready...only when you're..."

Guy wanted desperately to join them, but his feet felt frozen and unmovable. Their voices continued with their pleas, getting louder, finally waking him up. He was shivering and sweating at the same time, sitting up to grab the blanket at his feet. He turned to his side and looked at Anna, who was dead asleep, and then pulled the covers around him, thinking about the dream and the two great players that he honored for their play and courage. He wondered if he would be ready in a year to be drafted to play professional football. The dream was about his anxiety at the next level, he thought, a warning to be ready.

He laid his head back on his pillow as he pondered having to play college football for another year, even though the college game seemed to be in his rearview mirror. He turned his eyes to stare at his redheaded queen, who was carrying his baby. She looked so peaceful and content. He felt so lucky to be with her, and now that school was done, he could not wait for the birth of his girl.

· · ·

They packed quickly, deciding to leave early on Memorial Day to avoid the traffic home. The three days together and the serenity of the farm had been spectacular. Anna had two more weeks of desk duty before she would take off for over six months of maternity leave until the new year.

She drove out slowly down the gravel road, trying not to disrupt the darkness of the morning, and then pulled out onto State Road 602 heading north toward the James River. The Dodge Charger rolled on the unlined road through the countryside as the couple

177

settled in for the three-hour ride home. Suddenly, a Ford Focus appeared from a driveway in the pre-morning darkness. It pulled in front of them at the last second, causing Anna to brake quickly, pulling to the right side to avoid a collision. A white Dodge van pulled out from the same driveway to block her in from the side.

Anna realized immediately that this was no accident, but an attack. She yelled at Guy to get down while pulling her Glock 19 pistol out from the glove compartment. Within seconds, five men with socks over their heads emptied the van to attack the car in the darkness. She punched a button on her steering wheel to contact Brooks on her car phone in speaker mode. Quickly, Anna opened the door as she heard Brooks answer. "Five gangbangers in white Dodge van and maybe more in a green Ford Focus on Route 602, Buckingham County, Virginia. Need backup!"

"Get out of the car, now, hands behind your head. Throw us your gun, Agent Cobb," yelled the leader of the gang, who obviously knew her name.

Anna knew it was the Turk's men. "Brooks...it's the creep's men; they have us pinned." She tried to buy time from the gang leader.

"You're making a big mistake fucking with an FBI agent. They have your position and will hunt you down."

"Throw down the gun, or we will kill both of you...now."

Anna nodded to Guy to get out as she threw her gun under the door. Guy moved out of the car slowly with his hands up as Anna followed suit. Each was quickly surrounded by a pair of the Turk's soldiers.

Before they could tie her hands, she landed her elbows in the gut of each soldier and spun around to kick them both in the face. She then dove for the gun. Guy followed suit, flipping both soldiers over his back and slamming them to the road. He then tried to tackle a fifth soldier leaning over the gun, but it was too late; he got his hand on it as Guy reached him. They rolled on the ground with the gun. Guy grabbed his wrist just as Anna arrived, knocking the gun away again.

Their leader jumped out of the Ford Focus and started yelling instructions in Arabic as he grabbed the gun from the ground that was kicked in his direction.

In the dark, Guy and Anna continued to inflict damage on their assailants. Finally, three of them had Anna pinned on the ground with a stranglehold around her neck and each leg held down separately.

Guy had one soldier knocked out and the other just about finished when he saw Anna being pinned down. He applied one last punch to his second victim as he jumped in Anna's direction, blindsiding the one applying the neck hold. Anna was freed and sat up as she tried to wiggle out of the leg holds.

Crrrrack. The sound of the gun echoed in the silence and darkness of the predawn. Anna fell back down, reaching for her abdomen and turning to the side. The burning smell was as present as the pain from the hole in her right groin. Guy finished with his final punch to his third victim and immediately headed toward the gunman, who was walking closer to Anna to finish her off. Guy leapt at the gunman, punched away the gun, and started beating him. The two unbeaten soldiers rose from the ground to wrestle Guy for the gun and their leader. The leader was freed, grabbed the gun, and headed to the car. He barked out orders for the other five to get into the van as he sped out into the night.

Guy collected himself and rolled over to Anna, who had blood pooling between her legs. He ripped opened Anna's shorts and found the bullet hole in her groin. He rammed his finger into her wound to stop the bleeding of the shredded femoral artery. Anna was barely conscious, heading into shock. He found his phone with his left hand and called 911. He kept the phone on speaker and shouted instructions as he felt her weak pulse.

Anna was whispering something to him. He stretched his long torso over her chest to listen as she repeated over and over until consciousness left her, "Save the baby… my king. Save the baby."

Part III

The Future is Now

The Finelli- Angelluci Family Tree 2014

Geraldo Finelli and Philomena Finelli   Phillip Angelucci & Rosina Angelucci
(Died 1/19/53)   (Died 1984)   (Died 1955)   (Died 1967)
            Children   Children
Gaetano (Guy I) Finelli / Pietro Finelli / Helen Finelli   Ernesto Angelucci / Rose Angelucci
(Died 8/21/93)   (Died 6/7/2013)   (Died 9/4/2012)   (Died 7/7/2010)

Guy I Finelli married Rose Angelucci 1944   Ernesto Angelucci married Helen Finelli 1951
            Children   Children

Anthony Finelli   Phillip Finelli   Joseph Angelucci   Philomena (Philly) Angelucci
(Born 1944)   (Born 6/7/53)   (Born 1952 Died 9/4/69)   (Born 6/7/53)

(Anthony, Phillip, Joseph, Philly are known as Double First Cousins. All with the same Grandparents)

Anthony Finelli married Florence Gray 1966   Phillip Finelli married Carol Werner 1986
            Children   Children
                        Child w/ Leah Raines 1976)
Melissa Finelli   Joseph Finelli   *Alex Santucci   Grace Finelli   Gaetano (Guy)Finelli
(Born 1967)   (Cousin Joe-Born 6/4/70) (Born 8/8/76)   (Born 11/2/91)   (10/04/94)
                        **Charlotte Roberts
                        (Born 8/8/83)

*Adopted by Dr. Gene Santucci and Laura Santucci
**Step-Sister to Alex, fathered by Dr. Gene Santucci   Alex Santucci married Sally Keegan 2012
            (Died 8/15/91)   Children (Twins- Born 6/7/2013)
                                    Phillip II Santucci Philomena (Philly II) Santucci

Guy Finelli child with girlfriend Anna Cobb (murdered 5/26/2014)
                        Annie Finelli

CHAPTER 29

GUY FINELLI LEANED forward in his Ferrari, flying around turns, focused on the

flow of traffic ahead on Route 97. It was April 2019, and the Maryland countryside was beaming with the delicious display of spring-growing grasses on the green hills, exciting flashes of flowers busying the bees, and a triumph of trees exploding with new cover. As the extravagant vehicle surged with speed, taking advantage of the suddenly straight street, he witnessed the expansive back lawn of his cousin's mansion coming up on the right, perched on a hill overlooking the prominence of western Howard County. The remembrance of that special Christmas Eve with Anna and his family over five years ago still warmed his memories but would forever haunt him with the sadness of her loss.

He had been daydreaming, during the first half hour of the drive from Bethesda to northern Maryland, about the past dozen years since he became a teenager-the traumatic murder of Sean Taylor, falling into the drug world, returning to football, finding love, losing his lover, gaining a daughter, becoming the best defensive player in professional football, and winning back-to-back professional championships.

He had another twenty minutes of driving back routes to Sykesville in Carroll County for a private meeting with the Baltimore Banners' general manager, Aaron Michaels, and head coach, Neville Chambers. Then maybe he'd drive to Philadelphia and New York in the coming two days. It was the first day of free agency for the 2019 season, almost five years since Anna's killing, and he was still trying to make sense of it.

• • •

The murder, now known within the FBI as the "Memorial Day Massacre," was also the birthday of his daughter, Annie, who was born on May 26, minutes before her mother stopped breathing for last time.

The attack was assumed to be ordered by the Turk as a kidnapping or a physical attack that turned into the murder of an FBI agent. There was no evidence to confirm the connection; only Anna's gun was taken.

Guy had tried to stem the blood loss for ten minutes while waiting for help. He performed CPR for five minutes on Anna after her heart and breathing stopped. He could not find a pulse, so he found the pocketknife she always carried in her shoe and performed a perfect C-section to give his daughter life from her mother's abdomen, following her final whispers.

Following Anna's murder, Guy spent the month of June 2014 in seclusion caring for baby Annie at his parent's house in Kensington. She had spent a short time in the hospital but checked out fine after the amateur C- section. Guy had saved her life as the FBI and emergency medical team found him lying next to his dead girlfriend, who had quickly bled to death from the shot from her own gun.

Guy realized after a month that he could not cope with the violent loss of Anna and the sudden responsibility of fatherhood. After talking with Phillip, Carol, Alex, and Sally, he decided to head out West. His brother handed him $20,000 in cash and a credit card. He handed over Annie to Sally Keegan, who had a staff of six manning the house, doing security, being nannies, cooking, and cleaning round the clock.

His parents would sometimes host Annie and her twin cousins, Phillip II and Philly II, on the weekend, with the security and nanny services following closely. Over the next five years, the three cousins would grow up together as close as brother and sisters. When Guy did return, he eventually bought a high-rise condo in Bethesda, close to Alex and Sally, and focused on his football career. He adored his daughter and his niece and nephew, but he knew they were in better hands with Sally Keegan.

For the first two weeks of July 2014, Guy went driving on old highways, stopping at off-beat motels, shooting pool in bars, eating at diners, reading books near streams and rivers, and trying to stay invisible. He landed in Sweetwater, Texas, one night and called his father to tell him that he had visited the high school that Washington great QB Sammy Baugh had attended. He talked in a solemn monotone, mentioning that he was heading toward California.

Guy had taken a collection of Phillip's books for the trip, including philosophical books like *Zen and the Art of Motorcycle Maintenance, The Celestine Prophecy,* and *The Teachings of Don Juan: Trilogy,* as well as autobiographies of musicians Eric Clapton and Levon Helm and a biography of John Lennon.

As Guy talked to Phillip, he had trouble describing his ideas verbally, but Phillip learned that he was in a mood to learn about experiences from people and how they dealt with adversity. Guy had reached a pinnacle in his life and a path to greatness, and then in a moment, he was in a desperate fall that had no end insight.

183

It warmed Phillip's heart to hear Guy pour out his thoughts and feelings. He decided after an hour of listening to make a bold suggestion. Three years before, he had extracted the promise from his son to give up his drug involvement. It had worked and led Guy to experience greatness in sports and love in a relationship. Now, half of that was gone, and the rest was in peril. He disagreed but understood his son's comfort zone that had helped him cope with the death of Sean Taylor, and now he thought it was time to let him learn from it again. It was painful to advise him to stray into a mind-altering experience, but Guy was expressing desperation, and he knew that with his maturity, Guy would come out on the other side. The books were a start for him to learn about himself, but now he needed to experience it with someone that Phillip trusted. He decided to give him the phone number of a high-school friend who lived in Santa Fe, New Mexico. If he needed a comrade to expand his experience, Rhonda would help him on the way.

When he met Rhonda, Guy was immediately captured by her combination of ski-blond hair and surfer-tan skin for a sixty-year-old, hippie-styled woman. Her engaging personality, full of laughter, was like a breath of fresh air. After a tour of her home and some hot tea, Rhonda's first suggestion was that he dress in some local clothes that fit in better, and her second was to die his hair strawberry blond for a better disguise and to honor Anna. Guy immediately agreed to both and was excited by the feel and sight of it.

The next day they drove southeast of Santa Fe to view the Sangre de Cristo Mountains and to smoke the best marijuana of his life. It was his first toke in over three years and his first time with an experienced adult. It turned out to be the right medicine for his troubles. Later that afternoon they stopped by the Pantry restaurant and ordered carryout. Guy was in his element, having grown up on Chipotle food. They ordered the carne adovada, a Frito pie, grilled tilapia, stuffed sopaipillas, chiles rellenos, and guacamole. He ate for hours, while Rhonda told him stories about his dad and her current life, laughing most of the time. When Guy finished devouring most of the carryout, Rhonda brought out some hashish for dessert. She pulled it out of the freezer that kept it fresh for a special occasion like this one. Before he lit the bowl, he noticed the fragrance of the black rock of hashish permeating the room. Once Guy inhaled, it sent him back to heaven. Luckily Rhonda had ingredients for hot-fudge sundaes to finish the evening on a sugar high.

During the next month, Guy stayed with Rhonda off and on as he traveled the mountains. He managed to smoke marijuana daily and talked with Rhonda and sometimes Phillip on the phone. But he wanted something different, something to experience alone. Rhonda suggested doing some mushrooms with the natural hallucinogen mescaline by himself in the mountains. Rhonda loaded him up with food and drink before sending him to a friend's cabin in the mountains an hour away. There was a landline there if he needed her. She also lent him a CD influenced by her friendship with Phillip.

The experience was scary at first for Guy, but it changed his perspective of life, especially after a twenty- four-hour stretch of replaying the CD. It contained great tripping songs like Donovan's "Hurdy Gurdy Man," Tommy James and the Shondells' "Crimson and Clover," The Box Tops' "The Letter," The Band's "This Wheel's on Fire," The Beach Boys' "I Get Around" and "In My Room," Cream's "The White Room" and "Badge," and several Beatles songs, including "My Guitar Gently Weeps," "I Am the Walrus," "Strawberry Fields Forever," and his favorite, the slow version of "Revolution" off the *White Album.*

The response from the mescaline in the mushrooms kept him awake long enough to make him realize that he had never really experienced an intense, lasting feeling of anger about Anna's death. After finally getting some sleep, he downloaded the CD to his headphones and went hiking. Gaining confidence as the drugs began to wear off; he found a ridge thousands of feet high after hours of climbing. He sat and looked at the miles of country. It inspired him to scream out, "I play football, and I don't get angry; my hero was killed, and I never got angry; my queen was murdered, and I can't get angry!"

He sat for hours pondering his feelings, starting to sense some comfort with what had always been a scary feeling. His father displayed bursts of anger at times that he isolated himself from, deciding that he did not want that behavior to be a part of his personality. He realized that he had become comfortable with seeing the behavior but never internalizing it. The act of becoming angry or feeling anger for any length of time was just not in his playbook, but now he decided that he could trust himself with anger.

As dusk arrived, he headed back down the mountain toward the cabin with little light. On the way, before the tree line, he reached an open meadow illuminated by the by the moonlight. He lay down to look up at the stars and started planning out his "Revolution of Change." It took a while to focus, but during the eighteenth playing of "The Hurdy Gurdy Man," a game plan became clear: he needed to expand his personality to include anger and love, war and peace, fear and kindness, silence and language. A whole spectrum of personality was necessary to be a great person and an agent of change. It would take discipline, commitment, and most importantly, winning.

He rose to his feet and felt the final energy of the mushrooms fleeing his body, sensing that they were the last recreational drugs he would ever take. They helped him release his fear to wonder and dream, and now he could trust himself to discover the scary world of anger. Suddenly the words easily came to his mind, and he sat up to articulate them to the universe. "I will become the greatest-winning player in football," he shouted with vented anger. "I will take down the drug empire of the Turk and his soldiers, but most importantly, I swear on my child's life, and I promise Anna, wherever she is in the universe"-he felt the fire in his eyes as the stars seemed to swirl above him-"I will find your gun and help convict those feeble minds who killed you!"

Guy rose from the ground and dusted himself off as he felt the anger in his body find a place of memory in his brain. As he started to walk, he realized that anger was like a wild horse-once you trained it, you could ride it whenever it was necessary.

CHAPTER 30

THE SPRING OF 2019 was full of hope. Continued peace and prosperity had solidified

cooperation on so many levels of society. After showing great leadership in solving the football crises In 2017 and brokering peace in the Middle East in 2018, the madam president was enjoying an unprecedented popularity in the nation, leading a cooperative path of governing to solve the economic and environmental problems of the day.

The United States had finally reversed the years of being the world's greatest importer, and now, because of new battery technology that turned Detroit into the biggest maker in the world of hybrid and electric cars, meaning that massive oil supplies were not needed in the United States, the country was becoming the world's greatest exporter of goods.

The president had won a massive revaluing of the dollar with the WTO (World Trade Organization) that had put a stop to the US budget deficits. In addition, Congress had passed long-term legislation to shore up Social Security and Medicare, Immigration Reform that created millions of jobs with much-needed infrastructure projects, and righted problems with the health-care legislation. User fees for transportation, food and environmental safety, stock trades, and so on were lowering rates of income taxes and corporate taxes on the federal and state levels.

But two exciting projects announced by the president in the 2018 State of the Union had led the country to a groundswell of patriotic pride. The most exciting was the Mars mission program that was planned to start in 2020, with the first Mars manned landing slated for 2035. The twenty-year program would include building a manned outpost on the moon and three crew landings on Mars through 2040.

Secondly, a groundbreaking environmental project was announced that could save the planet. It was a fifty-year program to develop carbon-dioxide converters that would solve the global weather crises by the twenty-second century. The new technology, developed through funding by the Department of Energy, would have giant, land-based inhalers storing CO_2 deep in the oceans and atmosphere-based converters that would send CO_2 into the upper atmosphere to help repel the heat of the sun. The project seemed like science fiction to most people, but it was exciting news just the same.

For the Washington, DC, area, there were three important developments. The first was the 2022 World Cup being moved to the United States, with DC becoming the host city after Qatar was forced out as host. The second was the 2024 Olympics being awarded to DC after teaming with the states of Maryland and Virginia.

The third development came after the president saved football in the first month of her presidency in 2017, which turned out to be politically brilliant and assured her reelection in 2020.

Football had no choice but to declare bankruptcy after the 2016 season. The Supreme Court upheld three different class-action lawsuit decisions before the 2016 elections that totaled $123.5 billion in damages. The suits covered many areas but mainly involved mishandled medical care, including concussions, illegal pharmaceutical interventions, and discrimination that included mistreatment of minorities and sexual harassment of women and gays.

These final court decisions had a cascading effect on all levels of football, from professional to youth. Most football organizations had no choice but to declare bankruptcy, threatening that organized football would never be played again in the United States and North America.

The outcry across the country led the new president to broker a negotiated settlement of the lawsuits without appeal and to organize a presidential commlsslon to "make sure football continued as safe entertainment in North America and the world." Quickly, the new president collected professional team owners from the United States and Canada, college presidents, high-school principals, and youth-league coordinators, and guided them to come up with new, safe solutions to continue competitive football. Most importantly, she convinced Congress to financially guarantee it.

A new thirty-six-team premier football league simply known as GAF (Global American Football) was formed within a month. In addition, four Bleagues were organized and funded by the GAF to play in the United States, Europe, Mexico, and Canada, with expansion planned worldwide. The four B league champions would meet in playoffs for the Global Grey Cup Championship (G2C2). Players could enter the B leagues directly from high school and play for two years before entering the GAF.

College football no longer gave out athletic scholarships. Players were given academic scholarships to major in football if they finished their degree. If they left early, the scholarships would turn into loans paid by their first football contract or first job.

Mexico City, Monterrey, Montreal, and Toronto were awarded new premier GAF franchises. The franchise in Jacksonville was moved to London, and St. Louis moved back to Los Angeles. The premier league formed into six divisions of six teams and opened sixteen spots for the playoffs to reach the new championship contest.

NASA had **bought** the naming rights for the championship contest to start in 2020 for twenty years. It was called the Mars Mission Championship Contest (M2C2). They collected $1 billion from contractors, whose names would be prominently shown during the years leading up to the first Mars launch and until 2039. Part of this money was used to help fund high-school and youth football development.

As for that third development; the reorganization of football needed a centerpiece to look forward to the future, especially with the planned celebration of the one- hundredth anniversary of professional football during the 2019 season. Potomacs owner Burton Parker, who emerged as a leader and spokesman for the presidential commission, stepped up and announced in May 201 7 that he would build a new $2 billion stadium on DC land at the site of RFK Stadium, and it would be named the World Space Stadium (WSS).

The flamboyant Burton Parker had taken over the Washington football franchise in the late nineties and had changed the name to the Potomacs (pronounced PO- toe-macs) to honor the first known American Indians to inhabit the DC area, whom John Smith met as he traveled up the then-unnamed Potomac River in 1621.

A multibillionaire, Burton Parker had secured the rights to hold the first 2020 Mars Mission Championship Contest (M2C2-1) from the GAF owners as the first event to open the stadium. To fund construction of the new stadium, Parker secured $900 million in naming rights from the billionaire owner of World Space, the builder of the new Mars mission space rocket, who also owned ThE- Car (The Electric Car Company) and USolar (US Solar), two of the fastest-growing companies worldwide. Parker also had secured funding from the Olympic and World Cup organizations, making his final cost to build WSS about $400 million. The positive public relations received for his leadership on the world stage would be priceless.

The 2019 season would be the first, with all thirty- six teams competing for the new Thorpe Trophy in the M2C2-l. Parker was excited that his two-time, defending champion Potomacs might compete and host the M2C2-1 for a chance at their groundbreaking third championship in a row at the sparkling new WSS on February 2, 2020.

There were rule changes to open and speed up the game in the new GAF, and several more to limit injuries. The playing field was wider by five feet, and the end zone was now twelve yards deep. Kicking extra points was eliminated; a team either passed for one point or ran for two points from the three-yard line.

All kicking and punting had to be done by position players. Because of this new rule, goal posts were returned to the goal line and replaced by computerized, hologram-looking goal posts; highlighted by laser lights coming out of the ground. Three points would be awarded by computer after the football traveled precisely through the colors of the home team beaming infinitely toward the heavens.

Any punt, kickoff, or field goal not run out of the end zone earned a point for the kicking team. This was known as a Rouge (from the old CFL).

The offense was now allowed to have up to three men in motion at once, but no player could be moving forward before the snap of the football. Teams were allowed only thirty seconds between plays.

To limit injuries, blocking below thigh level was eliminated and stopping forward progress within a tackle ended plays immediately. Players were encouraged to go through a new knee ligament preventive surgery that virtually eliminated major injuries in 20 minutes and a 300lb. weight limit was imposed on players. Helmets were now concussion-proof with new air-bag type technology; and new uniform engineering added protection for pulled muscles and bruising.

Professional football had changed drastically since Guy Finelli signed his rookie contract before the 2015 season. As the fifth pick in the draft, his contract was predetermined by the collective bargaining agreement (CBA), $27.5 million for four years. Now with the new GAF, the sky was the limit for the size and length of contracts, because there were no salary-cap restrictions.

· · ·

Guy Finelli had the M2C2-1 on his mind as he guided his Ferrari under the overpass of 1-70 in northern Maryland, before downshifting to pass three unhurried cars. The smell of the tires added to the sweetness of gaining speed. The ease of reaching a higher cruising velocity for his vehicle forced Guy to crack a smile.

Blue spruces in the forest of evergreens emerged on his left. It reminded him of the years his family would come this far north to cut down their Christmas tree. The memories gave him hope that he would do the same with Annie sometime soon.

After fifteen more minutes of enjoying his vehicle dominating the road, Guy pulled into the parking lot of a deadbeat-looking strip mall in Sykesville and flew the Ferrari around one last corner to the back entrance of a bar with pool tables. The bar was closed this early in the morning, but Banner GM Aaron Michaels knew the owner. Michaels was standing at the door, waiting for Guy to park in a private spot behind the building next to another black Ferrari.

Michaels knew that it was unlikely that Finelli would leave Washington in free agency, but he had begged Guy's brother, Alex, for a chance to talk to Guy in person. Besides Coach Neville Chambers, Michaels had brought a secret weapon to meet Guy, a real fan and the owner of the bar.

Aaron Michaels and Neville Chambers first met with Guy while they shot a game of pool. It was a nice touch, Guy thought, to make him feel comfortable playing a game he had mastered.

Chambers was starting his second year with the Banners. He was the most successful CFL coach in history, guiding the Montreal Alouettes to five straight Grey Cup titles. When Canadian football went bankrupt, Baltimore had signed him to a five-year contract. In his first year, he led them to the playoffs, and his "Canadian Freeze" offense led the league in total yardage. The "Freeze" was named because it was designed to keep the defense from moving a second before the snap from center.

Chambers was able to take advantage of the new rule changes involving up to three men-in-motion, similar to Canadian football. He was an exciting personality with charisma that dominated a room. His friendly Canadian demeanor helped him with the media and the Baltimore fans.

Guy had not faced the "Freeze" offense during the 2018 season but had been intrigued by the use of motion. It had some of Tom Landry's offensive line shifts, the Notre Dame Box backfield movements, and Otto Graham's moving pocket passing.

The Potomacs won their second straight championship contest with an exploitive defense led by "The Safety." The great defense complemented a ball-control offense. To win an unprecedented third straight championship contest, Finelli knew they would face the onslaught of "the bomb" in the second year of the rule changes. Every team in the league was ready to copy some part of the "Freeze" offense in their game plans for the 2019 season.

"We are very excited that you would personally come and meet with us on this informal basis," Aaron gushed with sincerity. "Guy, we think that you are the most dynamic defensive player in the league. I'm sure as shit glad I didn't have to play against you in my career." As a former All-Pro tight end, Michaels had made his living catching the football as opposed to blocking.

"I think Aaron's right; with our offense clicking like it did last season, we need a leader on defense to complete our team," Coach Chambers chimed in with north-of-the-border charm. "Let me ask you something, Guy... how did you decide to not to play that last college season and then perform like Superman at the draft combine?"

Guy smiled and looked down at his favorite casual shoes, black New Balance that he got from his dad. It reminded him of returning from New Mexico and deciding not to play football in the fall of 2014.

· · ·

His face was still as red as his hair from his time in New Mexico. He had no shoes, just a couple pairs of shorts, T- shirts, and sandals. The drive back took several days. He wanted to get home to see Annie and talk to his parents about his experiences in New Mexico and his future.

"I think she missed you, Guy," Carol announced as she hugged her son and her granddaughter. "Isn't she precious? I mean, when the three cousins are together, it is way off the cuteness chart. Little Phillip has taken to her, trying to hold and feed her, but Philly is still a little scared of her, or maybe a little jealous."

Guy was stunned how big Annie had grown in six weeks, now almost three months old. "Thanks for all of your support, Mom and Dad. It would be great if we could talk." Phillip and Carol felt at peace having their son back, even if it was the hippie version. "But first, Dad, I need some shoes, socks, and a T-shirt maybe."

Phillip was glad to comply. They had the same shoe size, so he took off what he was wearing and flipped them to his son. "I've been looking for an excuse to open up the box to my new eight forty-sixes; these are a little worn." For years Phillip had ordered the same shoes from New Balance because they offered extra-wide shoes and had great support for his flat feet.

Guy gladly put on the shoes, feeling their comfort immediately. Soon they would become his favorite pair.

After talking all morning and through lunch, Guy finally realized that he was finished playing college football. He then called Coach Brown with the news, who waited until the start of practice to announce the stunning decision to the press.

Finally, Guy returned to College Park, after cutting his hair to remove the bleached look, in time to finish his degree in the fall semester. He cheered the team on at home games and otherwise kept to himself by attending classes and knocking out another eighteen credit hours to get his degree in business and a minor in film production by December 2014.

By his twentieth birthday, October 4, Guy started running and swimming, rediscovering his athleticism and his desire to play professional football. The perfect football weather in early November enhanced his workouts to include a private trainer for yoga, agility drills, and weight work.

Alex Santucci moved in with Guy five days a week to be that trainer and personal cook, after he announced his retirement from baseball in early November 2014. The Washington Presidents had missed the postseason after two trips to the World Series. Winning his second MVP Award at age thirty-eight was a nice consolation prize and eased his decision to retire at the top of his career. Now he wanted to focus on his brother's preparation for professional football while he finished school. Alex's team, led by his step-sister Charlotte Roberts and friend Patty O'Neil, would handle all media relations and negotiations in the future.

Guy had stayed away from the press since May, and the professional scouts did not see him prior to the football scouting combine in March 2015, where he was measured just a hair above six feet six and pushed the scales to 242 pounds. His hair was groomed like a movie star to go along with his tanned, muscular body. He performed in every running and agility drill, including a jaw-dropping 4.38 seconds in the forty-yard dash, a thirty-eight-inch vertical jump, and thirty-three reps on the standard 225-pound bench press.

The Washington Potomacs held the number-five pick in the draft after a 6-10 year in 2014. Most of the negative rumors about Guy had been leaked by them to various reporters throughout the country, especially Clark Battle. The "Macs" hoped that "The Safety" would drop to the fifth pick in the draft.

Clark Battle had taken his licks on the Guy Finelli hysteria over the past eighteen months. His conspiracy stories were mainly true but were ignored by the mainstream media and most of the adoring sports fans. The murder of FBI agent Anna Cobb, pregnant with her boyfriend's child, had only made a further hero of Guy Finelli. Battle was certain it proved Finelli's involvement in a drug world, but his sources had dried up to report on it. He also had to ignore reports of Finelli's drug trips during a month in New Mexico because they were being hailed as Internet nonsense. Besides, most of the public thought Guy Finelli deserved a binge or two after what he had been through.

193

Battle wanted to be cautious about the combine workout story, but he wanted back in the spotlight, so he bit on the unconfirmed source information.

While on the *Gang of Four*, he spouted, "Guy Pinelli may be on performance-enhancing drugs. His body looks like it, and his times in the forty-yard dash show it. According to my source, he didn't play last fall because of failed drug tests." He felt powerful being on national television again and went on with a further accusation. "The murder of his girlfriend was retaliation from his drug connection." Even the other right-wing members of the panel squirmed in their seats. Battle answered with protests about Guy Finelli's heroic actions in saving his baby. "Well, how do Finelli's heroic actions in saving his baby. "Well, how do dead? There were no witnesses. Maybe he had enough of her."

After a silent response from the panel, the *Gang of Four* went to commercial, and the next day, Clark Battle was fired from the *Nation's Times*. The next time he was heard from in the future was on a blog appealing to the fans of the Glenn Beck Conspiracy Theory Generator.

CHAPTER 31

GUY SPENT THE next few minutes in the bar with Aaron and Neville talking about rediscovering the love of playing football after two tragedies in his life. "It was the winter of '08 after Sean died. Nothing was important, food didn't have taste, video games seemed trivial, sports were a burden, school was a drag... my buddies were my only lifeline, and they introduced me to pot. I felt reborn and alive. It got me through over half of high school." Aaron wanted to hug him but kept seated. Neville was stunned at his honesty and remembered many friends who got through the Canadian winters the same way in high school.

"After Anna's murder, I went west to find freedom. I had no idea that I would end up in New Mexico, but I think it saved my career and my soul."

Guy was looking straight at both of them now, talking with certainty. "I understand the need to do drugs, but now I know I don't need them. Maybe when I retire, after my kid grows up, I'll buy a bong and the most expansive hashish in the world and store it with my liquor in the freezer to smoke for special occasions, like drinking a good scotch." Guy laughed out loud at the thought. "Anyway, I've been blessed to have a supportive family, beyond any in the world, and a daughter who is the most beautiful child in history. So, playing football is a privilege to me that I take very seriously."

Aaron stood up from the table, towering over the small room at six feet five. "We love your honesty, Guy, and I agree with you about the hashish!" He slapped the table as Guy rose to hug Aaron and shake hands with Neville. "But more importantly, I agree with your view of football, and that's why we are taking this meeting so seriously...by the way, if you don't mind, I want you to meet the owner of this place. He's a big fan of yours." Aaron pointed the way and put his arm around Guy-one of the few people that could see his face at eye level. "I have to warn you, he's a real pool shark."

Guy looked surprised. "Sure...! could use some competition."

The rack of balls on the green felt of the table exploded as the shooter walked around the table, watching the balls spin off the bumpers, colliding like coverage and blockers on a kickoff, fighting for an alley to score or land short of the end zone. This set of collisions filled none of the pockets for the shooter, Baltimore Banners owner Gus

Romano. He looked up from the table, gripping the custom-made pool cue, and reluctantly offered Guy the next shot. "Well, damn...I wish my defense shut me down like that. I cracked that break like Mike Curtis hitting a running back for the Colts. Didn't that crazy son of a bitch play in Rockville near your neck of the woods in high school? Best linebacker that ever played for Baltimore. I hear you handled those Rockville boys pretty well in high school. Not like the greaser crazies in the sixties."

Gus Romano was a sixty-five-year-old, second- generation Italian American; the son of a dock worker in Baltimore; and a self-made billionaire. He was a tort attorney and had invested millions in a construction business that built a great deal of "new" Baltimore in the late eighties. Then, profits from stock sales of the right tech companies in the nineties led to great investments and profits in commercial real estate before the 2008 crash.

Romano had many friends on the East Coast, from the blue-collar union workers in Baltimore to the Wall-Street money changers in New York. Some right-wing bloggers had suggested that after donating millions to Democratic PACs in 2012 and 2016, his money was connected to the Baltimore drug wars. All this talk was ignored by the Baltimore fans and media, because they loved Gus.

He grew up a die-hard Baltimore Colts fan and had offered the Indianapolis franchise $100 million for the nickname and the horseshoe on the helmets when he bought the team a dozen years ago. The publicity stunt gave him momentum to change the name of the team to the "Banners" and to reinstate the blue and white colors.

Romano built a life-sized replica of the USS *Constitution* battleship, used in the War of 1812 and named it the SS Banner, and placed it next to the south entrance of the football stadium, which was renamed the Star-Spangled Banner Stadium. It became the most visited tour in the Baltimore Inner Harbor.

Guy took the pool stick and ran seven straight solids, purposely missing the eight ball and leaving an easy tap-in for the boss. "I am honored to meet you, Mr. Romano."

Gus tapped in the eight ball, relishing the gift victory. "Gus, please, Mr. Romano was my dad, God rest his soul... another game, Guy?"

"Sure, I'm in no hurry, Gus."

"I hear you come from quite a sports family."

"Yes sir, my brother Alex was quite the ballplayer, probably a better overall athlete than me."

Gus paused before breaking the next rack and stood straight up to look very seriously at Guy. "I doubt that very much!" This time the rack explosion sent three balls into the pockets, all stripes. "No, I'm talking about football, which is the only sport I really care about. I mean no disrespect, because I love Alex Santucci and his lovely wife, Sally Keegan; they are great Americans. But football is the only legal battlefield left in this country, where players really put their lives on the line."

Guy stood at attention listening to Gus, captured by his emotion. Surveying the table for his next shot, Gus stood across from Guy, barely five feet nine, and put down his stick on the table. He stretched out his fingers on the bumper pads and leaned forward. "I believe your grandfather was the greatest New Jersey high-school player for his size...ever! New Jersey is the birthplace of football, for Christ's sake...and that seventeen-year-old, violin-playing, blind-as-a-bat little punk shows up to play on the line in the meanest game on Earth as a senior!" Gus paused for a moment to let the memory sink in.

Guy was well aware of his family history, and now, before the hundredth season of professional football, he was looking to complete that legacy of greatness that had started ninety years ago. His eyes moistened, remembering the stories, some tall tales by now, that his father told about his grandfather, Guy I, and his great- grandfather, Geraldo. They had laid the foundation for greatness in his family, and now it was his turn to make it a certainty. At this moment, he knew his decision.

"You know, people always say, 'It was a different time; they could not play today,' and all that kind of horseshit. But numbers don't lie. If you're the only person that, did it at that time, then that speaks for itself. Who notices a lineman when you play football? *Barely anyone* is the answer. Well, with no preseason write-up and no publicity, your grandfather's playing did the talking against all kinds of odds. A defense unscored upon! Are you kidding me?"

Gus walked over to Neville Chambers to present a joint front. "I know about your dad-a high-school football star who ruins his knee and then comes back as a QB in a county touch-football league and wins a couple of championships. Right... so what, some would say. And your uncle...a great baseball player and running back... but your dad wouldn't let him play because of grades, even though he was the starting running back as a sophomore. Then, after his knees are savaged playing baseball, of all things, he gets into running these touch-football teams. Becomes a biologist at NIH and runs into that college star, the quarterback...hmmm...went to Columbia... saw him play a bunch of times, baseball too, hit left-handed, had a great swing. At QB, he played like

197

Fran Tarkenton or this Seattle kid. They could never catch him, and he had a great arm...yeah, Archie Roberts! What a shame he wanted to be a heart surgeon. Christ...some people have too much talent." Gus chortled like a kid finding gum in his baseball-card package. He slapped high fives with Neville and hugged Aaron, buried in his huge torso.

He turned toward Guy as he put his arm around Neville. "Well, it's a small world, Guy Finelli. Coach Neville here played with the "Frederick Flash" in the CFL in the seventies, and guess where he got the foundation for the 'Freeze' offense."

Guy was now really listening. He knew all about the Frederick Flash. Every year when he practiced the "Flanker Delay" pattern with his dad, he heard the story about watching the Flash score several times from this seemingly simple pattern. The story would always make him hungry, like hearing a recipe for a great meal. Start with a three-step hesitation off the line of scrimmage; then measure the perfect angle for seven yards and pour into the perfect spot between the linebacker, the corner, and the safety; and then turn up the heat, and before you can count to ten, it's a touchdown.

"Tell him, Neville." Gus slapped Neville's back, who stepped forward excited to get the spotlight.

"Well, Guy... Mr. Romano-I mean, Gus-had just hired me, and we were on his plane back from Canada, drinking some great scotch, and he says, 'Neville, when did you start thinking about the Freeze offense?' And I told him that this black guy named Randall 'Flash' Rudolph from Frederick, Maryland, who was the fastest human I ever saw play football, would show me these patterns and plays when we played together in Toronto. I was QBing, and we ran them in practice, and they were unstoppable if you ran the patterns correctly. So then Randall and I got to talking after a few weeks, and I asked him where he learned about them plays, and he says, 'These Kensington guys, the Finelli brothers, when I played with Archie Roberts in the Montgomery County touch-football leagues.' And I said, *'Who?* What do you mean, *touch* football?'

"So then the season ended in early November, and he invites me down to Maryland for Thanksgiving. And I said, 'Flash, I'm Canadian!'" Neville enjoyed the punchline with a friendly laugh, knowing that some young Americans did not get it. "Oh geez...well, anyway, that Sunday, before I head back home, we drive down to Bethesda and watch these touch-league playoff games on two adjoining fields. It was 1978 and pretty nice weather for a Canadian."

Neville was getting more animated. "Randall tells me to watch these eight teams and guess which team is running the plays he showed me. Well, the first two games we watched took under two hours and had some fine throwers, standing fifteen yards back from center, slinging the ball downfield. Then the second set of games start, and this team comes out on the field looking overmatched and ends up going down the field to score."

Guy was ready to sit down, but the story was too good to interrupt.

"The QB didn't throw the best spirals, but his ball was strong enough to get it downfield. He had great timing, throwing to spots before receivers made their last move. After the first TD drive, where he went eight for eight to six different receivers, I turned to Randall and said that's him. He smiled and said, 'No shit!'" Neville loved telling that part as he got into Guy's space. "Guy... your father wasn't the best pure QB on the field, but he ran the offense like a general. Quick hooks, outside screens, backs up the middle, rollouts, timing patterns, flags, posts, fly patterns -all thrown within three counts after catching the ball from center.

"When I got home, I wrote out each pattern on every play, sometimes using four, five, and in the CFL even six receivers. That off-season, I worked them into the offense and convinced our coach to change the offense. He agreed, and the next two years, we won the Grey Cup." Neville was happy with himself as he sat down to finish his story. "Then my arm went south, and I went into coaching." Neville chortled loudly as he watched for Guy's reaction.

Guy's legs were feeling a little numb as he unlocked his gaze from Neville and laid his stick against the wall. He was perplexed by the story. Was it possible that the brothers (his father and uncle) never knew the effect they'd had on professional football for some forty years? He had so many questions to ask but could articulate only one. "Can I get some water?"

"Of course, my friend, hey let's sit at the bar; we can talk more over there."

Guy took a stool and sucked down the glass of sparkling water as Gus looked comfortable behind the bar, waiting to refill his glass. The daunting connection had been revealed. The history of his grandfather had been researched to make an impressive narrative. Guy sensed that the tort lawyer knew how to make a final argument for the jury-or could it be that he cared enough to find out about his family to make him feel special?

The water satisfied Guy's thirst and helped him gained some balance in his thinking. He admired the passion and the tenacity of an owner like Gus Romano. The Banner organization felt like a family that extended to the city and maybe all of Maryland. It seemed like a dream to play for someone that understood his roots and respected the role that football played in society.

Gus stood alone behind the bar, ready for his summation, as Coach Neville and GM Aaron Michaels sat next to Guy. "I think, my friend, that you were meant to play for your home state and this organization. You could finish your career here without moving away from your family. Our fan base is all over Maryland; and DC for that matter. Money will be no object. We are prepared to offer you the biggest contract in professional football." Gus reached out his hand as he tried to close the deal. "I believe in destiny. I believe we are meant to be a part of football destiny together. I think this will be a special year. You will look great in the 'Banner blue and white'...yes sir. God bless you, Guy Finelli."

Gus leaned over and said his good-byes with Guy, Neville, and Aaron. He expected Aaron to lead the discussion about the team and some parameters for a contract over the next hour. Then he expected Guy's brain trust, including Alex, Charlotte and Patty, to come to their head quarters to hammer out a deal.

Gus felt complete contentment as he headed out the back door to enjoy the ride in his favorite performance vehicle. He stopped for a moment as he saw Guy's 2015 version of the Ferrari 458 Italia. "A fellow paisano with good taste," he chortled to himself. He pulled out a cigar to celebrate the victory during his ride home, certain that he had hooked the biggest 'Finelli fish' in free agency.

CHAPTER 32

GUY FINISHED HIS talk with Aaron and Neville in the next hour and was eager to

head home. He felt comfort sliding into the Ferrari as he headed south on Main Street out of Sykesville and turned-on Forsythe Road to head through the Hugg-Thomas Wildlife Management Area. The next five miles of challenging terrain let the experience with the Banner owner settle into his ego. He hit the accelerator on the ramp to Maryland Route 32 south to a quick 120 before coasting down to the speed limit to get off on Ten Oaks Road.

Guy finally realized the emptiness caused by hunger in his stomach. The adrenaline rush of the Sykesville meeting left him needing the challenge of eating at Crabs in Clarksville. With one-hundred-dollar tip, he quickly secured a dozen Maryland blue crabs before the restaurant opened. Several fans hurried to cook and serve him his meal as he sat alone waiting. He signed a couple of autographs and then started to fill his craving. He devoured each crab with a viciousness usually saved for tackling running backs or receivers crossing in front of him.

The crabs were no match for him as he sucked the moisture from the lungs, carved out the yellow guts with his fingers, and licked them dry. Then ripped out every bit of pure white meat from each crab, dipped it in hot butter and Old Bay spice, and kept the taste in his mouth until his lips burned. When he finished, he sat with contentment and started to feel his energy return.

The Ferrari spun out of the gravel lot and headed west on Maryland Route 108 toward Ashton. The route recalled memories of his grandmother Rose as he passed the Brooke Grove Nursing Center. He felt her still watching over him and wondered if she was happy seeing all of his success.

The car purred like a cat as the 562-horsepower engine idled at the traffic light in Ashton. Guy turned south on New Hampshire Avenue for the ten-mile ride to his old neighborhood of Oakview in Silver Spring. He passed the road to the garage attic where he had smoked weed with his high-school friends, reminding him of how much, five years later, he still missed Anna.

• • •

The FBI had a helicopter at the murder scene minutes after Annie was born and scooped up father and daughter after EMTs had stabilized baby Annie. The helicopter whirled them directly to Georgetown Hospital in less than an hour. Dr. Natalie Woodson met them, along with the head of nursing, Athena Edmonds. A private suite was quickly secured under FBI protection. Natalie and Athena attended to the two patients, one covered in blood and over 240 pounds, and the other clean, tiny, and less than five pounds.

Brooklyn O'Malley arrived at the crime scene by seven in the morning. The trail of the "gang of six" was lost quickly in the vast woods of Virginia after the shooting. The crime scene was secured before the local sheriff arrived, who was then relieved, seeing the FBI presence. Special Agent O'Malley imposed FBI domain over the 911 call from Guy's phone and instructed the sheriff to secure the tape for his seizure.

He knelt next to the covered body, noticing her beautiful, red hair sneaking out a couple of strands from under the blanket. As he pulled down the cover, the red of her hair still grabbed his attention as the rising sun highlighted the color. His vision became blurred with tears as he saw her face, full of scrapes and bruises, imagining the vengeance it took for someone to kill this beautiful creature. As he covered her face, it felt like losing a family member, more like a daughter than an agent he had mentored from the first day she came on his unit. He knew it was he that made her familiar with the world of evil and put her in this danger. He felt responsible for letting her do something that she loved so passionately, knowing that her love for Guy might complicate the amount of danger. Guilt filled his mind as he realized he may have used her to achieve his personal goal-trying to eradicate the Turk.

He tried to put those feelings aside as he stood and collected himself. His life would be different now; from now on, he had one purpose-retribution!

• • •

Eight lanes of twenty-four-hour traffic pounded out a cadence of echoes in the space above him as the Ferrari crawled under the Washington Beltway. He turned right at the next light inside the beltway at Oakview Drive and headed slowly down the long hill, finally ending up in front of his old house and neighborhood. It felt different and more crowded with cars that he did not recognize. He moved on quickly, not willing to notice the results of less attention to the once-immaculate yard, pleasant patios, colorful flowers, and plentiful gardens.

He headed toward the pool and the school field, crossing the creek bridge on Oakview. Guy made the turns into the parking lot; to his left he recalled the great memories of the pool, and to the right, the field where he caught and threw thousands of footballs.

He remembered the throwing session with Hank Harrison and then getting into the car with the FBI agent in July 2011. It was the first time he had met with Regional Director Brooklyn O'Malley in Beltsville. The numbing expenence made him realize how close he came to destroying his life. It was a matter of luck and connection to get a supervising agent who changed his life.

It was directly ahead of him that he first saw Anna, in her bathing suit and shorts, looking like a high-school swimmer, just hanging outside the gate of the pool and talking on the phone. Suddenly, he was there, seeing their eyes meet for the first time as he entered the gate. He remembered smelling her scent as he passed close by her. A sweet smile beamed from her face as she played a teenager role to perfection, twirling her hair with a free hand. Quietly, she said into the phone, "Guy Finelli's here." He took another step, wondering if he heard his name, and then kept going before he came to his senses and turned to view the redheaded beauty. Her hair was hiding her face, but instinctively she looked up from the phone and put it on her chest. Brushing aside her hair, she said confidently, "Goodluck, Guy Finelli!"

He wanted to say so much more but only nodded and uttered, "Thanks." Turning away, he walked toward the nicely mowed bank of grass, remembering that he wanted to see her face again. But now, looking for the last time, he finally realized she was gone

CHAPTER 33

THE SEARCH FOR Anna's killers became an obsession for FBI Assistant Director Brooklyn O'Malley over the next four years after the murder. He spent every waking hour combing over evidence to implicate the Turk and his men. His wife left him for months at a time, spending as much time as possible at their vacation house in Rehobeth Beach, Delaware. He stopped playing golf, his favorite hobby with friends, and lost forty pounds from a shrinking appetite. Other than constantly exercising when not working, he had no social life. Before going to sleep around midnight, he would watch the opening monologue on *The Tonight Show* and ESPN's *SportsCenter* and then wake again at five to review evidence from all informants in the Baltimore drug trade before working most of the day.

The media were never informed after the murder that Guy Finelli was the focus of the attack by the gang of six. His relationship with Anna and the fact that she was an FBI agent had never been public. And as far as Buckingham County was concerned, the attack never happened. One hundred thousand dollars of new surveillance equipment to the sheriff's office had certified their silence. The media were never informed after the murder that Guy Finelli was the focus of the attack by the gang of six. His relationship with Anna and the fact that she was an FBI agent had never been public. And as far as Buckingham County was concerned, the attack never happened. One hundred thousand dollars of new surveillance equipment to the sheriff's office had certified their silence.

The media only learned of her existence several years after Guy was drafted by the Potomacs. His team of Charlotte Roberts and Patty O'Neil controlled the story from the time of the murder to the present day. Guy Pinelli was the most-loved Washington football player since Sonny Jurgensen. With the representation from Charlotte and Patty, Guy Pinelli and his brother, Alex Santucci, were sports icons in the DC area. They had both brought championships for the DC sports fans to celebrate, and they could do nothing wrong. The fact that the Potomacs had allowed Guy Pinelli to hit the free-agent market was causing pain and misery to all DC sports fans.

The evidence from the white van leaving the crime scene was minimal. There were no cameras on State Route 602, and back roads were plentiful in Buckingham County. There

204

was some DNA captured from the scene but nothing to match in the system. It would be held in storage in case the gun, the van, or the gang of six ever showed up. Brooks still had no physical evidence of the Turk's existence-no pictures and no idea of his location.

But four years later, Brooks finally received a break in the case. It was an exceptionally lucky one, but one that was made possible by a veteran FBI agent keeping his eyes open. Special Agent Angelo Randle was driving back from his beach house in Ocean City on the Maryland Eastern Shore when his car broke down while taking a back route off State Route 404. Randle, who had worked under Brooks on the Anna Cobb murder case for four years, was affectionately known as Julee by his family and closest associates.

Julee loved to turn right onto State Route 309 at the little town of Queen Anne, just south of the beautiful Tuckahoe State Park, as a pleasant bypass of traffic that would take him to US Route 301, which merged into US Route 50 to cross the Chesapeake Bay Bridge. It was a five- mile diversion on a well-maintained two-lane road that rarely had another car or police radar.

The sun was close to setting behind him in the west on this humid Saturday night in August, when his radiator started to spew steam from the front of the car. He guided the vehicle around a bend in the road, slowing down from eighty miles per hour. He finally pulled over and turned off the engine, just short of the only intersection of houses with a town name on this side route.

He walked in front of the car, watching the steam rise and cloud the colorful sky of the setting sun, and decided to let his car cool down before assessing the damage. He grabbed his cap and wallet from the vehicle and walked the quarter mile to the town intersection. A smaller side street appeared past the intersection, with several houses situated down the thin road. Heading down the street, Julee adjusted his cap, hoping to find a neighbor before darkness who was willing to lend him some antifreeze that might get him over the bridge and home to Annapolis without a tow truck.

As he passed the third house, he noticed a garage behind the house in the backyard with a side shed that had lights on. There was a small sign on the shed that read, "Nick's Gun Repair." Not seeing any activity in the house, he slowly headed down the driveway and knocked on the shed door.

"Come in... please come in," pleaded Nick Fuentas from behind a counter. Julee opened the screen and then the solid door and walked into an air-conditioned paradise for a gun owner. The short Greek immigrant behind the counter was happy to see a fellow human enter his domain. "Please come in ... how can I help you?" Nick asked as he sat on upright on his stool in front of a door that led to a back room in his garage. Around him were stacks of rifles and shotguns that were being cleaned or repaired. On the walls hung his collection of antique rifles and handguns collected from the last four centuries, some dating back to the Revolutionary War.

"Thank you...my car is steaming some antifreeze on the side of the road, just before the town. I was letting it cool down. Would you happen to have some antifreeze around?" Julee was relieved to find such a pleasant character on his side of the bay.

"Of course, my friend, can I offer you some water or some tea?" Nick took off his heavy magnifying glasses, hopped off his stool, and walked Julee outside to his garage to look for some antifreeze. "You know, it has been years since anyone has stopped by here for something, other than my regular customers, but that is always during the week. They all know I repair on the weekends, so they do not bother me then."

"Well, thank you, Nick; I won't take up much of your time if you have some antifreeze."

"No, please...this is a nice distraction to speak with a fellow...Mediterranean?"

"Yes, my mother was Italian, from Atessa on the Adriatic, a small mountain village with stunning views of the sea."

"How wonderful...sometimes it is a small world to be from the same waters, Mr   ?"

"Oh, excuse me... Angelo Randle, but my good friends call me Julee!"

"Yes, Ju-leeeee! How wonderful. The last gentleman
that stopped several years ago had spent lots of time in Greece and Italy but was from Turkey, I believe, even though he looked very Arabic."

Julee stopped in his tracks, suddenly needing some water to swallow. He coughed and collected himself, now waiting to hear more of the story.

"Hear it is...almost a full gallon. I hope this will arrive you home."

"Yes, thank you...! will try in a half hour or so. Can we sit for some tea, maybe?"

"Oh, perfect, I was hoping that you would stay. Back in my private room, let us go." Nick opened a door at the back of the garage to his private room off the shed. It had a sitting area with some books and storage shelves behind it, up and down the wall. Unlike the shed, it was neat, clean, and well- organized. For the seventy-eight-year-old immigrant from Greece, it was an oasis. As he sat, Julee looked on the walls and saw pictures and paintings of the Greek countryside and waters.

Nick served the tea and again brought up his past visitor. "I hope you become a friend like my last visitor. We have become friends from his visits every six months or so."

"That would be my pleasure. I could repay you for the antifreeze and bring you some guns of mine to fix."

"It would be my pleasure, so funny that it's the same way my last visitor became a regular customer. My Lord sometimes watches me well."

"You repair his guns for him?"

"Well, really just the one gun, but to him it is really special."

"I can understand that. I have a gun that is really special to me that my dad gave me. I will bring it to you to see."

"Very well, I can store for you if you like, the same as I do for my friend. I show it to you. It is right behind me here. I kept it away from dust and dirt of my shop."

As an FBI agent, Angelo Randle lived on hunches. This one was way out there, but the puzzle was now getting interesting as he waited to see the weapon. They had obtained very little evidence on the Turk over the years, but they knew he was an eccentric and hoped that he would keep the gun as a trophy in winning his battle against "The Safety."

The FBI also believed he lived or spent time on the Eastern Shore, possibly near the bay. Based on that profile, Randle had spent hours traveling through small towns and shops looking for any clue of his personality. It was a crazy ordeal, but it kept him thinking about the case and helped him believe that one day, he would catch the killer of an FBI agent.

Nick pulled out a carved wooden box and opened it. The gun was covered in a velvet pouch. He untied it carefully and pulled it out.

Julee had held the gun model so many times, he was certain without a closer glance that it could be Anna's gun. Only getting the serial number would confirm it. Nick held it delicately, using the velvet pouch to avoid touching it with his fingers. It was too much to believe that DNA or a print was left on the gun, but Julee could always dream. "I see...that is in perfect condition-a Glock nine, I assume?"

"Yes, my friend...many law enforcement use it. It looks like a special model; I do not know for sure."

Nick sipped his tea with his new friend for the next fifteen minutes, excited to talk more about the Turk. After some carefully crafted questions, Nick described the Turk's appearance and said that he came in every six months, right before Easter and after Labor Day, to see his gun in storage. Nick treated the visits like a customer checking his safety-deposit box. He would leave him alone in the back room for some time with his gun. He did see the Turk at times take it in his hand, pull the trigger, and smell it like it had just been fired. They would then chat and finish some tea together. The Turk would hand back the gun to Nick with $1,000 dollars to clean it and store it for the next six months. Nick complained about the overpayment but felt special that the Lord Almighty was looking out for him.

Angelo left with the antifreeze and the luckiest find of his career.

Taking no chances, Brooklyn O'Malley staked out the Nick Puentas property starting the next day in August 2018. Within two weeks they were able to break into the special room in the garage and confirm the serial number on the gun. The surveillance waited patiently until after Labor Day, when the Turk finally showed up to see his gun. For the first time ever, they had a picture of the drug lord that ran Baltimore.

They followed his vehicle but lost him quickly after the Bay Bridge. He was a master at switching vehicles. Brooks learned his lesson after that meeting and vowed it would not happen again.

According to Nick Puentas, the Turk had showed up on Good Friday every year for the past four years. Brooks waited for over six months for his next chance to follow the Turk to the source of his empire. April 19, 2019, would finally come, and Brooks would be ready to watch his target drive to China if that was what it took.

Chapter 34

AFTER THE TRIP through Oakview, Guy headed to Bethesda and drove his Ferrari through the gate of Alex's mansion, parking on the circular driveway in front of the house. He was early for the noon meeting with Potomacs owner Burton Parker and general manager Frank Alexander.

The morning meeting with Baltimore had given Guy a perspective on his talent that he had not considered before. Alex had convinced him to take the meeting, even though he had never considered playing anywhere other than in DC. "Hey, brother, how did the meeting go in northern Maryland?"

"It was amazing! Thanks for making me go."

"So you're ready to be a Baltimore Banner?"

"Hell yes...I mean, I am a Maryland native!"

"Any numbers?"

"Apparently anything I want."

"Well, that should help with the Macs. I think Charlotte let it slip that you had a meeting this morning when they scheduled this meeting. I think they wanted to meet at midnight to sign you."

"Yeah, like I was going to ruin my sleep over this nonsense; they had over two months to do the right thing."

"Well, let's go inside. I think Sally has the kids coloring hard-boiled eggs for Easter. Apparently you were never very good on the Easter egg hunt with Grace. Somehow she always whipped you pretty bad."

"I think my mom gave her hints." Guy laughed loudly at his own joke. "You know how engineers are...she thinks she's a lot smarter than me, and she was always able to figure out the little things better than me."

"Are you saying you would let her win?"

"After a while, it was hopeless to beat her, just like in chess and Sudoku...you know games like that. So I liked that she won, but I would try my hardest just to put pressure on her."

"Wow, that's pretty funny. I'm glad that I didn't have any siblings near my age to distract me."

"Apparently, you didn't have anyone your age to play with-just your mitt, a bat, and a ball." Guy playfully drove a forearm into Alex's chest, still rock hard, on a body still close to playing condition. As they walked inside, Guy wrapped his arm around Alex and hugged him with his taller and more dominant frame. He felt the power of their brotherhood. But they were more than half-brothers; they were best friends, closest allies, and trusted partners. They had something in common other than the Pinelli heritage. They had experienced and survived the immense pressure of performance as hometown heroes.

Seven years ago, during a remarkable summer season, Alex had learned how to fall in love and feel his emotions. It made him a complete player, a superstar.

He knew that Guy was on a different journey, one that forced him become comfortable with the difficult emotion of anger. The murder of Anna had made him more serious and determined to become the best defensive player of all time. While riding the force of anger, he still had to avoid the negativity of hate. It was a slippery slope, one that could lead him into an abyss of rage. But Alex could see that Guy was steady on his journey, one that would lead him to winning the chess game against his opponent. To take down the Turk would mean ascending above being a superstar to becoming a superhero.

Alex enjoyed the embrace and kissed his younger brother on the cheek. Sharing affection with his brother and father was always a special moment not easily put into words for him-"Let It Be," a song title from the Beatles, was close enough. He pulled away as they walked into the family room. "You know...! hope Annie didn't inherit your subpar detective skills for the egg hunt this year."

Full of curly red hair, little five-year-old Annie came running up to her father; smiling and too excited for words. Guy scooped her up like a fumbled football and swung her above his head as she shrieked with joy before bringing her down to his face for kisses. She went on to tell him about the eggs she dipped with her favorite color, red.

He put her down, and they held hands as they walked toward the kitchen to join Sally and the twins. Guy answered his brother's concern about Annie's performance the upcoming Easter-egg hunt. "I wouldn't worry too much about that...remember, her mom was a pretty good detective."

Alex laughed, "Good point!"

Sally greeted them wearing an apron and colored hands. She kissed each of them and complained about the mess in the kitchen. The mess did nothing to confuse her appearance. It was sight to perk up the senses. Her elegance and style had not been altered by mothering three young children.

At thirty-seven, Sally was becoming a superstar in her own right. After giving birth to the twins in 2013, she returned to teaching at Park University for a year, commuting to Kansas City for fifteen weeks each semester. She took the kids and the nanny to her house in Riss Lake from Monday mornings to Thursday afternoons. The following summer, she accepted an associate professor position at Georgetown University. It was a public-relations coup for their School of Public Policy.

She had become great friends with Alex's advisor from Princeton, Dr. Brightman. He had become the leading progressive voice supporting the economic-stimulus legislation in the first Obama term. Once she became situated at Georgetown, he mentored her on becoming a pundit on the news airways. She could present a moderate view of public policy and economics that he could not. Suddenly, she became a voice of reason for both the right and left in the media. Now she taught only one class a semester and was a guest on a number of news shows several times a week from a studio set up in her office.

"So nice to see you Guy, this is your big day...huh?" Sally said with joy as she washed her hands and removed her apron. [11] I hope you're planning to stay through dinner and getting these rascals to bed."

"With pleasure...thank you Sally, for everything."

"Anything for my little brother-in-law." She snuggled into him for a big hug. With her jet-black hair and petite body, she felt like a feather in his arms. "Now, you guys have a great meeting and make some money! Let me take Annie here and wash those red hands."

• • •

The greetings between the parties seemed to have a more serious tone than usual as they exchanged pleasantries in Alex's office suite in the back of the house. General Manager Frank Alexander was feeling the heat from the fans and local talk shows about letting Guy Finelli reach free agency. On the ride over, he revealed the information of the morning meeting with the Baltimore Banners from his source at Banners headquarters to hyperactive Potomacs owner, Burton Parker, who nearly jumped out of the back seat in anger to attack Alexander after hearing the news. He finally calmed down by the time they reached the Santucci estate.

Burton Parker entered the grand foyer and immediately found Sally and the kids

211

in the kitchen and family room area. He loved Sally Keegan and gave her an enthusiastic hug and kiss. He enjoyed every second of her scent and feel. He found her to be his right size as a woman -unfortunately his wife was blond and tall.

He could not stop talking about the three children or Sally after his visit in the kitchen. "Sally has done such a great job with the kids-of course, with a little help from you guys, I'm sure." Burton laughed awkwardly at his own jokes, often in isolation, but his talent was to switch on his charm to focus on others. "This is such a fine family. Washington, DC, is blessed to have the legacy of your careers to witness. We want that legacy to finish with the Potomacs."

"We appreciate your words, Mr. Parker, but Guy plays a violent game and has paid his dues to get to this point of earning free agency. To be honest, the Potomacs have not presented an offer that appreciates his career," Charlotte finished with authority. She and Patty O'Neil were in charge of the meeting, and it was their chance to directly attack Burton Parker. Up to this time, General Manager Frank Alexander had defended a home-time discount contract to them that fell way short of their expectations. Winning the second Super Bowl in a row had short- circuited their strategy to wait until the off-season to get serious in a contract negotiation.

"Miss Roberts...Charlotte, if I may? I am here now to finish this negotiation. I take responsibility for not getting involved earlier. This organization has become very successful over the past few years with me staying out of these matters. Frank and Gerry have been masters as architects of this team, but signing Guy Finell is different. He is the franchise...just between the seven of us here."

"Thank you for your honesty, Mr. Parker, What do you have in mind?"

"Please, Charlotte and Patty, call me Burton...Frank will handle the details of the offer and will listen to your concerns on matters of personnel, but this part I will present."

Burton Parker stood and walked up to the whiteboard that was on the wall in the office. He picked up a marker and asked Alex, "May I?"

Alex nodded as Burton unbuttoned his double- breasted suit jacket, tailored to highlight his very fit waist. He hung the jacket on the back of his chair and undid his Chesapeake-blue, gold, and burgundy cuff links-shaped like Potomac helmets-and then he rolled up his sleeves to show that he was ready to work. He stood at the whiteboard in silence for a defining minute, thinking about the importance of this meeting. Guy Finelli had turned down their generous offer a week after the championship contest victory in February. He had been living with the shame of having let his best player reach free agency. It had been the worst two months of his life, reading and listening to the rhetoric from the media about failing to secure Finelli after last year's championship win. He did not care about the ascending price tag for his mistake. The publicity he received from a big contract would only help him sell tickets and merchandise for the new stadium in 2020. No, it was not the money, he thought; it was all about squashing the competition.

The offer had to be like an earthquake in the deep ocean, causing the fear of a tsunami on every coast. He took the blue marker and wrote three numbers and one word in gigantic print across the board: "$100 million." Then he took out the red marker and wrote underneath in capital letters, "GUARANTEED."

Burton Parker looked for a moment at his masterpiece on the whiteboard and smiled to himself, hardly keeping from bursting into an awkward laugh while he rolled down his sleeves, slipped on his cufflinks, and put on his jacket. He slowly turned around and stared at Guy Finelli for a few moments, and he felt proud. He sat down, crossed his legs, and let out that awkward laugh. He lowered his head to regain focus and turned to the right to face Charlotte and Patty. Finally, he felt some relief and took a deep breath to smell the air of success before he asked, "Any questions?"

Chapter 35

SALLY KEEGAN HAD finished the serious task of dying three dozen hard-boiled eggs and sent them to the garage refrigerator for a few weeks of storage until Easter morning. After sending the kids upstairs for their naps, she joyfully set up the dining room with several dishes delivered by the Pines of Rome restaurant now just a fifteen-minute walk from their newly inhabited mansion in Bethesda.

The smell of sausage and peppers ready for hoagies, the beauty of a whole rockfish from the Chesapeake, and the redness of the tomato sauce covering the manicotti and meatballs filled the room, causing the negotiators to descend like hounds finding their next target.

Smiles and hugs were exchanged as celebration toasts circled the table. Burton Parker and Frank Alexander each backslapped each other over closing the deal as they struggled to eat their overloaded hoagies. Eating like pigs seemed an appropriate exercise for signing their best player for the rest of his career. Burton was all but certain that his legacy would be sealed as the greatest football owner in history if they won a third straight championship contest this season.

GM Frank Alexander at times cringed at Burton Parker's awkward behavior, but he had forged a close relationship with the brazen owner over the last seven seasons and thought his legacy would be that of a great owner someday. When he was hired, he insisted that Mr. Parker stay out of personnel decisions unless he was invited, as in today's negotiation. During his seven years as GM, he had kept his word.

Burton Parker and Frank Alexander excused themselves to head to the office and get the lawyers to write up the contract. Frank Alexander promised to be back by dinner for Guy Finelli's signature.

Family and friends came by to eat and give their congratulations to Guy. Cousin Joe, Furrey Favarro, Uncle Anthony, and Phillip all stopped by.

Guy's and Charlotte's phones had a series of text messages from GM Aaron Michaels. Charlotte phoned to update him on the contract agreement with Washington. An hour later, a call came through to Guy from Gus Romano. He decided to answer. "This is Guy."

"I hear congratulations are in order for you and the Potomacs!"

"Well, sir...yes, we hope to sign the contract this evening, but everything is agreed to," Guy said as his hand holding the phone starting to shake. "I appreciate your great enthusiasm for me, Gus; you made me feel special."

"It was my pleasure, Guy. Let me know if there is anything I can do for you or your family in the future. You will always be welcomed here as a son of Maryland."

"Thank you, sir..." Guy felt a gush of emotion but held back in midsentence.

"Listen, we plan on meeting you in the championship contest this season. It should be a short ride to DC. Wouldn't that be something for this area?"

"Nothing would make me happier, sir."

"Best of luck, Guy, on the season, but between you and me, I think our offense is going to Freeze you in your tracks!" Gus said with gusto and a big laugh through the phone.

Guy paused to let the laughter settle, and suddenly his hand was not shaking anymore. "Well, Gus...! guess we'll see about that. You know we are playing indoors at the new stadium. Tell Coach Chambers I'd hate to see his offense melt under pressure."

■ ■ ■

Guy sat on the couch with Annie on his lap, Phillip II on his right asleep on his leg, and Philly II fidgeting on his left, trying to stay awake to watch the movie. Annie usually outlasted her cousins and rarely fell asleep without being put to bed. Tonight, she was comfortable on her dad's chest and about to head into slumber.

The contract had been delivered by Frank Alexander at six-thirty as promised. His face showed great relief when Guy penned the document. It was quite a historic deal. In the re-formed league, there was no salary cap but still rarely guaranteed salaries. Only the bonuses were usually guaranteed, but they were based on years of playing out the contract. Usually, after year three, the whole bonus was doled out.

This contract guaranteed the whole $100 million bonus no matter how long Guy played. The contract was set for ten years with an average salary of $20 million a year, including $30 million in the first year and then descending salaries in the next nine years. All of the bonus would be paid the first year, so Guy Finelli would make $13 0 million in the first year of the contract. The total package of $300 million for ten years was the largest contract in professional football history.

Guy felt the quiet of the room as all three kids fell into unconsciousness. Soft violins were playing over the credits of the movie they had watched. Sally moved quietly into the room and picked up Phillip II from the couch. Alex was right behind her, laughing at the sight of Guy surrounded by children, and whispered, "Now that's a great picture of a dad!"

Patty O'Neil, who had dozed off on the side couch, rose to help with the children picking Annie up off her father's chest. The trio headed upstairs to file each child under their covers.

Guy waved and mouthed "Thank you" as Annie slightly opened her eyes to check out her new carrier. She fit nicely into Patty's chest and matching curly red hair. Patty had become the official, comfortable girlfriend for Guy during the past couple of years. She had become overwhelmingly attracted to him the first time he showed up at Presidents Park with Alex in 2012. She was somewhat embarrassed to be so captivated by a seventeen-year-old, but after becoming friends with Charlotte, they enjoyed laughing about their guilty Guy-candy pleasure.

Alex and Sally had become her second family after they rescued her from a bout of pneumonia in 2012. She became a part of Alex's support system, first handling public relations for the couple and then going to law school to handle any legal issues in the family.

Sharing one night of intimacy, even impaired by alcohol, on the night of his eighteenth birthday, gave her an anchor in Guy's life, even as he soon fell for Anna. Since Anna's death, Patty had become a close friend and now a companion. Guy was still just twenty-four, and she was thirty-two, so she was still patient as she waited for the next step of commitment.

Guy switched the movie screen to *SportsCenter*. The main topic was the news of his signing of an enormous contract to stay in Washington. Even on this late Saturday night, the football pundits interrupted a weekend date night to comment on the news. In the background they were playing highlights of his four-year career, when Patty appeared and snuggled up to him on the couch. Most of the time, she was cautious to ever show PDA with family or friends unless Gus initiated it, but when they were alone, she helped herself.

"Just in time to see some great highlights," Guy pointed out.

"There's our client, number twenty-one in Chesapeake blue, gold, and burgundy forever!" Patty exclaimed, rolling back into Guy to give him a big kiss.

Physically, Patty was quite different than Anna. At five feet eight and 145 pounds, she could playfully dominate him. She had a striking resemblance to a young Maureen

O'Hara, an actress who always presented a handful of problems to John Wayne in the five movies they did together.

Rarely did Patty dress to feature her full breasts and fit waist. Her muscular thighs and behind gave her a full but striking figure. Only recently had she learned to highlight her strong cheekbones and eyebrows with makeup. Sally Keegan had slowly introduced her to the concept of putting on her face in the morning. Sally always said that it was private time for her to begin the day. The next step was to change her wardrobe, which involved Patty wearing mostly baggy sweatshirts and jeans and putting her great amount of hair in a ponytail. Sally had brought several New York fashion experts to the house to revamp Patty's wardrobe after threatening to nominate her for the show *What Not to Wear.*

Guy loved Patty's body but was more impressed by two physical features that she possessed: excellent hands and a great arm. She was a gifted athlete but had never excelled in team sports, except basketball. She loved tennis, but most importantly, she loved throwing and catching the football with Guy.

They sat together on the couch, feeling satisfied at seeing the results of their work being played out on a stage of ESPN highlights and punditry on the big home- movie screen. Guy noticed something in his pocket and pulled out the pen that Alex had given to him to sign the contract. It was the special blue-ink pen he had received from Presidents owner Frederick Meyer when he signed his contract in 2012. At the signing, the smell of the ink had jumped off the paper, and the blue color had a lively look. Quietly he opened the pen and smelled the ink. The memory got him very excited.

Watching the highlights of his career being replayed on all the sports channels gave him a chance to review his four years of playing for the Potomacs after being drafted in 2015. At the time, the honor of being the fifth pick in the draft and signing a $2 7.5 million contract did little to fill the void of losing Anna. It seemed important to build a wall around his emotions with the public, and he resolved to never talk to the media until after the season, going against the advice of his brother, Charlotte, and Patty. Luckily, his father supported him in his decision, saying that Sean Taylor had let his playing on the field do the talking for him.

The rumors about his life swirled, and the stories mounted that first year, as did the fines he collected for missing mandated press conferences. In the first half of his rookie season, Washington continued to play poorly like the previous year. Finelli was beaten early and often, playing in a cover-two system that seemed to not cover anybody or take advantage of his skills. Finally, at the midseason bye week, he implored the

217

defensive coordinator to make him the single safety, with man-to- man corners and eight in the box defense. It was similar to the Chicago "46" defense.

It was an instant success as Guy intercepted ten passes in the last eight games to give him a dozen for the season. More importantly, the team went 6-2 toendup8-8 for the season. But Coach Shannon Dellums resigned at the end of the season when owner Burton Parker refused to extend his contract past the 2016 season.

Parker was happy to save the $7 million for a coach he did not like. His main quarrel with Shannon was him not recognizing the greatness of Guy Finelli. He had taken half the season to use him properly on defense and refused to use him in the return game until the last four games of the season, when he finally relented and watched Guy return two punts and two kickoffs for TDs.

Guy turned to Patty, trying to ignore his arousal. "Remember when we met with Burton at his house to talk about the new coach in January of '16?"

"Yeah... wow, what a surprise that this billionaire was asking you, just finishing your rookie year and only twenty-one, about who to hire as head coach."

"I think I freaked him out when I said Coach Brown from UMD, hoping my cousin Joe and Coach Favarro would come as well. I was shocked when Mr. Parker told me he knew all the starters on the UMD championship team and all the coaches. He knew Alex, Joe, and my uncle Anthony

-and was in love with Sally Keegan!"

"That was sweet. You know he can be awkward sometimes, but he knows his shit."

"Yeah... but he even knew my Sprint DMC boys!" "That was freaky...drafting Cary and Duran in the third round together and signing Mark as a free agent. That was an awesome coup for the defense."

"Well, they should have drafted Excel in '17, but the Banners got him, and the rest is history."

"Coach Chambers loves that guy. He plays like he has skates on in that Freeze offense."

Guy looked hard at Patty and those light green eyes. She had dressed in a nice-fitting blouse and tight jeans for the evening, making her seem irresistible. "Did you just make that up or hear that on ESPN? That's a pretty funny comment for a lawyer."

She held his arms down, forcing her chest onto him. She hovered over him, landing kisses on his face and neck. Guy enjoyed the mugging and the breast feels for a minute but finally escaped to the side of the couch. "Just tell me if you're bored watching my career highlights!" Guy said sarcastically.

218

"All right, I'll behave for a little while." She adjusted her bra and blouse back into place. "So, how did you convince Parker to hire those guys?"

"Well... I told him that Vince Lombardi's only head coaching job was at St. Cecilia's High School in New Jersey until he got the Packer job at age forty-eight."

"Nice touch to bring out the Cecilia reference. Wasn't that the name of your first girlfriend?" Patty quickly jumped off the couch, expecting retaliation. "By the way, how does that relate to Coach Brown?"

"Not having pro experience, I guess...anyway, it seemed like a great story at the time...You know I love Coach Lombardi." Seeing that Patty was distracted, Guy went straight for the molesting move from behind that he loved to do to her, quickly ending it by tickling her until she begged for freedom. "OK... OK, you are so sensitive."

Once again Patty made wardrobe adjustments. "Didn't Lombardi at least coach in the NFL as an assistant?"

She had escaped from Guy and turned toward him while sitting on her knees on the carpet, extending her chest toward him. He smiled at Patty's playfulness and recognized her power position, as he refocused on his thoughts. "You are such a tease, but to answer your question-yes, he was, and yes, it was a poor comparison, but it seemed to work on Mr. Parker."

"Well, yes, that is the point of the story, I guess...Somehow, he bought the idea."

"Yeah, he wanted Joe to be defensive coordinator, but Joe knew that he didn't have the patience to deal with the media, so he told Mr. Parker that Furrey always ran things better with him as his assistant. So then he ended up as special teams coach. How about that for honesty?"

• • •

For the 2016 season, new head coach Gerry Brown and two of his UMD assistants, Furrey Favarro and Joe Finelli, kept the momentum of the previous year and led the Potomacs into the conference championship game against Philadelphia, coming short of victory on the five-yard line as the clock ran out.

Guy Finelli became the breakout star of the defense and special teams, almost tying the record for interceptions in a season with thirteen, and had four TDs on returns. Their "Surprise Sprint" offense, named by Coach Brown, in which Guy ran with his defensive backfield after designated punt returns, averaged ten yards of offense a play.

Normally only four plays a game, it scored four TDs and converted four two-point conversions during the season.

Guy made his first Pro Bowl and was named as the league's first-team, All-Pro free safety. He started to dominate the way QBs called a game. Most would still challenge him by throwing deep consistently, but after he was averaging close to an interception a game, that idea was scrapped. Eventually, in the playoffs, Philadelphia took advantage of the defensive line giving up too many yards in the running game and on-screen plays. It was a defect on defense that Washington took care of before their 2017 Championship season.

The 2017 season played out like a fairy tale. The defense did not play well early in the year, and then the offense sputtered late in the season, but they made it into the playoffs as a wild-card team.

It came down to the last half of the last game of the year to get into the playoffs. The offense and defense finally jelled, coming back from a 24-0 halftime deficit to win 27-24. The defense held New York to a negative- twenty-yard offense in the second half with the help of the rain and wind at the Meadowlands. Ironically, it did not seem to bother Potomacs QB Marcus McNeil III and the offense as they churned out 350 yards, scoring on five straight second-half possessions to win the game.

Guy Finelli ended the last New York threat with his record-tying fourteenth interception of the season. The excitement in the locker room gave him reason to break his almost three years of silence with the media after the final regular-season game of 2017.

He stepped to the podium, towering over the room of reporters. The first question asked the obvious: "How did it feel to tie the interception record for a season?"

The rush of the post victory adrenaline go this throat as he felt the annoyance of the question. "It's an insult to the great Dick 'Night Train' Lane to believe that I tied his record. He did it in a twelve-game season, during an era when they threw the ball half as much as they do now. I figure that it would take nineteen interceptions to really tie his record and twenty to break it."

"Do you think you will ever break his record?"

"Will I ever get twenty interceptions? If it helped the team, then maybe, but that would seem improbable. What seems probable is getting to the championship contest this year and winning it...and then in 2019 and repeating...and then again in 2020 in DC for three in a row. Now, that would be a record for the ages."

Guy's directness and controlled anger seemed to permeate the room. He waited patiently for the next question, remembering Patty O'Neil's advice not to be mean to the reporters personally, just assertive with his answers.

"Are you predicting you'll win three championship contests in a row?" reporter Kelly Browner with Big Atlantic Sports Network (BASN) asked quietly.

Guy noticed her soft smile and decided to go with some charm. "Well, maybe getting twenty interceptions would be easier." Guy beamed with a million-dollar smile that the public rarely saw. He shifted his weight behind the podium as he started to feel his energy wane from the fierce battle of the day. He became serious in his next reply, hoping to be understood. "I'm a team guy and maybe a little old-school, you might say. So, to me ... winning three championship contests in a row to tie Coach Lombardi's record of three NFL titles in a row is the pinnacle of greatness. That's why they named the NFL trophy after him." He tried to finish his thought and suddenly remembered to stand up straight and smile. "Now... no team has won three championship contests in a row, including back in the days of the Super Bowl. As a player, that's the way to football immortality."

Like a politician creating a sound bite, Guy Finelli unknowingly began a campaign that would lead him to the edge of transcendence. He walked from the podium with a wave to the crowd of eager reporters.

•••

"How did the players react to Coach Brown?"

"It was a relief at first, because the year before had been such a struggle, and then halfway through the season, things on offense got pretty weird. A big power struggle came about between Marcus and Coach Brown about play calling. The defense felt a lot of pressure while they sorted things out. Luckily, nothing made it to the media. Everybody stayed together in the locker room, and the rest is history."

"So, one last question before I take you to bed."

"I'm all ears." Guy was ready to answer as quickly as possible to accept the invitation from Patty.

"How do you get Burton Parker to sign Hank Harrison for the 2018 season after three teams let him go, and that deaf guy you played with in high school?"

"Oh, you mean Albert, one of the Christian Brothers. Yeah, that was amazing. You know Mr. Parker...he likes to hang out with his best players, like Marcus and myself... I mean we just do what we're told, like show up at his Potomac palace for a cookout or fly to Atlantic City to hang out. So, we're on his private airship, and Marcus started complaining about the third-down offense protection breaking down, stalling drives, and whatever. He loves to complain to Mr. Parker...who loves to listen!

Anyway...! was like, hey, my man Hank Harrison is a third-down catching machine. I said, put him next to my deaf boy, Mr. Christian, at right tackle, and I guarantee you'll get the pass off to Hank. So Marcus was like, 'Yo man, how does that dude hear me?' And I said, 'He doesn't...' So I stared at him a minute and told him, Albert is the smartest guy on the field, and he always knows what to do. I didn't tell him Hank always signs to him.

"Anyway...so, Mr. Parker chimes in like a girl left out of the conversation and says, 'Let's go get both of them.' Marcus was like...'Hey, that's cool with me'...even though he's all born again about Hank being gay and shit."

"So, the first deaf guy and the first openly gay guy on the team-boy, you are a troublemaker!"

"Sometimes I think these guys believe all this macho crap they spout until a teammate or two calls them out on it. Anyway...the next day, Hank and Albert are picked up in Canada at workouts in Saskatchewan for the new B division in Canada. Mr. Parker signed them after a workout with Coach Brown, and they helped us win a second Super Bowl."

"You're something, Guy Finelli...you're really something, but how did Marcus deal with it?"

"Oh yeah...he fell in love with Albert on the first day after seeing him reading Bible verses at lunch. Albert is a PhD candidate in religious studies at Notre Dame, so they started to hang out, and Albert taught Marcus sign language, and then the whole team. It was really awesome. It raised the level of the meaning of *silent counts.* Eventually, Albert raised Mac III's level of thinking about Christianity, like, to a Jesuit level of thinking. It has helped him become a more tolerant person."

"I can see that about Marcus, becoming definitely less of a *me* person. As for you...how about you make me *more* of a *me* person by entering my domain, if you know what I mean?"

"I'm only a ballplayer, Patty, so this is getting way too complicated for me. I believe you should love who makes you happy. Now… speaking about making me happy…"

Chapter 36

IN AUGUST 2014, Guy Finelli's trek home to Maryland f r o m New Mexico started with

a fifteen-hour marathon of driving twelve hundred miles from Santa Fe to Nashville. He had not planned it that way, but he rolled out of bed before three in the morning and hit Interstate 40 for the great plains of Texas. The sun had been beating down for an hour or so when he first stopped for gas, just east of Amarillo, Texas. He picked up some coffee but no food as he resumed his march into the central lowlands of Oklahoma City.

The heat of the pavement challenged the coolness of his vehicle as he traveled down the interstate. As noon arrived, he passed Fort Smith, Arkansas, and the beginning of the interior highlands that headed into the Ozarks. His appetite seemed to rise with the altitude, and he finally stopped in the town of Clarksville, Arkansas, off US 64 for lunch at the Catfish House on West Main. The lunch buffet of fresh fish, chicken, gumbo soup, and his mom's favorite, hush puppies, was starting to attract a crowd. Guy drew little attention as he sat in a corner, ordered an ice tea, and helped himself to fill a large plate.

Not realizing his depth of hunger, he finished the hush puppies and chicken in record time. He sat back for a moment to enjoy his ice tea while noticing a toddler stuffing his mouth with the delicious hush puppies. The deep-fried balls of artery-clogging material filled his mouth as his mother and her friend were deep in conversation, enjoying the few minutes of quiet from her four-year-old motion machine. Guy could see trouble brewing as the young boy held his head up, trying to catch a breath while clearly choking. Guy sprang up, ran across the room, grabbed the boy in his left arm, hung him head down, and swatted his back with his right hand. In moments, the balls of cornmeal exploded onto the floor. Guy flipped up the boy to face him and cleaned off his face with a napkin, still in his right hand.

After messing up his hair and telling him, "Don't forget to chew," he had the boy back in his seat within fifteen seconds. The mother pounced on her boy as Guy threw twenty bucks on the table and headed out the door. The women yelled out "Thank you" as Guy looked back with a wave and a smile.

The rest of the day's travel was literally downhill and matched the settling of Guy's feelings from such a rush of excitement in Clarksville. The Ozarks in the distance seemed like a beautiful place to visit sometime as he followed the drainage of the highlands through Little Rock and, finally, the Mississippi River. He stopped for gas in Memphis after the river crossing and felt a tinge of being home in the East, but he still wanted to drive through until the end of daylight. Finally, he entered the Music City of Nashville and found the tallest hotel in the downtown skyline, the thirty-one-story Renaissance Hotel.

By ten at night, Guy was feeling refreshed after room service and a power nap. He left the hotel on Commerce Street for a block and headed down the steep hill on Fifth Avenue to Broadway, passing Ryman Auditorium on his left, the home of the original Grand Ole Opry.

Once on Broadway, he faced four blocks of music with a surprising multitude of voices and instruments that spilled onto the wide avenue. He walked down Broadway toward the Cumberland River, imagining himself on some Sunday afternoon, playing in the stadium across the river against Tennessee.

He decided to enter the Whiskey Bent Saloon and sit at the bar to order some shots of Jack Daniels, kept alive in Tennessee by those "whiskey runners" during Prohibition. The fact that he was just nineteen was never really questioned because of his size and a month of beard growth.

The crowd was growing restless with the solo singer/ guitarist playing a current country/rock crossover hit by Keith Urban. Most of the crowd was looking for some traditional country singing, and they were shouting their disinterest. Things escalated quickly, causing the first glass mug of beer to come flying across the tiny corner stage. The singer stayed down low and finished the verse but then moved quickly across the wall to get cover behind the bar and find the back exit. Several more beers hit the wall behind him as he yelled out "Motherfucking, drunk rednecks" toward the crowd.

The singer, Bobby Gentry, felt enthused about standing up for himself, but he realized quickly that it was a clear mistake as another trio of drunks, fitting the redneck description, stood up and fired three beer bottles from the table toward the escaping singer.

Guy was finishing his third shot when he saw the young singer scream his final curses to the crowd and then duck his head while heading behind the bar for shelter and exit. Guy turned left and saw the trio launch slightly empty Bud bottles end over end toward the mirror in the back of the bar. He jumped off his stool with both feet and started a dive toward the bar. As he reached parallel, two of the bottles were knocked away with his left arm, but the third was gaining altitude. He spun in mid-leap, reached up with his right hand over his head, and caught the third bottle. Landing on the bar, he slid on his back and quickly jumped into the bar area, handing the empty Bud bottle to a wide-eyed bartender, who cried out, "What the fuck... are you kidding me...who are you?"

Guy shook his hand and said, "Sorry for all the trouble; I'm getting out of here."

"Hey, no problem, just head out the back door where Bobby went, and thanks, man, for saving my bar."

Guy followed the singer out the back of the bar and met him in the alley. They quickly exchanged greetings and decided to get something to eat. They hurried a couple blocks to a quiet Japanese restaurant on Second Avenue. Guy bought a bunch of sashimi and teriyaki, along with some Japanese beers. The singer was only nineteen, like Guy, and was down to his last couple of dollars. They talked until midnight, and then Guy took him to a Best Western near the capitol building and booked him a room for a couple of days.

Guy loved his voice and could see talent in his eyes. He handed him a wad of hundreds that he had left from his trip and gave him some advice.

"Don't give up, Bobby. Write a song about tonight; call it 'Three Buds in a Bar' or something. Then drive out to LA and write a bunch more on the way about all the people you see. Get in touch with Jeff Lynne and beg him to produce an album for you."

"Now, that sounds like a plan. Is he the ELO guy that played with the Wilburys?"

"Yeah, he's my dad's favorite, along with Roy Orbison and the Beatles."

"I can dig that...sorry about your girlfriend, but I think you're doing the right thing."

"Thanks, Bobby."

"Hey... I'll be following you when you get to the pros. I'll look you up if I get to DC."

"You'll owe me some sashimi, dude."

"Man, I love that stuff, yeah...next time on me. But really, the money...man, I expect to pay you back. It feels like you're like an angel for me. Shit...like a guardian angel. Listen...do you mind if I write a song about you and Anna? 'My Angel Anna' or something like that, I'll make you proud of your investment."

"I'll be looking forward to hearing it on the radio."

"By the time you make All-Pro safety." "You got a deal."

Guy towered over Bobby as they hugged and exchanged phone numbers to stay in touch.

"Oh, by the way...nice catch on the Bud bottle." "Thanks...but I thought the two I knocked away saved your ass."

Guy enjoyed the smell of the fresh sheets of the hotel bed and the softness of the

225

pillows in the first room he had splurged on during the trip. He quickly fell into a deep sleep until seven in the morning. After a slow wake- up, he went downstairs for a morning workout and then showered to hit the road.

He headed out a few miles toward the Vanderbilt campus and got some breakfast at the Pancake Pantry on a recommendation from his buddy, Mr. Gentry. As he waited for a table, he saw a brochure for the Cheekwood Mansion about six miles away. He had heard about the estate from his parent's recent trip to Nashville in May.

As he headed out on US 70, he noticed a couple of nice golf courses in the well-established Belle Meade community, surrounding the fifty acres of the Cheekwood Mansion. Unlike plantation mansions built mainly in the nineteenth centuries by slave owners, Cheekwood was built in the early 1930s by Leslie Cheek. He sold his family's grocery stores to General Mills for $40 million and then made additional fortunes investing in his cousin's fledgling Maxwell House Coffee company and IBM.

Guy realized as he entered the grounds of the mansion that before his New Mexico experience, he would not have appreciated the beauty of the estate, including the grounds, gardens, waterfalls, and residence. After touring most of the grounds, he found a spot overlooking a series of ponds that collected water flowing downhill from the residence. The sound and visual flow of the water had a trancelike elegance. It helped him zone into finishing the last few chapters of the book *Zen and The Art of Motorcycle Maintenance*. The story follows a father trying to emotionally connect with his son and his lost years of memories as they ride on a motorcycle journey through Montana and other states to the West Coast. Guy had to reread the first fifty pages three times before he understood the philosophy of the story. Now, as he was finishing, he did not want the journey to end.

The quiet of the morning surrounded him, with the sun warming his shirtless back to a toasty level. Reading his book in isolation, he wondered whether he would take a trip like this with his father and brother, or if this would be his last chance of being unnoticed if he achieved the fame that he wanted. A light morning breeze came through the Japanese garden just to his left as he lay on his shirt at the edge of the lower pond of the Robinson Family Water Garden, distracting him enough to look up at the view of the mansion on the hill several hundred yards in the distance.

He noticed two mothers with four daughters working their way down a path from the mansion, following the busy water heading to the ponds. He could hear laughter and giggles from two of the young children, hand-in-hand with their mothers, as they spoke out directions of safety.

There was a playful calm in the air as Guy returned to the last pages of his book. His volume of reading over the past six weeks had superseded the total in his lifetime. Somehow, he was able to digest almost a dozen books that he had taken for the trip.

The serenity of the environment created a stoppage in time that allowed each moment to seem like an eon. Guy hardly noticed the sun increasing the crispness of heat on his back, the grass grazing his toes to a slight tickle, or the wind lightly throwing a strand or two of his hair in his face. His consciousness at times felt separated from his physical being. He was learning to attain a sense of self above his physicality that made him feel alive. He was beginning to separate himself from the tragedy. He could feel a door of time opening, yet slowly, to help him discover his mission in life and fulfill the greatness for his love as "The Safety."

Feeling a great emotion open in his heart as he finished the last page of the book, he knew his task in life would be greater than just playing a game. His position as "The Safety" would be in real life as well, and not just in front of a big audience. He would sometimes have to play a role that was not planned, but it was always in the moment. The key, he thought, was to pay attention to the world around him and not just pass it by in a fast car or wearing a helmet.

As he completed that thought, Guy closed the book and shut his eyes. Quietly, his thoughts came to rest as he gently laid his head down on the grass. The smell in the air was sweet summer before the heat of the sun would sour the day. He felt at peace with his long journey toward healing. It was time to go home and be an adult. The numbness of the murder was something he now understood not just as a football fan but as a friend and lover. As a father, it would be a new journey to understand and follow a path for success. Having a great family gave him confidence that he would never get lost again.

The peaceful quiet as Guy was deep in thought was broken up with a soft splash. Instinctively, he knew it was bigger than a rock and smaller than an adult. The moment of silence afterward was enough to connect him with his physical being, and it was followed by a solitary scream of help rippling above the ponds, and then another voice, and now a joint panic of yelling.

Guy sat up and saw that no one was in the area except two mothers with their babies. One was in misery, stuck with a fallen ankle in a parade of rocks. The second mother was grabbing the two infants and corralling her other children as she pointed to the pond, screaming endlessly in a loop of language that sounded like gibberish, "She's in the water!"

The mother stopped her screaming and attended to her friend held by the rocks. She suddenly felt peace as she knew that the shirtless, shoeless, giant male leaping up from the ground and hurtling toward the pond below her was an angel sent by God. He had been hiding in the grass, ready to protect God's children, she thought.

Guy ran like a jackrabbit, passing the first two ponds in under ten seconds before soaring into a perfect dive into the third pond. The screams had stopped and were replaced with quiet sobbing as he entered the quietness of a familiar substance. He felt the instant refreshment of the morning water, like it was a swim meet on a Saturday morning, as he powered through the water with a ferocious leg kick and breast stroke.

He could see some little feet kicking without lift, near the bottom of the pond. In two strokes, Guy glided in that direction without creating a ripple, grabbed those young legs, and rose to the surface with one leg kick.

The four-year-old girl was not breathing as he laid her on the grass. Confidently, he quickly gave her CPR and had her coughing up water and breathing within thirty seconds.

Refreshed from the cold of the water, Guy looked up at the trapped mother and ran to her. He picked up a hundred-pound rock to release her from her peril and tossed it away like a pebble stuck between his toes. He lifted up the injured mother, who could only stare at God's angel through the tears covering her eyes. Guy carried her down to the saved daughter, where the two mothers and three of their children crowded around the coughing daughter as she sat up crying.

Two security men pulled up in a car in the distance up the hill. They called in for an ambulance before they left the car. Guy slipped away from the two families hovering over the coughing girl and headed in the opposite direction to recover his shirt, shoes, and book. He walked into the quiet shade of the Japanese garden and found a bench. He smiled as he dried his face, put on his shoes and shirt, and then wandered through the garden, knowing that reality was just around the comer. He looked down the hill from behind the security car as he made it to his car and saw happiness flowing beside the ponds. He was 660 miles from completing his journey, but he had already found a home, now a protector of lives as "The Safety."

Chapter 37

F OR THE DEFENDING two-time world-champion Washington Potomacs, training camp

in Richmond in July 2019 was a steamy summer start to a stormy season. Everything the team and players had worked to avoid during t h e i r t h r e e -year c l i m b t o g r e a t n e s s , l i k e distractions and selfishness, would take root in the sleepy Capital of the South in the Civil war and grow like weeds during the season. It had been a century and a half since the last northern siege on the city, in this case by over one hundred thousand fans that camped out during the weeks of training camp. Every practice was open to the public, with festivals, concerts, and car races before and after, in and around the city to keep the crowds entertained.

Owner Burton Parker gazed at those crowds of youthful fans wearing hundreds of dollars' worth of Potomacs jerseys and hats, and he smiled at his future net worth. The signing of Guy Finelli to the largest contract in sports history had sent a magnet through the country that doubled the Potomac Nation. Tickets to every sold-out home or away game could be sold for at least triple the face value on any secondary market. The excitement of the first Mars Mission Championship Contest (M2C2-1) to o p e n the new World Space Stadium on February 2, 2020, had some tickets going for ten grand, based on the assumption that the Potomacs would be defending their two-time championship and playing in DC for a historic third crown 1 n a row.

Th   e bumper stickers on thousands of cars read:

MACS TRIFECTA M2C2-
1@WSS 0202-2020

The Potomac players were celebrities everywhere they went in and around Richmond for the four weeks of training camp. Guy Finelli was the rock star of the team, but he had little interest in playing that role with the fans. The media avoided criticizing the league MVP, and the fans rarely complained about having little interaction with their hero, who in their minds was a part of football royalty. It was an aura of invincibility he had achieved with two league championships and rumors of intrigue in his life.

Never giving interviews since his prediction of three championships in a row, he projected the stylish confidence of Joe Namath and the mystery of Greta Garbo. Every once in a while, he would stop and sign a single autograph. It would always be a woman that looked in her mid-twenties, and most looked to be natural redheads. A rumor had spread about this anomaly in the back, back chat rooms of social media, which the press had never reported. Only die-hard fans knew about the anomaly and sought out redheads in the crowds outside the player exits. In July 2019, the city of Richmond seemed to have more and more redheads springing up as Macs fans sought for a close look at "The Safety."

After two early, embarrassing losses in the exhibition season, Coach Brown was discussing the distractions of training camp with his trusted defensive coordinator, Fury Favarro, and special teams coach, Joe Finelli. Personally, the head coach was confident that the leaders on the team would focus once the season started. The three of them had traveled north on a Sunday morning to find some quiet and privacy to talk on his boat cruising across Lake Anna.

Dipping some fishing lines in the water, Coach Brown was the first to break from the pleasantries of talking about their families and discuss business. "Boys... any ideas to get these guys refocused at Monday's practice?"

"Yeah, let's bring them out here on the boat and dump them over to see who can swim back to the shore," Joe commented with a deadly serious look. He'd had to watch four fumbles by his return teams and shoddy tackling on punt returns in the first two games.

"I agree; we may have to rent an eight-ton barge to get rid of about five dozen of those worthless pieces of shit that are parading around like ballplayers in Macs uniforms!" The normally even-keeled Coach Favarro was fuming with frustration at Coach Brown.

Gerry Brown had never exploded on his team in the three previous years of coaching the Macs. He frowned on his assistant coaches ever yelling disparaging comments at his players. He believed in positive reinforcement while teaching about football-playing mistakes, especially if it was going to be in a loud tone.

This was a slight change from his college coaching years, when he was known to have hit the roof at times. He had a graduate degree in sports psychology and did his thesis on "Motivation in Professional Football," which involved researching coaching techniques and argued that constant yelling and degrading statements to players had a long-lasting negative effect on their performance, much as torture did on terrorist suspects.

Coach Brown calmly answered his defensive coordinator. "Well...we may need to intensify the practices this week. These guys are having too much fun in Richmond with all this attention to listen to us yelling at them.[11] He cast his fishing line in the lake with a smooth throw. "But if we add some drills and increase their repetitions while we smile at them and shout out pleasantries"-pausing for effect as he intensified his focus on the beauty of water and his fishing line with a recast-"there we go...I think somehow that we'll get their attention rather than flogging them." He felt a twitch on the fishing line as he finished his last word. Standing with a wide stance like a linebacker readying for a running back, he pulled out a good-sized rockfish with precision and focus. "I'm glad somebody was listening out here." He delicately removed his hook and softly lowered his catch back into the water while praising the healthy-looking fish. "You put up a nice fight, fella...next time you may want to notice that metallic look on the hook and run a different pattern!"

The third game of the exhibition season was the only home game at FedEx Field before the season started. The last home exhibition game was sold for $10 million and would be played in Montreal Olympic Stadium against the expansion Montreal Metros.

Joe and Fury knew that the last exhibition game would be a media circus and played almost exclusively with backup players. This game would be their only chance to right things on defense and special teams. During practice, they followed Coach Brown's directions and wondered if the team would respond.

Guy Finelli had played two dozen plays in the first two games, made two tackles, and never touched the football. The first teams, on both sides of the line of scrimmage, were scheduled to play the entire first half. A thunderstorm had come through the area in the afternoon, bringing a front that dropped the temperature a pleasant twenty degrees. For the Macs, who had trained in the heat and humidity of Richmond for four weeks, it felt like November football weather.

The Baltimore Banners would be the opponent this year, visiting FedEx for their annual exhibition game. After twenty-three seasons, the rivalry between the two teams had clearly been established. The announcers for the national television audience were touting the game as a preview of the M2C2-l.

Guy felt the excitement of the crowd as he stood on the field. The kickoff team surrounded him, full of regulars getting together for a reunion. Tackle Albert Christian, who had become the first deaf player ever to start a game for the Macs, spoke. His voice was articulate and strong, even though he rarely used it. "We do not need to make a big deal about this." This shy giant of a man looked up at every one of his teammates' eyes. "But...let us take this right up the middle of the field. Straight blocking... everyone should be *pan-caked!* Do not bother blocking someone unless you can *land* on *top* of *them!*" The players joined hands and quietly departed.

The football came floating down the middle of the field, with the perfect, blue sky behind it. Guy was looking forward to getting smacked. He knew that the middle return with straight blocking was not for success but to make a statement about the use of blunt force. He secured the ball five yards deep in the end zone and proceeded to race a forty-yard dash with his head down and his arms pumping in a sprint. The quiet of the crowd had given way to the sounds of crashing in front of him, like cars in an intersection accident piling up around of him. He crossed the twenty at full acceleration and reached the thirty untouched. Guy was about finished with his sprint and wanted to end his fun by finding a victim to go down with him. To his left at the thirty-five was a linebacker type about his size, trying to make the team as a 245-pound, stand-up rusher converted from a defensive end. He was learning his professional chops on special teams, now in his third game, as he planted to stop this monster of a runner coming at him. All he could do was close his eyes as he established perfect technique with his shoulders, neck, and helmet. The initial contact seemed to go well as he started to wrap his arms around Guy's backside. What he did not expect was the thrust of force from Finelli's thighs and knees, which seemed to be injected with high- octane fuel. He held on with the tips of his fingers as he experienced an instantaneous direction change that defied gravity. The air in his body left, along with his mouth guard, creating a calming feeling of suspended animation for a micro-second without oxygen before he landed on his back. In cascading order, body parts hurtled into the manicured grass, creating a divot with his butt, upper back, shoulders, and back of his helmet; then final force of a 242-pound man of steel, moving at twenty-five miles an hour, came to crash-land into his chest. The final collision forced some of the new sod into the linebacker's shoulder pads and helmet.

Guy quickly rolled off after the tackle and flipped the ball to the umpire as he surveyed the war zone and counted seven Banner players lying on their backs, struggling to get up. He adjusted his shoulder pads and righted his facemask as he joined his teammates on the sidelines. Albert Christian came into his face, looking possessed. He did not utter a human sound but signed something to Guy that was clearly some quiet trash talking. He remembered it from his high-school days, watching the Christian brothers communicate. Once he asked Albert what he signed to his brother after he got all pumped in a game. Guy always remembered it because it was so funny: "Game on from the Christian Brothers! Can you hear me now?"

Chapter 38

THE FIRST-TEAM OFFENSE and defense played with the precision and force of a two
ime defending champion, leading the Macs to a 35-0 halftime lead over the rival Banners.
They finished the exhibition season with a lackluster performance in Montreal, just
edging the expansion Metros 33-31, and then started the season with four uninspired
performances and a lucky 4-0 record by the end of September. The offense, led by
Marcus McNeil III, outscored teams with a passing offense not seen in the three previous
years coached by Gerry Brown. The normal ball-control offense with a strong running game
and short passes, complemented with play action for deeper throws, had turned into a
weekly highlight reel of Marcus III running around the field making spectacular plays
and throwing bombs downfield. It also created offensive turnovers and sloppy play, and
it put the defense on the field a lot, causing an overworked defensive line.

A 4-0 September led to a horrific but predictable October with four straight losses.
Suddenly, with half the season gone, the team stood at 4-4, with a nationwide fan base
wondering if they had jumped on a broken-down bandwagon.

The next three weeks would put the Macs on the road, with games in London,
Toronto, and Mexico City. The international tour was set up by the GAF as a quirk in the
schedule to highlight the defending champions touring the new international franchises.
Most teams would hate playing on the road, much less foreign travel, but the Macs needed a
new challenge to shake them up. Each game was like a mini World Cup final. They arrived
Wednesday night in each city and practiced in front of large crowds. A parade was held
every Saturday morning, followed by meeting the local heads of state.

Most sports pundits had predicted that Washington, with all of the distractions,
would be in danger of losing one or two games and ruining their chances for the playoffs.

With the limited but public practice time for each game, Coach Brown decided to
simplify the offense and reinstall the Sprint DMC offense after the first punt return of
each game. Mac III was not pleased initially but trusted Coach Brown's instincts.
"Coach, it's not the offense causing all the trouble. Man, our D-line can't hold a cup of
coffee. We've been scoring enough points."

"I hear you, Marcus, but the defense needs to get off the field. They can't play thirty-
five minutes a game or defend turnovers inside their own twenty. You got to help them,
Marcus."

"I feel you, Coach. I do, and I love those guys on D like brothers...but I got a contract next year, and Mr. Parker thinks I don't do nothing special on offense. He loves Finelli. That's his boy."

"No way, Marcus...you've been here eight seasons, and it was you that brought excitement back to DC. You started the Mac Attack! Without you, our offense is nothing. They would play eight in the box all the time, but with you as a weapon, we can play like the old-time Packers and beat teams up. Then when think they got us surrounded... boom! You explode."

Mac III fought back tears. Hearing Coach Brown talking about him was like taking oxygen after a big hit. He could not get enough of that special feeling flowing through his body. It gave him tingles from head to toe. He sat up and tried to compose himself. "I hear you, Coach. I see it. We're all champions-just like Coach Lombardi told you, right?"

"That's right, Marcus, just like Coach Lombardi."

Coach Brown sat back for a moment, recalling his stellar athletic career at UMD as an All-American in two sports, followed by two years of professional baseball and then being drafted by his hero, Coach Lombardi.

After one conversation with Lombardi, he had signed with the Packers and made the team as a backup linebacker in 1964. Lombardi switched him to strong safety before the 1965 season, and he went on to start on two Super Bowl championship teams. He played one final year with Washington in 1969 when Lombardi came to coach and then retired as a player and got into coaching after Lombardi died in 1970.

He thought about him every day, knowing that as a player he would eat dirt for him, but as a coach he wanted his style of coaching to be different. He realized that Lombardi's effectiveness was his intimacy with each and every player, not his yelling and screaming. In private, Lombardi treated Brown like a son and got the most out of him athletically.

"You're right, Coach; I've been trying to do everything myself. But something has been missing. You know...that special feeling about knowing you're the best. We've been chasing it instead of trusting it to come back."

"There it is, Marcus...that's why you're the leader of this team. Let's trust it and be the best."

"Thanks, Coach... and I appreciate those kind words, but...you know and I know and the American people know who the leader of this team really is."

Coach Brown laughed, grabbed the back of his QB's head, and hugged him.

"I mean...I'm cool with it. He deserves everything he got and more, as far as I'm concerned. He is a big monster out there, and he's just as fast as me! I thank God he's on my team so I don't have to play against him."

"That's a good point, Marcus."

"Thanks, Coach... one more thing-make sure you keep putting in a good word with Mr. Parker about my next contract."

"Mac, I have a feeling, somehow...that will work itself out."

• • •

Aztec Stadium in Mexico was rocking, with a record 130,000 fans creating waves of songs and drums that pounded the field like sonic booms. It was the first Monday-night football-game kickoff on foreign soil.

Washington had played like a new smash musical in London and Toronto, blowing the doors off the world stage. The combined score of 73-0 won over fans in both countries, while the local media wanted to portray the defending champions as domestic terrorists taking their teams hostage.

Marcus McNeil III led a balanced offense that took control of each game in the first half with three long touchdown drives. In the two games, Guy Finelli had a record eight interceptions. Four he returned for TDs, and the other four led to great field position. His interception total for ten games so far in the 2019 season was eleven, three short of the record of fourteen in twelve games.

Surprisingly, the Mexico City Marauders were putting up quite a battle as they led at halftime 7-3. They were the only expansion team to build their team around the running game and solid defense. Being a soccer country, the fans were happy with low-scoring games and offenses that moved methodically down the field.

Mexico City took the second-half kickoff and moved successfully into Washington territory. The drive had consumed over nine minutes off the clock in the third quarter as they faced a third down and goal inside the five- yard line. They lined up in a two-tight-end set with only one wide out.

Guy read pass all the way as the QB turned to fake a handoff to the tail back. The fullback had dived into the line to fake a block and was now pulling himself through the line like a prisoner of war seeking an open field after surviving the tunnel. The QB rolled right after the fake and then threw back across the field to his left to the wide- open fullback inches from the goal line.

What happened next could only be reported by the hometown announcer on the radio broadcast. The pass sailed in the air, suspending time for the fans. The veteran announcer was on his feet, ready to make his TD call.

"El finge el traspaso y rollos derecha. Pasa de nuevo a la izquierda y el gran fullback es pulgadas de ancho abierto de la linea de gol... atrapa el balón y se vuelve a marcar, pero esperar es como una ley! Ahora el se levantó con las piernas corriendo en el aire y ahora cae hacia atras. ¿Quien puede ser este defensor? Oh si... por supuesto...es veintiuno...se trata de 'la Seguridad'! Si, el gran Finnnnnnnnnneeeeeeeeeeeellllllllllllli!"

On *SportsCenter* the next evening, the local broadcast was found and played with English subtitles, almost unnecessary because the translation became obvious:

"He fakes the handoff and rolls right. Passes back to the left, and the great fullback is inches wide of the open goal line...he catches the football and turns to score, but wait, he is like a statue! Now he is lifted up with his legs running in the air and now falls backward. Who can be this defender? Oh yes...of course...it is twenty-one...it is "The Safety!" Yes, the great *Finnnnnnnnnneeeeeeeeeeeellllllllllllli!"*

Mexico City went for the field goal on fourth down to make it 10-3, but the momentum had returned to Washington. The Macs responded with a nine-minute drive of their own to tie the score with less than eleven minutes to go in the game.

The Marauders once again controlled the clock for most of the last quarter but decided to open up their offense after entering Washington territory with less than four minutes to go. But they continued to run the ball, even with three wide receivers. Guy Pinelli had made six tackles in a row when he called a time-out and went to the sidelines. "I'm not playing the run anymore," he announced to Coach Favarro and his cousin Joe. "It's time for me to play centerfield and get our front seven to stop them from running."

The coaches looked at each other, a little stunned, but agreed with their superstar player. "We're with you, Guy... just make a fuckin' play soon so we can get back home. No overtime...got it? My back is killing me sleeping on these hotel mattresses for three weeks." Joe broke into a big smile as he pushed Guy toward the field.

After the huddle, Guy settled into his spot on the field, twenty yards from the line of scrimmage. He grabbed his facemask and felt his mouth guard against his teeth. He noticed number eighty-four in motion from right to left. It was the FCU star that he had played against in a practice game in high school with Hank Harrison. He was hanging on as the Marauder's third receiver but still had great speed. The ball was snapped, and the receiver ran up the slot straight at him to make contact. Guy slipped by him as the runner was tripped up in the backfield.

On second down, Guy played farther back as he felt the sweat of his shoulder pads for the first time. He adjusted his supposedly moisture-free undershirt as he watched eighty-four miss a block on Mark Pelligrini, who made the tackle for another loss. It was third and sixteen at midfield at the two-minute warning.

The coaches were calling Guy to the sidelines. He ignored them as he sat on one knee, looking at the massive crowd in the stadium. Their energy was contagious as they continued their song and drumming all night. Now they were exchanging "Mexico" and "City" shouts across the stadium. Guy closed his eyes for a moment to take it all in. It felt like the peaceful eye of a hurricane before the storm resumed.

The official blew the whistle as Guy found his spot on the thirty-yard line. He knew the play would be a turn- in around the thirty-five, either for the first down or field goal range. Eighty-four went in motion in the same direction and headed up the slot again. Guy watched the catch at the thirty-five as he decided to keep his spot, five yards deeper. He enjoyed watching Pelligrini again make the tackle.

It was fourth and inches as the clock ran down. They came out with two tight ends and eighty-four in motion. Guy felt refreshed and confident as he knew that the post- flag pattern was coming. It was the only play that made sense to him. He had waited four plays for this move and mapped out where he would catch the football.

As they broke the huddle, he whispered to Pelligrini, "Make sure the boys block inside on the pick." Mark acted like he did not hear him but felt relieved that Guy had figured out something to stop these guys.

Guy stood on the twenty-yard line as eighty-four went in motion again and cut up the slot. Bodies at the scrimmage line made contact in every direction, but noise from the collisions was drowned out by the crowd noise that hovered over every wavelength.

Guy stood his ground in the middle of the field. The receiver thought he had him beat as Guy seemed stuck. Predictably, eighty-four got careless and cut off the extra step on the post part of the pattern, because he was too excited about being wide open in the corner.

The QB settled in the pocket after the fake handoff and threw to the perfect spot toward the front corner of the end zone. Eighty-four was three steps into his flag part of the pattern, with his eyes on the spiral of the ball just reaching its peak in the air.

The Safety had retreated to the goal line on the near hash mark. Finally, he put his head down and bolted the twenty-two yards to catch the ball. He had timed this play a thousand times in practice and in his head. He knew the wind at his back would swirl the pass down enough for him to aim for the five-yard line, and the slight angle gave him a better chance to keep his feet after the interception. Guy slowly lifted his head as he reached his cheetah- like speed. Suddenly, the weight on his shoulders felt like a feather as he watched eighty-four passes in front of him. The receiver thought the ball would carry deeper, leaving the five-yard line to Guy, who snagged the dying pass with two hands.

Pelligrini emerged from the pile of bodies on the scrimmage line and started to yell out assignments for blocks without penalties. Guy hit the ground inside the ten-yard line. He hurdled a lineman near the twenty, sidestepped a linebacker around the thirty, stiff-armed a cornerback as he passed the forty, and blew past the quarterback at midfield.

Eighty-four had landed on the goal line and saw the interception in front of him. He was determined to run a "Bob Hayes" one-hundred-yard dash to catch Finelli. After an eighty-yard sprint, he got within a dive at the twenty and caught him at the ten. His 170-pound frame seemed like a mouse on a greyhound as he tried to hang on, but he fell off as Guy crossed the goal line.

On the radio, there was no need for translation of the winning TD.

"Finelli esta en los cuarenta, el treinta, el veinte, los diez, los cinco, es un scooooooooooooooooooooore!"

239

Chapter 39

THE TEAM'S RETURN flight home was split between a low-key get-together in the front of the plane that lingered with tired energy the entire flight, and those asleep in the back or the "slightly awake" in the middle. The slightly awakes joined the low-keys for an hour or two in between unsuccessful bouts of sleep, as though they were keeping watch for any reportable action. The get-together was being hosted by the unique pairing of Guy Finelli and Marcus McNeil III.

Even though they were recognized worldwide as the leaders of the two-time defending champions, in truth they never spent time with each other as friends. Their only time together was before or during a game, discussing strategy, mainly with Mac III seeking Guy to give him a read on the opposition defense. Mac III knew that Guy was a genius at seeing plays on offense before they happened. And after Guy played QB in the sprint offense for a handful of plays early in the game, he would suggest a half a dozen plays to Mac III that would work later in the game.

Coach Brown knew that at times, Mac III listened to Guy more than the offensive coaches on play calling. As long as they won, he put up with the grief from his coaching staff and stood up for his players.

Guy loved Mac III's pure energy, especially before the game. It was rare, but at times Guy had trouble getting "pumped up" for games unless he really cared about beating the opponent. Most of his teammates' chest thumping before and during the games meant nothing to him, but when Mac III showed leadership, it always pumped him up. Deep down inside, Guy Finelli wanted to be as cool as Mac III.

He may have been influenced by the fact that his father, Phillip, had loved Marcus McNeil III since watching him in college. The house oozed with the same excitement on draft day in 2012 as it did when Sean Taylor was drafted in 2004.

"That was some kind of a play today to win the game. You set the bitch up, didn't you?"

"I got tired of making tackles, so I took some plays off. I was trying to regain my breath, to tell you the truth."

"Oh man, why you try to play it like that? You know you set the bitch up. You knew that pattern was coming, and you knew you were going to intercept it! Hey, even your paisano told me after the play that you set up the blocking before the fucking play."

Guy was laughing as he listened to the Baptist-bred QB, who was drinking, cussing, and sitting next to him like a brother.

"You know that crap ain't human. Hell, that's supposed to be my job to be all superhuman and shit. You're the coolest, low-keyed, best fucking football player on the fucking planet." Mac III gulped down his fifth drink of Jack Daniels, his only vice, which he usually did in private. "Man... that feels good to get that off my chest.

How come we don't talk like this more often? We should be brothers. I don't have a brother, you know."

"All sisters, huh? Yeah, I grew up with one. I guess I was pretty lucky."

"Lucky... are you kidding me? Your family is the best. I mean, your brother is Alex Santucci! That must be way too cool. And his wife, Sally, she is way hot for a dark-haired white girl! Man, I'm speechless, bro."

Guy finished his drink and whispered to the attendants for two refills.

"She is something, that's for sure. She's probably one of my best friends. I'm pretty lucky, Mac, but we all have our problems." Guy hesitated as he sipped on his new drink of whiskey. "You know...things in the past try to catch up to us...and decisions to make about the future."

Mac III waited to hear the end of the silence. His whiskey buzz had opened up feelings, and he felt like he was listening to Guy for the first time. He turned and looked into his dark eyes and saw an opening for friendship. "I'm with you, Guy. I understand that every book has many chapters. Some are hard to read, but they're all important. Amen to that, brother."

They exchanged soul handshakes and man hugs. Mac III sat back in his chair and took a gulp from his new drink. He leaned into Guy and whispered, "I hear you have a little daughter. How old is she?"

"Annie, yeah, she just turned five and lives with Sally and the twins. She's as fiery as her red hair."

"Five years old and red hair? Hell, you just turned twenty-five...right? Wow, that must be a shit storm of a story."

"That would be an understatement. Maybe after the season, I can tell you the whole story, but for now we got a championship to win."

"No problem, bro...I'm good at zipping it up and throwing away the key like the fat

241

guy in *Uncle Buck* telling a secret to the *Home Alone* kid. God, I love that fucking movie. That last scene always makes me cry. You know, having sisters and shit."

"Oh yeah, bro... maybe the fucking funniest...oh hell, the best movie ever made! I love John Candy... God rest his soul." They clinked glasses to toast the dead and gulped their drinks.

Mac III held up his drink for one last toast. "No more losing this season, and you're going to tell me that story after the season!"

"You got a deal, bro!" The sound of glasses clinking sealed their deal, and a new friendship was started, as the dawn of a new day ended a night of celebration.

Little sleep was achieved by any member of the organization on that flight. To finish the three-week international road trip with three victories was a welcome change after the month of October full of losses. With a bye week scheduled before their next game, they could enjoy the Thanksgiving holiday without thinking about football. At 7-4, they had jumped back into the division lead.

Chapter 40

PHILLIP WAS TOSSING the football with his three grandchildren in the spacious backyard at the Santucci mansion during halftime of the eleven o'clock game from London, England. The London Monarchs were hosting their first Thanksgiving Day game (even though it was not their holiday) in history against an expansion team, the Montreal Metros.

With England able to stage a game in the morning because they were five hours ahead of Eastern Standard Time, the GAF was excited to broadcast four games on Thanksgiving Day for the first time.

Annie, at five and a half, was running circles around her cousins, Phillip and Philly, both a year older, to get open and catch the ball from her grandfather. All three grandchildren had been catching balls since they were infants and were exceptional at it. Listening to Grandpop about running pass patterns was another story.

Inside, Alex and Guy had taken over the kitchen to run Thanksgiving dinner, sipping on their first cocktail of the day. Their plan was to have a drink for every half of football they had to watch. Sally was stirring up the second round of cocktails.

"So, Patty, what did you do with yourself for three weeks not seeing Guy?" Charlotte inquired.

"Oh, the usual, a little prostituting, some drinking, and lots of drugs!" The room exploded with laughter as Patty continued, "Really, though...the time away was good for Guy; I guess he started missing me in London, so he bought me something." Patty revealed an eighteen-carat, white-gold, marquis-cut diamond engagement ring on her left hand.

"Did his knees feel good enough to get on and ask you the right way?" Carol asked, hoping to stir up some trouble.

"It took him a couple days to rest up...but then he took care of business Wednesday night...if you know what I mean."

"Patty, I couldn't be happier for you." Charlotte then showered her friend Patty with an emotional hug, followed by Sally, Grace, and Carol. Sally picked up the pitcher of the next round of vodka martinis. "Well, now we really have something to drink to!"

That weekend after Thanksgiving, Guy and Patty celebrated their engagement with a private dinner at his condo in Bethesda. Guy brought in a chef to serve steamed clams for an appetizer and veal chop with linguini for an entree. A nice Italian Chianti helped washed down the clams while a Pinot Noir savored the veal chop. After serving the dessert, the chef quickly slipped out, as instructed, leaving the newly engaged couple to enjoy the creamy tiramisu alone. With their appetites full and their emotions enhanced by the wine, they made love quickly on the dining table.

They showered together, got into robes and watched sports highlights for an hour before retreating to their bed for a slower round of love making until midnight.

Patty slept for several hours before waking at 3am and walking out on the balcony looking south into DC. The cold air felt fresh on her face and body that was unusually hot. She had been off the pill since Guy's birthday in early October and tonight had been the night of her dreams. She wanted a little boy and his journey had just started after dessert.

■ ■ ■

Brooklyn O'Malley pushed away from the dinner table as the third game of football was just starting. His family was used to him bolting into his home office after dinner, even on holidays.

He felt like he was closing in on the Turk's empire after almost a decade of pursuit. The problem was that he wanted to convict him for the murder of an FBI agent as well. It had been five and a half years since Anna's murder, and it was not getting any easier for him. Every time he saw Guy's little redheaded daughter, it sent daggers through his soul.

They had landed a great lead on the gun, but connecting the Turk to it was not so easy. The evidence had given them the location of his headquarters in West Baltimore and wiretaps.

Brooks knew that gambling was the Turk's Achilles heel. The MGM Casino just outside of DC that had opened in 2017 was feeding his addiction. The Turk had been identified by the FBI and was seen playing there on a weekly basis during regular surveillance. No more trips to Las Vegas just for legitimate gambling. It made him feel like a real citizen to be able to gamble publicly in his home state. On the inside though, it was feeding his need for a big score on game fixing. It had been several years since he had gone after a big game. Now the M2C2-1 was going to be in his backyard, and it was his for the picking.

With the season almost three-quarters over, the Potomacs were on track to make the playoffs. It was a certainty that the Turk would contact Guy Finelli if they got close to the championship contest. Brooks was positive the Turk had a plan ready to go, and somehow, Guy Finelli would be involved. The M2C2-1 could become more than a football game; it could become a match between good and evil.

•••

The bye week after the Thanksgiving holiday had allowed Guy to join his brother Alex for six days of running and swimming in Bethesda before his return to practice the following Wednesday. The aerobic conditioning had revived his strength and flexibility after eleven straight weeks of playing games. On early Tuesday morning, they headed out from the Glenbrook mansion for the last of their runs together. They turned on Hampden and ran slowly for several blocks across Arlington until Woodmont and then right two blocks to Bethesda Avenue.

Alex suddenly felt a buzzing in his back pocket and answered a call from Sally to head back home to help her avoid a domestic crisis. He told Guy that he would catch up with him on the Crescent Trail on his way back.

Guy man-hugged his older brother and lowered his hoodie-covered head as he entered the tunnel under Wisconsin Avenue to join the Crescent Trail. He powered past a couple of slow-moving, talkative walkers on the trail, otherwise void of humans. He felt like a lion on the prowl, smelling the crispness of the morning air, as he went out for his morning adventure. He accelerated through the tunnel under Air Rights Building as it opened up again paralleling Montgomery Avenue toward the next tunnel under East-West Highway. The east-only Montgomery Avenue contained a mixture of buildings and houses, now used as offices that backed up to the trail, some ten feet above it.

Guy was headed toward the last building on the left, feeling the power to slay the fantasy of an enemy ahead. The eleven-story Riviera Apartment complex, built in a modernism style in the late seventies, hovered like a Godzilla-type monster, with its C-shape design reaching like giant arms over the trail as it seemed to breathed fire to those exercising below. His legs churned powerfully on the asphalt as he entered the shadows of the hovering monster. He heard a scuffle from the back of the building and then a scream as a small adult body headed down from the third floor. Guy instinctively tracked the object at full speed, like a punted football coming his way, and laid his body out in a dive, trying to catch or disrupt the fall of what now appeared to be a small and thin elderly man. Uncharacteristically, Guy mishandled the body and hit the asphalt empty-handed. He rolled to the dirt on the side, trying to regain oxygen in his lungs.

After a short minute, Guy felt someone patting him on the back. At first it felt annoying because he was using all of his energy to regain his breath, but then he realized that the small human trying to escape the monstrous building was alive. He slowly turned over, feeling the welcome oxygen returning to his lungs, and looked up at the small, bearded man hovering over him, speaking some Arabic- type dialect. The man looked happy and full of energy. He bowed over Guy several times, clearly thanking him for saving his life. Apparently, the adventure of jumping off the balcony and surviving without a scratch had given him a reason to live.

Guy got to his feet and guided the man back to his building, where his daughter and wife greeted him with delirious joy. Guy took the moment of reunion to escape and headed back to the trail to finish his run.

He continued east through Columbia Country Club and into Rock Creek Park before heading back home. The more he ran, the less he felt the collision with the little gentleman. The superhuman action gave him a sense of floating on air. His breathing was effortless as he increased his pace into a forty-yard sprint every thirty seconds or so. Finally, after he finished returning through the golf course, he ran into his brother a hundred yards after he came through the tunnel under East-West Highway.

"Hey, there is some kind of commotion on the trail on the other side; maybe we should head back through the neighborhood instead." Alex noticed blood running down Guy arms, legs, and face. "What the hell happened to you? Did you get hit by a train or something?"

Guy looked at his arms and seemed amused to see the blood. Luckily, he thought, there had been nobody on the trail that noticed him.

"Yeah, it was something all right...I tripped and took a nice tumble on the asphalt."

"Wow...you football guys are always hitting the deck."

The conditions for the Sunday game at FedEx Field on December 8, 2019, were just cold enough to make throwing the football a challenge for the team from sunny California, the Los Angeles Rams. After playing twenty- one seasons indoors in St. Louis, the Rams were now playing in a new stadium in Inglewood. The franchise had started in Cleveland in 1937, moved to Los Angeles for the 1946 season, and stayed for fifty years.

Guy's scrapes from his Tuesday run had healed nicely but had led to a lot of ribbing from his teammates during the week of practice. It had also given Guy an excuse to miss practice for two days and focus on game film of the Rams rookie QB, who had led them to a similar 7-4 record and first place in the West Division of the National Conference. Some pundits had projected this as a preview of a playoff game.

Guy knew otherwise after two days of studying the rookie QB. He was more than just predictable; he had been downright lucky in four of their wins. Defenses had dropped eight interceptions by his count in those games. The rookie had dazzled opponents with his running and improvising nature. The offense also ran a nice package of screens and draw plays to a 270-pound fullback, Eli Cummings, who could scamper a quick twenty yards and was known as "the Tank." If a defense was beat up, they tended to miss or avoid tackling him. Guy knew that if they got a ten-point lead, then the rookie would have to throw downfield, and the football would be his to intercept.

Washington secured that ten-point lead just before halftime. The defense had been well prepared to control the rookie QB and tackle the Tank. With the clock under forty seconds, the rookie completed a long pass down the sidelines against Cary Collins, who had tipped the ball into the receiver's hand on the Macs' thirty-yard line.

With no time-outs, Guy knew the rookie would get greedy and run four "Go" patterns before trying a field goal. Guy came up to the line of scrimmage to fake a blitz, then Guy turned at the snap and headed to the intersection of the opposite hash mark and the goal line to defend the slot receiver. The rookie took his eyes off of Guy after the snap and stayed in the pocket, looking left and finding his wide-open slot receiver heading past the twenty-yard line. The football was thrown perfectly for the goal line as the rookie QB held up his left hand, pointing out the coming TD.

The slot receiver took to the air just inside the five-yard line to snag a score before halftime, but Guy was already airborne and politely secured the ball without contact.

The 10-0 halftime score held up until the Macs made another field goal before the start of the fourth quarter. Every player on the defense knew that Guy needed one more interception to tie the unbreakable record of fourteen interceptions in a twelve-game season by Dick "Night Train" Lane in 1955. Guy might care after the game, but he refused to let anybody acknowledge it during the fourth quarter.

Predictably, the defense went to a three-deep coverage to force the Rams to take time off the clock to score. Eli "The Tank" Cummings personally marched the Rams into scoring position by catching two screen passes for thirty yards and ran two draw plays for twenty yards. His blockbuster running style had the Macs defense reeling.

Coach Favarro called the inversion defense with the football on the Macs ten-yard line. The corners and the middle linebacker had deep coverage, with both outside linebackers covering the short outside pass. Both safeties came up to the scrimmage line to cover the rookie QB and the Tank.

Guy could see Eli breathing hard in the backfield as the rookie QB shouted out a fake audible at the line of scrimmage. The Tank was not listening but instead looking down, trying to catch an extra whiff of oxygen before another pass or run to him. Guy guessed the delay running play and stepped up into the hole at the scrimmage line to meet with this side-of-beef running back. But Eli Cummings played the fake handoff beautifully and headed directly into a surprised Finelli, who was back on his heels. The collision felt much like the one earlier in the week on the Crescent Trail with the falling body, but he managed to grab a foot and trip the Tank on his way over him. It caused the massive running back to stumble and finally hit the deck.

The rookie QB floated a pass toward the goal line in the middle of the field, expecting Eli to come into the opening, but instead the Tank was tripping to the ground and could only get a hand on it. The football flipped up in the air toward Mark Pelligrini, who was coming out of the end zone at the goal line. He anticipated the interception, only to be crashed backward by the smallish Rams slot receiver running across the middle of the field. The collision caused the football to spiral backward up into the air again and come down like a spinning top toward every lineman on both teams. The massive scramble on the five-yard line built a mountain of humanity with hands raised skyward. Taped fingers covered by dirt and blood made the cold pigskin uncatchable as it spun off the pile of bodies and tumbled backward toward Guy Finelli. The Safety was on the ground at the line of scrimmage, barely able to turn over to see the rumble. Instinctively, he extended his arms and cradled the crazy pigskin before it hit the ground. The record had been tied!

The last play of the game was discussed for the next few weeks. The rookie QB was asked if he had thrown the football deep down the middle of the field to Guy Finelli so he could break the interception record for twelve games with his fifteenth interception. He politely said, "No."

Pedro Carew with the *Washington Reporter* asked, "Being down by thirteen with no chance of winning, were you concerned about being the QB that might have thrown the record-breaking interception?"

"Well, I was just trying to score...but I guess in hindsight, it was a pretty stupid throw."

Ron Roswell with the *Washington Daily* followed up with the big question: "I guess you're pretty happy that he dropped It... maybe"

• • •

Washington Daily

Finelli Ties Int. Record - Drops Record Breaker

By Ron Roswell

Guy Finelli is the best player in professional football. As good as he is in football, he is a better curator and historian of the game than anybody in his generation. Finelli was well aware that the tipped football landing in his hands with less than five minutes left in the fourth quarter after he was bulldozed by Eli "The Tank" Cummings was a gift interception from the football gods. That it iced the game at the time was more important to him than the fact that it tied the sixty-five-year- old interception record by the great Dick "Night Train" Lane.

Finelli, like his fallen football hero, the great safety Sean Taylor, only cares about winning football games. So, assuming he mishandled the football on the last play of the game would be a mistake. What was important to Finelli at the time was ending the game. He knew that if he allowed the football to drop, no more running or tackling would be necessary.

It is true that Sean Taylor would have caught it, because he enjoyed running into people whenever possible. But Guy Finelli, now in his fifth season, has a different style of play. But what he shares with Taylor is that breaking the record on that play did not enter into the equation at that moment.

If you understand that, then maybe you can comprehend how great a football player Sean Taylor was then and Guy Finelli is now. All of Washington, DC, and the world should be watching for that, instead of worrying about breaking records.

Chapter 41

GUY LAUGHED AS he read the front-page article by Roswell about the reason that he dropped the ball in Sunday's game. He loved to read Roswell's columns because he thought outside the box with his writing. Though he never gave an interview to him on the record, Guy had spent many hours with him since he was drafted, in secret locations, talking about his life. And since he was twenty-one, he had learned to drink scotch from Mr. Roswell. That enticing drink had opened Guy up to share with him all the details about his past drug life, Anna's murder, and his problems with the Turk.

It made Ron Roswell one of few people that he trusted and that knew his predicament, along with Brooklyn, Alex, and Phillip. But even with all that insight, Roswell had guessed wrong on the last play of the game. Guy had dropped the football on purpose, that was true, but not because he wanted the game to end or because he never thought about breaking the record. It was actually the opposite, Guy did not want to break that record, because he had been lucky to tie it, and therefore breaking the Night Train's record under those circumstances would be unfortunate. He believed that the record itself represented such greatness that tying it, under the circumstances, would elevate and preserve Dick "Night Train" Lane's legacy.

What Guy wanted was to set a new record for the twenty-first century for the new GAF. Something never to be broken, that could stand alongside the Night Train's record, but for the sixteen-game, modern-day schedule. For the second century of professional football, he wanted to start a new Mount Rushmore of defensive records.

Guy Finelli wanted twenty interceptions in a sixteen game season!

■ ■ ■

After reading the paper, Guy picked up some running shorts on the back of a chair in his bedroom and put them to his nose to see if they were wearable. They smelled like the outside instead of his body odor, so he put them on. Guy knew that he was a smell freak. As a child, he had loved hanging out at Grandma's house before dinner to smell the garlic and onions cooking. Around the holidays, when his mom got a real chance to cook, he would sit with her for hours just to smell all the dishes cooking and the pies in the oven. He never flinched when his mom or dad hugged him, because he loved both their smells.

When he got into smoking pot as a teenager, he loved the smell as much as the high. When he first became aware of girls, he would neck for an hour, sometimes, just to smell her hair. He became a girl favorite because they thought he was just being romantic by enjoying the foreplay for so long.

His current favorite was entering the shower after a workout session with Patty followed by sex. The cornucopias of smells were like witnessing a perfect rainbow or tasting a perfect martini and chewing the olives at the end.

He had never connected his smell fetish with his need for hot sauce on his taste buds, but recently he had started to wonder. Was it because it actually tasted better with the hot sauce, or was it because he had a heightened, and just a somewhat freakish, sense of smell?

He grabbed a fresh running shirt out of his drawer, enjoying the whiff of cleanliness while fitting the shirt over his face. As he walked into his kitchen, he poured himself some coffee and then felt something in his right pocket. It was the card that Alex gave him last week from a visitor looking for him.

Guy looked at the card and recognized it as the phone number for the custom shoe store in Columbia Mall. He was curious enough after the big win on Sunday to see if it really was the Turk trying to contact him after all these years.

He pulled out his cell, dialed, and held his breath. "Yes, Mr. Finelli, my boss was waiting for your call. May he call you back on this line in a moment?"

Guy was heading downstairs for a workout but agreed to wait for ten minutes. Within seconds, his phone buzzed. "Mr. Guy Finelli, I am a big fan of yours. As you know, I have followed your career over the years. This is quite an honor to finally talk with you again."

"Well...yes...of course. What is it that I can do for you, Mr.?"

"Actually...Mr. Guy Finelli, I would rather answer that question in person...you know...more formally. I seem to draw such a crowd these days, as I am sure you can relate to...besides, it is hard to know who is listening in these days over the phone."

Guy tried to loosen the tightness in his throat and his death grip on the phone, as he envisioned the person who was responsible for Anna's death. "Is this...who I think it is?"

"Yes, I believe you visited my shoe store in Columbia several years ago. We seem to have a history together, you might say."

Guy ran his hand over his face as if removing water that had been sprayed on it, blinding him with anger for a moment.

"What did you have in mind?"

"If you would not mind, my associates could pick you up during one of your morning runs."

Oh shit, Guy thought, *this prick has his soldiers following me in Bethesda.* Suddenly, he realized that further indecision at this point would ruin his chance of meeting this monster. "Sure...Tuesday or Thursday morning of this week before six on the Bethesda Trail under East-West Highway."

"Sounds splendid, tomorrow I will prefer...say six in the morning. I promise to have you back to your run by seven, on my honor, my friend."

Guy gritted his teeth and uttered calmly, "I look forward to it!"

• • •

Guy headed downstairs and went into the condo manager's office. "Do you have a phone I could use in private for a few minutes?"

The manager could not believe his luck-having Guy Finelli come into his office was a dream. Seeing him walk through the lobby occasionally over the last few years was cool enough. He tried hard to stay calm as he handed him his cell phone and started to walk out the door.

"Sorry, I don't need this; I'll use your landline, if you don't mind."

"Oh, sure, Mr. Finelli; I wasn't thinking. Hey, great game Sunday. Please take your time."

"Oh, thank you...Mister?"

"Yeah...I'm Bob Volkman, a big...I mean...a huge fan of yours. Sorry to bother you, Mr. Finelli."

Guy realized he was not being mannerly and took a quick look at Bob, who looked to be in his fifties. "Please call me Guy. I should be just a moment." Guy remembered to show his rarely seen killer smile and give a bribe to keep Bob Volkman quiet. "Listen, Bob... would you like some tickets to the Dallas game after Christmas?"

"Oh Lord...you must be kidding...Mr....no, Jeez...uuuh...Guy, I mean...uh, yeah...absolutely!"

"I'll drop off four tickets and some killer parking right on your desk here in your office by Friday...but, Bob... please...you'll have to agree to one just one thing."

"You betcha...anything, Mr. Finelli. Oops, I mean Guy... jeez... oh yeah, no problem. I'll zip up the mouth here and throw away the key." The fifty-seven-year-old native of Canada did his best John Candy imitation, muttering between his sealed lips, "Oh oblm...ust eween ee an ooou."

Guy waved good-bye and lost the smile as he dialed FBI Assistant Director O'Malley on the land-line phone.

Brooklyn answered without recognizing the number, because he was feeling adventurous. He was in a good mood after watching the game on Sunday.

"Brooks, listen, we need to talk. I'm on a landline because I think I just talked to the Turk, and I agreed to talk to him in person."

"Is this Guy?"

"Oh yeah...I seem to be forgetting my manners today. How are you, Mr. O'Malley?"

"Did you get hit in the head or something yesterday? We have been tracking that guy for a while and still can't get close to him. Why would he want to meet with you?"

"I think he wants to bet for or against the Macs in the playoffs. That's a guess."

"That's what we hear. He spends half of his time at the MGM Casino at the National Harbor. Where and when do you meet?"

"I don't know, and tomorrow. He's going to pick me up on the Bethesda Trail under East-West Highway."

"What! Are you crazy? Tomorrow, that's too soon to set up a surveillance team."

"I know, I know...I don't care...listen, I have to go. Is there something I should know about the case? Any leads?"

"I can't tell you shit, but remember to keep looking for Anna's gun."

"What does that mean? You know something about

the gun? Holy shit! I would love to just...Jesus Christ... OK... OK. . listen, I'll be cool. I was just on the phone with him. He thinks I'm his best friend because he is such a piece of shit. It's like playing a good quarterback, but he's really a dipshit...you have to be patient, but at some point this jackass will throw into coverage. I have to go. I'll call you later."

"Stay safe."

"Don't worry. He still needs to beat me and win the ultimate chess game going on in his head."

• • •

Guy pulled his hood over his head as he slowly headed down the Crescent Trail from Woodmont Avenue. He wondered how stupid this would look if he ended up beaten up or killed by this megalomaniac. "I never really worried before about doing stupid things,

253

so why start now?" he chuckled to himself.

Two men in long coats stood on the deserted trail behind the Riviera Building. "Wow, twice in a row this monster is out to get me!" Guy said out loud. The two soldiers greeted him politely with slight bows and asked, "Mr. Guy Finelli?" They handed him a full-length raincoat to wear to help hide his identity. As he walked to the car, he wondered if either of these well-muscled goons had been involved in Anna's shooting. He quickly decided to end that thought as he entered a black Mercedes. They drove west on East-West Highway across Wisconsin Avenue to north on Woodmont before pulling over before Norfolk Avenue. Guy saw the back of the Tastee Diner through the window.

"Is this where we're going?"

"Yes, Mr. Guy Finelli. If you would get out and enter through the side door. Our leader is in the back booth."

"Well, this has been fun, boys, but I can get myself home from here. Thanks for the short ride." Guy smiled as he left the car and thought of the irony of meeting at the favorite restaurant of his still-living grandfather.

While he had never met his namesake, Guy I, he grew up seeing his other grandfather, James Werner, a brilliant engineer who had worked and lived in Bethesda. To say the least, he lived a conservative life-driving only used cars and keeping them going for twenty years or more, riding his bike whenever possible, and walking to work at NIH every day for thirty-five years. Most nights he worked in his basement on electrical projects or building model trains and doll houses from scratch.

Guy's mom, Carol, would tell stories about eating at the Tastee Diner every week for years when her mom had night classes. Her dad would order the meatloaf and mashed potatoes every week, until Carol quickly learned how to cook when her mom was not around.

As Guy took a few steps on the street before he entered the diner, he thought of the great weekend he had with Anna at his grandparent's farm in the middle of nowhere in Virginia before the shooting. Somehow, the Turk had found that remote location. Could he have known that the diner was the site of his grandfather's favorite meatloaf?

He realized that he was letting his opponent get into his head, so he focused for a moment about his world being so different than his grandpop James's. He started to smile when he remembered that he had learned to dance when he was young by going many times to Glen Echo for big-band music on Sunday nights with Grandpop James, his sister, Grace, and sometimes his mom.

Otherwise, their worlds only intersected on one thing, and that was football. He loved that Grandpop James was a huge football fan who had gone to games at Griffith Stadium in the forties and fifties to see Washington play. He was dazzled by his grandpop's stories about seeing Sammy Baugh play many times in person. It gave him chills replaying that memory just as he was about to open the back door of the Tastee Diner.

The Turk sat with his back to the sparse crowd in a booth in the back room, while the rest of the patrons were all up front and around the corner, sitting at the counter. He wore a dark wig and sunglasses. Guy noticed that he was bigger than he had imagined, with large shoulders and a strong handshake. He was trim and had a perfectly kept beard and manicured fingernails. The waiter, an obvious soldier, brought tea and took his breakfast order.

Guy was suddenly hungry and ordered the Western omelet with corn-beef hash, sausage, and coffee. He liked the idea of stuffing himself in front of the disciplined Iraqi native.

"It honors me that you agreed to see me." "You're welcome, Mr.?"

"Assante...Mr. Assante. Can I pour you some tea?" "No, it's pretty early. I need coffee if rm not running." Quickly the waiter came with coffee. Guy slurped it. "What can I do for you, Mr. Assante?"

During the next few minutes, Guy listened quietly to his adversary in disguise present his idea for making money on the Potomacs as they made it through the playoffs. Guy slowly ate his omelet and corn-beef hash, liberally pouring hot sauce on every bite just to freak out his opponent.

Mr. Assante could not help but notice this strange behavior, but he did not take the bait to comment. He wondered if it somehow helped him play with such great talent in such a violent game without ever losing control. He tried to stay focused on the topic at hand. Part of him was having trouble not being overwhelmed by the presence of Guy Finelli, but he had to remind himself that he too was a great presence-he controlled hundreds of soldiers and an illegal empire of crime to prove it.

Guy politely waited until he was done eating to say,"I appreciate that you would take the time in person to explain your proposal to me, but I am not interested. My goal is to find a way to end our relationship without fear of harm to me, my family, or my friends."

"My friend, once again thank you for meeting with me. I think it helps us understand each other better. I believe your team, led by your wonderful play, will advance to the championship contest at the new World Space Stadium. It will be a great moment for this country. Perhaps we could meet again the Monday before the game so that I can update you on my plans. I will be in touch, Mr. Guy Finelli."

Usually, it was a goon or two that sent his messages of intimidation or deals to throw a game here or there. Guy had managed to survive those tactics, always wondering what would be next. This time it was serious, the real thing, and the Turk was willing to meet in person to make it happen.

"Well, Mr. Assante, I appreciate your confidence in our team making it to the championship contest, but that is pretty far off. As for involving me in your little scheme to make money in the playoffs, you are free to bet on riding the right horse. I plan only on winning."

"Exactly, Mr. Guy Finelli, it will be quite a ride for you as well. It would allow us to end our relationship on a positive note for both of us. You know, my friend, even if you have bet on the best horse in the race, they do not always win. That is why you can bet to win, place, or show. In this case, it will only be a two-horse race, so betting to place eliminates all the pressure."

Chapter 42

T HE THREE GAMES leading up to the Christmas holidays were dominant wins for the

Potomacs. Offense, defense, and special teams took turns in showing their supremacy in each game. Marcus McNeil III led the offense with his trio of wide receivers, Lincoln, King, and Kennedy, nicknamed "the Targets"; tight end Hank Harrison; converted running back Amos Enos; and a mobile but muscular offensive line led by tackle Albert Christian.

Harrison was quietly leading all tight ends in the league in receptions and TDs. Whether he would receive All-Pro honors at the end of the season was way overdue, according to McNeil. After each win, he would make a point of discussing two players on offense-Harrison and Christian. On most running plays, the duo would either set the edge with their blocks for Enos or McNeil to run outside or pull inside with great deftness to open up holes in the middle.

Amos Enos was a former tight end at ACU and huge for a running back. When he joined the team before the 2017 season, Coach Williams converted the six-feet-four 255- pounder into a tailback. It seemed risky at the time, but he soon became the missing link for the offense. He had great hands, blocked like a tackle, and ran over people while carrying the pigskin.

He became roommates with Albert Christian and his brother Andrew after joining the Macs. His parents were hot-pepper farmers in the Louisiana bayou, and both were hearing impaired from birth. Being an excellent signer, Amos immediately connected with Albert.

His other expertise, hot sauce, made him an instant favorite of Guy and Hank. Albert and Andrew became hot- sauce freaks in the first month of sharing a house together. Amos would have a case of bayou-made hot sauce sent in once a week for Guy and the defensive players.

On special teams, Coach Joe Finelli had honed his players into master craftsmen on each unit. Now in his fourth year, Cousin Joe had convinced the best players on offense and defense to play special teams as well as seasoned backups. The Targets, Sprint DMC,

Albert Christian, Hank Harrison, and of course, Guy Finelli-all took their turns to cover the kicking game and block on returns

Albert was the snapper on punts and field goals, and Guy was the main return man, along with Mark Pelligrini. In addition, Guy was the backup punter and field-goal kicker. With the new rules, the punter and kicker had to have a number of plays from the line of scrimmage to be eligible to punt or kick. Luckily, Guy only had to punt twice during the season and never had attempted a field goal.

As dynamic a player as Marcus McNeil was on offense and in representing the team in front of the media, the defensive unit led by Guy Finelli had become the soul of the team. Coach Furrey Favarro had enormous talent on the defensive line, with Braxton Black and Chester Blue and linebackers led by Clarence Night and Horace Day. But the defensive backfield, with three All-Pros in Cary Collins, Duran Hall, and Guy Finelli, allowed the Macs to dominate offenses at times.

Games against division foes Carolina, New York, and Atlanta made the back end of the sixteen-game schedule important wins. The final game would be the last regular season game at FedEx Field against hated division rival Dallas. Washington had closed down RFK Stadium in 1996 with a 35-0 stomping against Dallas. Guy's teammates, the fans, and the local media were looking forward to a similar trouncing.

Christmas 2019 would come on a Wednesday, giving Guy two days to finalize his shopping for all the special people in his life. He had done most of his shopping in London in October in virtual anonymity and had the goodies shipped to his condo. On Monday, he would take the morning to roam the shops in Bethesda and the luxury stores in Chevy Chase and Friendship Heights, better known as the DC line.

After some window-shopping in Bethesda, he ran for a mile and a half down to the district line, just enough to stretch out his muscles after the Sunday game against Atlanta. It was a fun game, especially since it was indoors in December at the Georgia Dome. He had finally picked off two interceptions, giving him sixteen for the season after going two games without one. Both came in the second half as Atlanta rallied from a 27-0 deficit with three touchdowns in the final eight minutes of the game.

The backbreaker to the comeback was a one-handed interception by Finelli of an attempted screen pass that Chester Blue tipped. Guy was diving low to get the football under several blockers in front of the screen, with the ball tumbling down in front of him. He snatched the ball with his left hand just before the blockers ran over him, unaware of his magic act. Curled in a fetal position, Guy was willing to take some cleats on his back as he possessed the official interception that broke a sixty-seven-year record.

The last interception was a deep sideline throw with thirty seconds left that Guy had covered all the way. It was his easiest interception of the year.

Technically, Guy had set a new interception record, but he refused to talk about it or recognize it. Not meeting with the media was costing him plenty in fines, but the freedom it bought him was priceless.

He had called his friend Hank Harrison to help him with some gifts for the four important women in his life: Carol, his mom; Patty, his fiancee; Charlotte, his friend and agent; and Sally, his sister-in-law, friend, and caregiver to his daughter, Annie. First, they met at Chipotle for an early burrito before it became crowded. They found a table to eat at without being noticed.

There was a slight panic when the close buddies noticed that there was only one bottle of Cholula hot sauce on the table. At first, their right hands were impatiently waiting for the hot sauce to become available, but they soon found a rhythm that worked-eat with the left hand, allow for time to chew, and then douse the next bite with the right hand. The burritos were quietly obliterated in record time.

Unfortunately, Hank had picked up Guy's habit of hot sauce fever when they became friends in high school. Hank could drive as a senior, and he took Guy out for food after their seven-on-seven practice sessions. The Chipotle on Cherry Hill Road became the destination after one McDonald's run. Hank tasted his first Chipotle burrito with hot sauce and was hooked forever. Pretty soon, eggs, meat, hash browns, and even pancakes became targets for hot-sauce fever. Only cereal and PB&Js were immune. Phillip Finelli would tell his son, "Either you're going to die at an early age from stomach cancer, or you'll become immunized from all diseases."

Hank brought Guy through Neiman-Marcus at the Mazza Gallerie to point out several ideas for gifts. Then they walked across Western Avenue into Maryland and hit Gucci, Tiffany's, and Louis Vuitton before ending up at Saks Fifth Avenue, where Hank's partner Blair Montgomery now worked as a buyer. It was a job that he had always wanted, and with Hank's income, he was able to retire from work he did not enjoy. He welcomed the chance to get on the floor and spend Guy's money.

Blair gave Guy a real hug in his UMD hoodie and stepped back to size up Hank's teammate and his outfit. "My, my...are you ever going to stop growing? I know you're doing the undercover thing...being so famous and all...but if you ever need someone to outfit you, just give me a call. We have a great men's store over at Mazza

Gallerie that would do the trick." He nestled up to Hank. "As you can see, I did a pretty good job with Hank."

Hank released himself gently. "Blair, as you should know, Guy is not interested in being on the cover of *GQ* anytime soon." Hank grabbed the strings of the hoodie and playfully pulled them tighter. "Maybe when here tires, he'll jump into the whole metrosexual look. But for now, he needs you to do some women shopping."

"I see, my dear. I think our friend has a better sense of humor than you do, Mr. All-Pro!" Blair untightened the hoodie and pulled it off Guy's head. He pulled out a comb and quickly straightened up his hair. "Now there, Mr. Finelli, you look better already with that black hair showing." He slipped his hand around Guy's arm. "Now, let's get started." He then softly spoke into Guy's ear. "I understand that you know that I know several styles of fashion." He turned toward Hank and said in a louder tone, "I mean, I do work for Saks Fifth Avenue, for Christ's sake!" He turned back to Guy and patted him on the arm. "Now, if Guy wants to go for the Brooks Brothers look, I'm there for our friend."

Guy was all smiles as he enjoyed seeing Blair banter with Hank. Their relationship had survived a long journey, from being victims to hardly being noticed. "My friend Blair, you have always been a great help. Thanks for your time with my shopping. Now, you know I have four women to shop for, and other than some jewelry I bought in London, I need some special ideas for outfits or accessories. I have all their sizes and some pictures with their coloring."

"Wow, a prepared male shopper *and* a great athlete. What else could a girl ask for?" Blair took a moment to look at the pictures. "Ahhh...yes... Hank has told me about the redhead thing. Your mother is so lovely and still as petite as Sally. And what a gem Sally is with that dark hair...she and your brother make such a great couple; it gives me chills! And of course, Patty and Charlotte-so pretty...they could be sisters with the redhead, tall, athletic builds, and nice racks too! This will be fun!"

After thirty minutes, Guy parted with Hank and Blair and decided to run home, realizing that his Christmas buying was in good hands. Later that day, Bob Volkman sat in his office on the first floor of the condo building and signed for four large bags of beautifully wrapped Christmas presents. Little did he know that those gifts were worth more than His yearly salary.

He called Guy to see if he was in the condo. "Mr. Finelli...I mean Guy, this is Bob Volkman. Hey, I have four bags of gifts here that I wanted to run up to you if you were in."

"Thank you, Bob, but listen...no need. I'll be down in a few minutes to pick them up."

"Well...sure...OK... Guy. I'm going to run over to the bank to put in a few deposits, and I'll be back in ten minutes or so."

"See you in ten or fifteen minutes. "Guy threw on his hoodie and headed downstairs. He wanted to get some air and enjoy the feel of the sun for a few minutes in winter as he waited for Bob to get back. He headed south on Wisconsin Avenue toward the old farmers' market area. Unfortunately, there was no market in December, but it was an open spot to sit in the sunlight.

Across the street and on the corner sat Perpetual Bank, Bethesda's oldest bank. The scene looked pretty quiet for a Monday afternoon. Unexpectedly, Bob Volkman emerged from the front door like a rocket shot out into traffic on the busy avenue. For a second, Guy thought he was watching a movie as cars stopped and honked, and Bob showed some great agility finding running room between moving cars to cross the street.

Just behind him, a character with a gun stopped on the corner and fired a shot across the avenue toward Bob, which careened off a windshield instead. Quickly, the shooter, an apparent bank robber, fled after Bob, while carrying a bag of presumed stolen cash. He jumped on several car hoods, leaped over the middle island, and finally landed on the sidewalk, chasing Bob, who had turned north toward the condo building.

Guy had moved in Bob's direction as he crossed the street in front of him, expecting him to stop, until he heard the shot fired at him. He saw the shooter running a diagonal through cars trying to run down Bob, who must have been the only witness in the bank.

Guy could only think of the head-first shots, since banned by football, that Sean Taylor would take on unsuspecting receivers coming across the middle. It was all he could do to keep from smiling as he launched toward his target. First, his head slammed into the running target's spine, followed by his shoulder breaking three unprotected ribs, and finally his forearm causing a concussion with a winding blow. But the worst damage to the poor man's face was the taillight he smacked into on the way down to the ground.

Quickly, Guy rolled over, grabbed the money bag, and found Bob just fifty yards up the street, who had turned around to watch his new hero.

"That was awesome, Guy... are you all right?"

"Never been better...here, take this bag back to the bank and be a hero. And remember, this is between you and me!"

"Absolutely...you were never here."

• • •

Somehow, over one hundred thousand fans were allowed into FedEx Field for the last regular-season game against Dallas. Burton Parker had stuffed twenty thousand standing-room-only fans onto the upper-deck party platforms built four years ago in each end zone. Today's SRO crowd alone paid for the decks.

The fans on the platforms were liquored up and/or stoned by kickoff and led the rocking and cheering in the stadium. Dallas had not witnessed such an avalanche of power as the Potomacs brought to the field in the first half in decades. Guy Finelli led off the game with a kickoff return for a TD, followed by two interception returns for TDs before the Macs offense touched the ball. When they finally did receive the ball in the middle of the first quarter, Marcus McNeil led the Macs on two drives, each eighty yards and fifteen plays, for two TDs, which combined, took up fifteen minutes of the clock.

When Mark Pelligrini blocked a punt late in the first half and returned it for a TD to make it 42-0, Dallas put in their backup QB to run out the clock in the first half.

The only question for the second half was whether Guy Finelli would reach the magical twentieth- interception mark. In reality, his fantasy goal was to get to twenty-one, a jersey number he had shared with Sean Taylor since his second year in the league. Before he signed his rookie contract, Guy had held out for the right to wear number twenty-one, but Coach Shannon Dellums refused to grant such a request, so Guy chose number thirty-six instead, which Sean Taylor had worn in his rookie year. After Coach Brown was hired, his first phone call was to Guy Finelli telling him that he could wear the same number as he had in high school and college, number twenty-one.

Guy figured he would stay in the game through the third quarter before Coach Favarro would take him out. Dallas started the second half on their own twenty-yard line with their starting lineup, including the QB. Dallas moved the ball into Potomacs territory, with Guy guessing on every play and trying to make a turnover happen. On the eighth play of the drive, he guessed wrong on a turn-in pattern as the wide receiver faked inside and flew past him for a forty-five-yard TD pass.

The Macs punted on the next series after three plays, giving Dallas good field position. Guy had been burned last series but still guessed the wrong side of the field on two thirty-yard passes up each sideline.

With first and goal from the seven, he remembered the halfback option pass play that he had seen in the Cotton Bowl two years ago run by Baylor University with running back Fiddy Watts, who now played for Dallas. He had thrown a left-handed pass for a TD across the back of the end zone going toward the center of the field. He remembered it because it was quite a difficult throw.

Guy loved to watch old NFL games, especially with Lombardi coaching, and even better when they beat Dallas in back-to-back NFL championship games in 1966 and 1967 to get into the first two Super Bowls.

In the famous 1967 Ice-Bowl game, which he had watched at least twenty times, Dallas scored a short-lived, go-ahead TD on a running-back option pass from Dan Reeves to Lance Rentzel, but Reeves was right-handed and rolled left for the deception. It was a brilliant play-call that even Lombardi did not see coming.

The first-down pass was a corner throw knocked away by Cary Collins. On second down, Guy knew that the option pass could happen, so he played deep in the end zone. But when Watts went in motion to the right, it looked like an outside screen pass to the wide receiver on the left. Then, the QB faked a pass left, slid a couple of steps forward, and turned to fire a pass to his right to Watts, who was back on the fifteen-yard line. It was a clear lateral, making a forward pass still possible. Suddenly, the defense shifted back to their left and charged Watts, who faked two steps to the scrimmage line and then stepped back to find his target.

The whole time, Guy was patrolling the back of the end zone, hiding among the players heading toward Watts's side of the field. Guy saw a wide-out in the back of the end zone coming toward the middle with his right hand up, yelling for the ball. Watts threw a bullet just like in the Cotton Bowl. Guy Finelli rolled back two steps into coverage and snagged his nineteenth interception. He ran it out of the end zone to avoid a Rouge (a point against) and was tackled on the ten-yard line.

The Potomacs offense punted again after three plays, giving Dallas great field position at midfield. The defense ran back on the field, with linebackers Clarence Night and Horace Day establishing the huddle. They, along with the rest of the defense, now wanted the twentieth interception for their leader and would call a special defense for it in the huddle.

First, Clarence Night spoke: "OK, now listen, all of you. We do this thing like Day says, OK? So, be ready every second, every minute, every hour...I mean, all freaking Day...that's what I say!"

"Night's right...here it is, my homeboys." Horace Day looked up at all his players in the huddle. "We all blitz...! mean, all at once, but with a man in front of you...got that right? Of course, except for the front four and the middle backer, but each of you mothers take a lane and get those paws up. Especially you, Black, and you too, Blue! Force him to throw to his right. Don't let him slip past you like butter! Spread out evenly...now, do you feel me? Are we good? Night, is that right?"

"Nice, Day...nice! One more thing, Italian Man is going to be the only mother-backer doin' freakin' coverage, so do not-and I mean *do* not-let that mother-cow-sucking of a Dallas-freaking QB get outside...got that right?" Clarence Night paused for a moment, scowling at every face in the huddle to make his point clear. He jabbed his elbow to his fellow linebacker, Horace Day, to wrap it up. "End it, Day."

"Allll gooood, Night...all good. All right, boys, let's get our Italian Man-you know, the Big Guy-his interception number twenty. Let's bring it in now. Let's say it together and break...*all day and all of the night!*"

Guy stepped back from the huddle, loving the presentation of the defense by Day and Night, and watched closely as Dallas came out in formation. He thought quickly that the defensive call would be a disaster for the play, because they were loaded to his right. Suddenly, the wide-out on his left went in motion to his right, and the tight end shifted to his left. The slot on the right changed sides and became the slot on his left. Now he thought, *Whew...wow...everything is perfect!*

He was looking for a quick slant to his left when the blitz poured in. Dallas was set up for a screen to his right, but the QB would see the pressure and come back to Guy's left. Everyone crept up to the line; the Dallas QB was counting burgundy helmets-too many for the wide-out screen, he decided. The ball was snapped. Horace Day and Clarence Night powered over the guards. Braxton Black and Chester Blue knocked back the tackles. Cary Collins came in slow from the left side, holding the left flank.

Guy quickly hit full speed to cut off the slot route. The ball was released, just barely passing through all the defenders' outstretched arms. The football seemed lost in all the hands at the scrimmage line. Guy turned instead to the receiver, who had his arms outstretched, ready to cradle the football as it hit his fingertips. The football glided toward the receiver; inches away, Guy finally saw the football. His timing was perfect in the moment he had waited years for. His brain commanded a rush of strength, seeing the football needing to be rescued from the enemy as it started to settle in the receiver's gloves. Violently, Guy latched on to the receiver's gloves and the football with his bare hands. The receiver tried to slip out of it, but was no match for the power of "The Safety." He was pulled along for ten long and painful yards as this twenty-first-century "Night Train" left the station. With the naked football in hand, Guy found a lane past the mass of bodies in the backfield.

Free of any likely pursuit, Guy Pinelli was now all by himself with interception number twenty. It felt like holding his newborn baby Annie for the first time, as he gave her life from death. He roared with an unexpected exuberance, holding the football above him with both of his beaten-up hands, as if making an offering to the football gods. The crowd in the end-zone rows flew out of their seats watching him making history. The fans in the party decks above them jumped with their beers in their hands, showering each other with suds containing hops and barley.

The reverberation of noise cascaded from end zone to end zone, as Guy kept running down the field, not feeling his legs, just the air passing around him. Finally, he approached the goal line, and for the first time in his career, he dove, as his idol Sean Taylor had in 2005 to secure a playoff spot, into the end zone, rolled into a somersault, and stood high with the football above him. He took a few more steps and then collapsed down on one knee, closed his eyes, and shut out the world.

He had no prayer to recite, just a feeling of serenity that sent him back to a memory of his front lawn in Oakview. He touched the grass in the promise-land of the end zone with his left hand and put the football under his nose with his right, to smell the memory, seeing himself as an eight-year-old kid diving into the luscious zoysia-grass lawn, rolling around with joy, clutching a reception of a football thrown by his dad.

The three seconds in his head seemed like slices of The three seconds in his head seemed like slices of felt like being in heaven. Ironically, it could only be interrupted by a joyous pile of humanity. His teammates had arrived to celebrate his accomplishment!

265

Chapter 43

THE FIRST TWO playoff games were played at FedEx, and the Potomacs marched through Toronto and Tampa Bay with ease. The team engine was powered by the efficient cylinders of offense, defense, and special teams. By now the Macs were a well-oiled, tough machine that extended the regular-season eight-game winning streak to ten games overall. To return to DC for the M2C2-1, they would have to win on the road in Seattle for the conference championship.

An ominous fog was descending on Seattle from the northwest, surrounding the stadium just minutes before game time. The television crews were praying that the monster fog would not settle on the field. The coaches for both teams had little concern, because their offenses were built to run and rely on defense.

Seattle's core of players had won the Championship in 2014 and should have won in 2015 except for the worst play call in the history of football from the one-yard line on second down. This was their first appearance in a conference championship since the disastrous end in 2015 and most experts believed that it was the last chance for this group of players to get back to the big dance.

Guy Finelli had seen QB Randle Walton play in college and faced him several times in the pros. His success in the professional leagues had been unexpected, because he barely broke the five-feet-ten mark, but his strong arm, uncanny maneuverability, and fearless leadership made him a champion early in his career.

He became the highest-paid QB in the league after the 2015 season, but Guy had little concern about losing to him. There was not a play or formation he did not know by heart from Seattle's offense. His game plan would be to play deep most of the game and make tackles on obvious runs. In other formations, the defense would play man-to- man with him or fellow safety Mark Pelligrini, designated to spy the QB.

Guy wanted to take away the deep middle throw, because Randle Walton's once-powerful arm could not make the deep sideline throw with just a flick of his wrist anymore. But the real key would be which defense would stop the opponent's running game. Being late in the season, every lineman was beaten-up, playing with bruised shoulders, ribs, hips, and thigh muscles, along with sprained fingers, knees, ankles, and toes. These maladies would never make any injury list.

This time of year, passing teams would lose their edge to defenses because they would not dominate them physically or take advantage of their maladies. Offensive lineman backing up into pass protection fifty times a game, instead of being able to inflict pain on defensive lineman by blocking forward on running plays, would be the ones beaten-up by the end of the game.

The fog kept the scoring low in the first half, with Seattle taking a 12-3 lead into the locker room. Guy Finelli had fifteen tackles on forty-two Seattle plays, mostly running plays. Luckily, the Macs defense had held the Sea Monsters to four field goals. On twelve plays inside the ten-yard line, Finelli had made ten tackles. It was a performance that amazed and frustrated the Seattle twelfth man, their overwhelmingly supportive fans.

Marcus McNeil III had been hit hard in the first half and was limping noticeably by the end of the third quarter. Coach Brown made a decision that stunned the pundits after the defense stopped Seattle and forced a punt. He called a time-out and brought Guy to the sidelines. "Stay in after the punt, run the offense, and get us a score, somehow, someway!"

The offensive line looked up at Guy in the huddle, ready to kick some ass. Albert Christian spoke up with two words, "Zone read." He then signed the rest, which Guy read as "Been there all day, Mac hurt, can^{1}t run!"

"Got it...let^{l}s run it all day on the ball, no huddle."

He pointed to his fellow defensive guys playing wideouts. "Same five audibles, when we need it."

First snap, Guy reads the defensive end inside, fakes to Amos Enos, runs outside, and crosses midfield for a first down.

Snap two, Guy reads inside again, takes a shot from a linebacker, and almost fumbles.

Snap three, Guy hands off; Enos gains twelve for first down.

Snap four, Guy reads outside but rides Enos with the ball, hoping for an inside commit from the linebacker and the defensive end. He sees it, takes the ball from Enos, and runs down to the twenty-five.

Snap five, Guy sees the middle open just before the snap, takes the ball, and hurdles straight up the middle for fifteen yards to the ten.

Snap six, Guy calls an audible to Cary Collins for a quick post and runs up to the center for the snap. He almost fumbles the ball but recovers and throws high to Cary for an incomplete pass. The offense huddles; hard breathing is the only sound. Guy looks around for ten seconds, stalling, before uttering, "This is fucking great... isn't it? Let's have a fun play before we score. OK, T- formation, handoff to Amos up the middle. Let's beat the shit out of them on this play. Then line it up, and I'll go with a zone-read fake." He turns to his friend Hank Harrison without a catch in the game and laughs, "Hank, get open somehow. I'll read you, but I may be rolling right, all wide-outs tight on both plays."

Snap seven, Amos up the middle for no gain but defensive bodies are hit hard and dug into with fists.

Snap eight, on the ball quickly: Guy calls out "Blue fifteen... Ready... set ... go."

From the Washington Potomacs Radio Network: "Finelli fakes to Enos, starts running right, bundled up by Marberry, the defensive end, but no...he breaks away somehow. They are after him near the sidelines, but no, he stops and leaps ...it's a jump pass...my God... he fires across the field. The ball is in the fog...I can't see it, fans... but yes...I think it's Harrison running the opposite way, leaping...oh, my Lord... he caught it...he caught it...he caught it! Oh, my God, it came out of the clouds...from out of the heavens, and Hank Harrison caught it. Somehow, he held on after being crushed head-on by the defensive back. He was in-bounds...! saw that...but they're talking on the field...oh, Lord...I don't know...what can it be, folks? Yes, yes, yes, it has to be...they're signaling a TD.. it's a miracle play, what a throw, what a catch! Could it be the play from out of the clouds?

Here's the extra point play. Finelli under center, fakes to Amos, fires to Harrison in the back of the end zone for the point; it's twelve to ten, and the Macs are back in it."

The fog had covered the field by the fourth quarter, making the television broadcast come entirely from ground level. Seattle was convinced that it could protect their territory, like a lioness protecting her cubs, with their stout defense. The television audience was treated to seeing twenty of the twenty-two players on the field line up within two yards of the scrimmage and go at it with brute force.

Marcus McNeil III returned to the game and tried to move the Macs into Seattle territory for the go- ahead field goal but with no success. Randle Walton was running down the clock with short runs and scrambles. He was feeling a sense of success when they crossed the Macs thirty with another first down at the two-minute warning.

Coaches Favarro and Finelli met with the defense near the sidelines during the time-out, but "The Safety" stayed on the field watching Randle Walton in the Sea Monster huddle. Furrey started to walk out to the field to call in Guy, but Cousin Joe grabbed him.

"Let him be; he's figuring something out." "I hope so!" Furrey responded.

Guy looked across the field and saw Walton's eyes. They always looked confident, whether he was up by three TDs or down by three TDs. Just once, Guy wanted to see something different in those eyes, like fear, or maybe just uncertainty. He was the model of consistency, unflappable, and a great person to represent the game. Guy at times wanted to be more like him, being with the fans, always doing charities, giving interviews, and living a clean-cut life. But he knew that was not him; those things seemed exhausting. He was playing football, not badminton or ping-pong for Christ sake. Those things were distractions, and besides, he had a family to take care of-and those superhero things that kept coming up, so maybe he was giving back to the community. Getting the Turk was also on his mind for now, and that was something big. Something that Randle Walton wasn't doing! After football, he thought, he would give back to the community, maybe give his money away and become more accessible to the media, like his brother or Randle Walton.

Guy admired Walton going back to his career at NC State and enjoyed beating him in every meeting on the field. They were both professional champions, but Guy knew he was a better athlete and a college champion as well. Randle was standing between him and a third straight championship. Now, once, just once, Guy wanted a full shot at him. He was so elusive that hitting him flush in the ribs or back was almost impossible. Suddenly, Guy did not care about anything else. It was time for a rib shot on his adversary-nothing personal, but they needed the football.

The defense returned, and the expected "We need the ball back!" cries permeated the huddle.

In the next two running plays Seattle gained four yards, and were left with a third and six with a minute fifty to go. Finelli heard nothing in the huddle as he stepped back into deep safety position. He turned around to see the fog hovering around the triangular end-zone seats. He watched on the huge video screen above as Randle Walton came to the shotgun position.

The fans and the video screen disappeared in the fog. Guy turned and was hungry to eat some ribs. He started running toward the line of scrimmage, totally bypassing his teammates and un-phased by the signal call. Luckily the ball was snapped as Day and Night pinched inside the guards allowing Black and Blue to catapult the middle forcing Randle turned to his right, never seeing "The Safety" launching out of the fog toward him. Randle pulled the ball from his running back and started to get outside as his guard pulled to lead him. Guy flew through the opening and smashed into the 300-pound offensive guard like he was a simple beanbag. The guard flew backward like a discarded toy, and felt Guy Finelli's cleats use him like a stepladder as he sprung into the air, like a caped crusader, emerging from the fog and shocking Randle Walton with a direct hit.

Guy accentuated his target into his unprotected ribs with a clean shoulder follow-through while he punched out the football with his left fist. He finally landed on top of Randle Walton and looked straight into his eyes. The fearless warrior struggled to breathe as he helplessly watched the football fly into the fog and into the hands of lineman Chester Blue.

In the next few seconds, the two adversaries listened to the silence of the crowd as Blue rambled down the middle of the field with Braxton Black beside him, Day in front of him, and Night close behind.

Suddenly, Black looked back and saw Blue fall down at the Seattle five-yard line, where he went down completely out of oxygen. Day and Night protected their teammate as a posse of Seattle linemen caught up and showed mercy by touching him down.

Guy fell back to his feet and rose from his target. He bent over and helped Randle Walton up. Randle's eyes were glassy, but his smile was intact.

"Great tackle...Mr. Finelli. It looks like you got us again."

"Mr. Walton...we got lucky...you're the best!"

Randle took a deep but pained breath. "I think you're wrong about that, my friend; you're worth every cent of that contract-congratulations."

Guy led Randle slowly to his sideline as the trainers ran onto the field to rescue their leader. "Listen, Guy... remember, the Lord will be with you on and off the field... best of luck in the championship contest."

"I hope you're right, Randle. I'm going to need his help."

"I hear you, brother...but hey, you are "The Safety!" Randle winked at him after they exchanged man hugs. They separated slowly, holding on to each other, exchanging energy. Guy felt nothing but love from someone he had just laid out. He thought, *Maybe when I grow up, I can have that much class.*

The Potomacs took pleasure in running down the clock as Mac III twice took a knee. A tired Seattle defense looked on and could only watch the game-winning FG for a 13-12 Potomac victory. The celebration on the field was the first thing that was clearly visible to the television audience, as the fog had finally lifted just after the fumble. It seemed to lift the pressure of the year off the Potomacs' shoulders, now being able to defend their two-time championship at home. It would be a once-in-a-lifetime event in DC to open the new World Space Stadium against agreat opponent from just thirty miles north-the Baltimore Banners!

Chapter 44

IT HAD BEEN a gentle kidnapping on Monday morning on the Crescent Trail, and not unexpected. Guy saw it as an invitation to meet his real-life adversary on his own turf. Guy was curious and feeling adventurous as he rode in the back of a van with a bag over his head. He wanted this whole part of his life over with-it felt like a cancer within his body that was slowly killing him. This strategy seemed like an experimental treatment, untested on humans that could wipe out the cancer if successful. He was willing to take the insane risk to gain the evidence needed to bring down the Turk, or now, Mr. Assante. *This Is what superheroes do,* he thought.

After a forty-minute drive the van stopped, and he was led slowly out and down some steps. They moved quickly through various halls and stairways to a room where the hood was lifted. It was dark and only lit by candles with smells of incense everywhere.

Mr. Assante rose from his throne and came forward to greet his guest. "Mr. Guy Finelli, welcome to my... office... you might say."

Guy stood, after having his hands freed, and accepted the respectful handshake from his opponent. His large hands felt the grip of massive strength from this beast of a man, who stood just less than six feet but was clearly a solid 230 pounds. Sitting in the booth at the diner in disguise had hidden his physical size.

"Nice to see you again, Mr. Assante. What brings me here to your...office?"

"Please, call me Berker... that is my first name. It means 'Solid Man' in Turkish. May I call you Gaetano?"

Guy was a little taken aback but tried to stay cool by smiling. He had been called that by his mother, when he was a little boy, the few times he was ever disobedient. "Of course...Berker...whatever you like."

"It is such a powerful name, Gaetano-I believe it fits your...how do you say...your persona!"

"Thank you...maybe when I retire and become a movie star, I'll have to switch names." Guy laughed with unusual gusto considering the situation.

Berker politely smiled, hardly moving his facial muscles. "I believe, Gaetano, you were named after your father's father. Is it true about his talents?"

"Every bit of it," Guy responded defensively as he felt penetrated by a surge of anger. He felt his fingers extend, wanting to wrap them around Berker's thick neck and squeeze every ounce of air out of it. "Well, it was ninety years ago, so who knows, I guess." His fingers retreated as he thought of the Japanese garden outside of Nashville and guided himself to some inner peace.

"He was such a little man, with so much power. I believe you have that same power, but of course in a much larger body."

"That is true, but..."

"Yes, well, the record does speak for itself, I believe, just as your record will always speak for itself. Do you not agree?"

Guy recognized the resumption of the chess game in Berker's thoughts. He had played a gambit, Guy had fallen for it, and now he was on the defensive. It was time to attack. "Berker, you humble me with your compliments, but I am just a football player who plays a game; you are a businessman that runs an empire. What do you need from me?"

Berker felt alive at having his opponent bow to his wishes. "Gaetano, it is simple. I do not need you to lose the game-that will be taken care of-just do not try so hard when you find that things are hopeless!"

Guy was obviously confused by Berker's statement but did not want to know more about the bluff. Suddenly, he realized that a deal could be made for his freedom from this man by taking away Berker's freedom.

"How much do you plan to win?"

"I win every day, Guy. I see the game as an opportunity for a great achievement for my empire!"

"How about if I guarantee that achievement to be a certainty?"

"Cooperation would be wonderful, my friend." "Well, this way you can have both sides covered."

The strategy was working. He had Berker intrigued and curious.

"What do you have in mind?"

"I can't play in a game that I have no chance of winning. It would be too obvious...it will be a pick-'em game...no one would be favored. So, what if I guarantee you ten million dollars if we win?"

Berker was puzzled, but felt a jolt of excitement from the show of strength by Gaetano. Finally, he had found a challenger with an ego as brave as his. It made him feel powerful that a man of this machismo would pay him $10 million for a chance to win the game. His empire was so powerful that he had made Gaetano surrender part of his fortune to be free of his terror. "My friend, I understand your dilemma about obtaining your championship, but it will be impossible for you to win. But as a businessman, this money can be insurance to secure my investment." He became more focused on this man before him, someone of great standing asking for his help. It honored him to feel so important. "What do you gain by winning this game and guaranteeing this money?"

"I ask for two things, Berker: First, no more contact, or as you say, 'business between us or my family or my friends.' I will become free and clear of you. On this I will need your word." Guy paused for effect as he tried to emphasize appealing to his honor. He knew that Berker would eat that shit up. "And second, you will return Anna's gun to me! That would only be fair, considering she died in the line of duty. I don't want her name tarnished because she lost her gun." This was a delicate play, a bit dramatic, but he thought it should do the trick.

Berker thought quickly about his response, his next play for checkmate, as he laughed inside about the foolish demands. What would be the downside for him? Ending their relationship was a joke; it meant nothing to him. It had been a challenging game, but now he had won, so he would move on to the next challenge. As for the gun, it was a needless prize for a necessary murder. He had no use for it. But overall, nothing would change, because he would not have to pay up-Gaetano Finelli had no chance to win the game.

After a few more seconds of pondering, the strange intimacy Berker had felt a minute ago solidified into a feeling of a dominant achievement. A proud smile came to his face as he put his hand forward to shake on it. "I think we can work out a deal...my friend!"

In the next thirty minutes, Berker and Gaetano worked out a complicated agreement to exchange the gun and the $10 million as tea was served. It would happen the Monday morning after M2C2-1. There was no discussion about the wager or the tactics that Berker would use "to ensure," as he put it, a Potomacs loss.

On the ride back to Bethesda, Guy was unhooded and untied as they reached the Baltimore Beltway at the Catonsville exit. He thought that his strategy was just foolish enough, emotionally deceiving, and egotistically supportive to Berker that for him to just give up a gun would seem an overwhelming victory. Guy knew that giving up $10 million just to win a game and get his girlfriend's gun back played into Berker's huge male ego.

For his part, Berker was positive that the gun could not be connected to him in any way. As far as he was concerned, it was quietly held and cleaned by a well-paid friend over the big bay, far, far away. Little did he know that the FBI had connected him to the gun by the greatest of luck.

Guy's father, Phillip, had always taught him to think paradoxically when facing an unusual opponent. Direct reasoning does not work on proud, narcissistic men. Guy had met quite a few on the football field and had always figured out the edge to beat them. As far as he was concerned, Berker "the Turk" Assante was just another complicated opponent.

Guy had a plan, but he needed some help from his friend Brooklyn O'Malley. They decided to meet on a quiet street in Oakview, which was about halfway between Bethesda and Beltsville. Guy backed into the end of East Light, just in front of the sound barrier to the beltway. Brooks had parked on the other side of the creek and walked across the bridge to get into Guy's car. "I think you're watching too many detective shows. What is all the covert action? Oh, by the way...congratulations on the big victory. Don't you ever get tired of making big plays?"

"Thank you, thank you...well, it was just plain fun, doing what I love to do. Lots of tackling, got to run and throw the football, and I finally got to really lay a hard tackle on Walton's ribs after all these years of chasing him around."

"That was more than a hard tackle; it was like diving into the pool from fifty feet high and hitting him with a butterfly stroke."

"Thanks for noticing-that was my best stroke years ago."

"Years ago, shit...you're only twenty-five!"

"Well, sometimes it feels like several lifetimes."

"I hear you, my friend. Well, what can I do for you?"

Guy turned up the volume on the car radio as he heard the familiar chords from Lee Michael's organ. He had borrowed the car from his new friend Bob Volkman, the manager at his condo, to avoid being followed. It was tuned to the XM Seventies channel, and Guy could not help himself when the great song came on. Luckily, Brooks recognized it as well and patiently waited out the interlude. He did love listening to the song as he thought of driving his '67 Mustang with Phillip, each with girlfriends next to them.

"Do You Know What I Mean?" began with a plea: Been forty days since I don't know when I just saw her with my best friend Do you know what mean?
Lord... Do you know, know what I mean?

Guy turned down the music. "In two weeks, I'm going to have the gun that killed Anna!" After a few moments, he turned it up the volume again.

You haven't noticed that I held back my tears and now you have, but it's really too late Better find yourself another girl Better find another girl Better find uh, another place.

Brooks knew that Guy was not usually a jokester, so he waited patiently for the punch line. After listening to another verse, he turned down the music and finally asked, "What the hell are you talking about?"

"I'm talking about delivering the murder weapon to you."

"And how is that going to happen?"

"You would rather not know, but whatever surveillance or information you have on this guy, be ready to take him down the morning after the championship contest." Guy turned up the sound for the great ending of the song, feeling Lee Michaels's lyrics, stroking the emotion of losing his woman. It always made Guy surrender to his emotions. He was lost in his past as he heard Lee Michaels end with his final plea: "Hoooo...help me."

Being probative in nature, Brooks found it difficult to not ask any questions. He looked at Guy, lost in a song, who was a boy of seventeen when they first met. He wanted to trust that it was worth the gamble to set up the operation to take down the Turk. If they got the gun, it would be over for him. Maybe it was time to roll the dice. At least he had two weeks to stake out everything. Christ...right in the middle of the greatest two weeks in Washington Baltimore sports. No matter what, though, he was going to watch the game. "Let me ask one question-am I supposed to cheer for the Macs or the Banners?"

"Well, that seems pretty obvious to me. I would make sure to bet a lot of money on the winner."

As they talked further about the details, Guy wanted to have his friend Mach returned from New Mexico to stay with him for the next two weeks. He needed him and his expertise with computers to make the exchange work. Brooks agreed and made arrangements to bring him back in the morning. Guy had a town house on MacArthur Boulevard, just northwest of Georgetown. No one except Patty knew about it. It was purchased under a corporate name, "The NC Group." Guy knew Mach would be safe there.

Chapter 45

AFTER RETURNING FROM his meeting in Baltimore, Guy was able to spend the rest of the week with his family and Patty. She was starting the third month of her pregnancy and feeling great. The reality of a coming baby gave Guy the reason to tell Patty he wanted a wedding over the weekend. "Listen, let's do it this weekend before all the craziness of the championship contest starts. I could talk Sally and Alex into hosting it, and we'll keep it simple and small."

Patty was speechless but wanted to know more. "Is there something I should be worried about? Or should I shut up and just agree?"

Guy grabbed her, lifted her onto the couch, and kissed her. He went down her chest to her slightly protruded stomach and kissed her tummy until she started laughing.

"OK, OK, I'm in. But is it just for the baby?"

"I want us to be together forever, and yes, I want us to get married for the baby as well."

"That sounds like a deal to me. So we're a team, right?" "Absolutely!"

Sally and Alex held a small, magnificent wedding party on Saturday night. A crowd of fifteen, including the three children and Father Higgins, who performed the ceremony, were in attendance. Privacy was asked of all those attending. Cousins, friends, and teammates would be told after the championship contest.

Patty looked lovely in her mother's wedding gown, flown in from Ohio, with her red hair shining like the sun on her shoulders. Little Annie was the flower girl in a green dress, followed by Phillip II and Philly II, the ring bearers.

Most of the night, Annie sat on Guy's or Patty's lap. Patty hoped the adoption would go through soon- she would become Annie's legal mom, and the new baby would have a sister.

• • •

In the depths of the right-wing blogosphere, Clark Battle, since his banishment from the *Gang of Four* years ago, had carved out a nice living with online subscriptions to his writing and video pieces about the crazy, liberal- dominated media world. He had put his nemesis, Guy Finelli, behind him and focused on politicians to bring down, like the popular president.

But lately, the rumors were swirling like tornadoes coming through his world. For years he had ignored reports of Finelli's drug exploits in New Mexico in 2014 and the reports of superhero events in Texas, Arkansas, and Tennessee on his drive home. There was once a grainy picture roaming the right-wing Internet of Guy Finelli in a bar catching a beer bottle as it headed for country singer Bobby Gentry. The next year, Gentry become a national sensation with his song "Stranger Things Have Happened" about a bar fight in Nashville that described how he escaped an unhappy crowd with the help of a stranger. The CD cover had a drawing of the escape, with the singer and his handsome smile, guitar in hand, running behind the bar. Only the back of a large body catching and deflecting beer bottles could be seen. By coincidence, Bobby Gentry was singing the national anthem at the M2C2-1 and happened to be a friend of Guy Finelli.

Now there was a rumor that his girlfriend was pregnant, and his daughter, whose mother might have been murdered, was almost six. There were more about wild times in Bethesda. First, some crazy old man of Syrian descent was found shouting in the lobby about being saved by a monster-sized runner behind his apartment building after he jumped from his balcony. Second, a bank robber was literally knocked out and almost paralyzed, supposedly by an un-athletic, overweight, sixty-year- old guy, who happened to manage Guy Finelli's condo building.

Battle knew it would be political suicide again with the lame-stream media, but the insanity of the article would attract new readers paying each month to get his blog. He decided to write the article anyway-it would cause media frenzy before the M2C2-1, and it was a good chance to get interviewed by Fox News, One America Network, and if he got lucky, CNN. Someday, Clark figured, something would stick to Guy Finelli. Take your pick-a drug user and seller, one child or maybe two out of wedlock, ignored GAF mandates for press conferences and fans, and the thing Battle could not stomach, his liberal championing of homosexuality. His friendship with Hank Harrison was probably sexual, and Battle wouldn't be surprised to hear rumors about him and the Baltimore drug lord again as well.

As he sat down at his computer, he wondered if he should make some calls about the Baltimore drug scene, even though all of his sources had gone cold for years. He realized he'd better stick to current rumors for now.

• • •

As Guy had predicted to the Turk, the game between Washington and Baltimore had landed on even money. Money from Richmond to Boston was pouring in to illegal bookies on the East Coast, as well as record-breaking amounts into legal gambling in Las Vegas. Oddsmakers had started Washington as a six-point favorite, which most football pundits agreed with, but the overwhelming amount of betting on Baltimore made the game even. Guy and Brooks O'Malley knew why, even though they had maintained radio silence between each other since their meeting last Monday. The Turk and possibly the whole East-Coast drug world were in on the scam that moved the spread back to even. Now it was the Tuesday before the M2C2-1, and the media day would start off the festivities.

Guy Finelli had decided to end his self-imposed boycott of the press and avoid the six-figure penalty. From the roof of the new World Space Stadium, the field looked tilted in one direction as Guy played host to over a thousand journalists for his media obligation. He sat comfortably in the third row of an end-zone seat, with some media around him but most of them below him on the field.

ESPN, Fox Sports, Local News Channel, CNN, CNBC, and even Al Jazeera were covering the reclusive football star live. The interior of the beautiful new World Space Stadium was the perfect venue for such a circus. The fake-grass field was the surface for all the thousands of media personnel walking around for interviews. It was used for all athletic events except for Potomacs games and other special events, which merited use of the perfectly manicured, real-grass field. The grass field was usually kept outside in a protected, temperature-controlled area that could be opened in perfect weather. When used, it was named the "RFK Memorial Field." It had been perfected from seed from the old stadium field and was a living tribute to Robert F. Kennedy.

The inner carbon-fiber roof was able to open in less than a minute, making it available to expose or seal the outside environment conveniently during games. The three decks of the ninety-five-thousand-seat stadium were higher on the sidelines and lower in the end zones, allowing for the outer roof line to appear like the curved RFK Stadium that it replaced. On each end zone was a large, continuous concrete deck just under the roof that could hold up to fifteen thousand SRO fans. Each had phenomenal views of DC behind it. In another tribute to RFK Stadium, the two lower end-zone levels were able to rock if most of the fans stomped and jumped.

Guy Finelli lay back to watch the inner roof open like the eye of a camera. It was hard to get enough of it. The sun was shining over his shoulder, as though he had ordered it, making it difficult for members of the media to see him without a glow around him.

279

Clark Battle's article had been flourishing on the Internet since Monday and influenced the first couple of questions.

"Guy, were you involved in any of the rescue attempts described in the Battle article?" Veteran DC reporter Pedro Carew shouted out the first questions among many.

Guy leaned forward and put up his hands. "Pedro, if this is important to you, I did meet my friend Bobby Gentry in a Nashville bar, before he was a star, and I did help him escape from a rowdy crowd." Guy smiled for a moment. "If I remember correctly, they didn't like his playlist."

"So, did you actually catch a beer bottle thrown at him and deflect a few others?" Pedro asked with determination.

"I'm a pretty big guy, Pedro, so it wouldn't be the first-time things were deflected by my body and something fell into my hands." Guy's grin expanded, and his eyes opened to full exposure. "Now, did I plan some kind of rescue for Bobby? No... I just thought he was a cool guy that could sing. So, we got out of there and hung out for a while. Have you ever been to Nashville, Pedro? Things like that happen all the time. It's really a fun place."

"Guy Finelli...Guy Finelli..." ESPN reporter and family friend Bonnie Bramlett was shouting through the throngs of media. Guy saw her, stood up, and pointed at her. "Guy, can you talk about your family? I know, being a family friend, how wonderful they are, and I think the public has too many rumors about your life that aren't correct. Would you like to set the record straight?"

Guy sat down as he felt the billion people around the world inch closer to their screens, dying to hear information about him. His stunned reaction to the question would wipe out any thoughts of Bonnie Bramlett being a Finelli family setup.

"I guess you're right...that is pretty important. I'm just getting used to the idea of being a celebrity. Now, I think of my brother, Alex, and his wife, Sally, as being celebrities, but me...well...I'm a pretty boring guy, Bonnie. I live in a condo in Bethesda. I run, I swim, I work out, I play football, and I eat burritos with hot sauce."

The crowd laughed with great relief as Guy leaned forward and dropped a bombshell. "I just got married over the weekend to Patty O'Neil, my girlfriend of several years. We are expecting a child in July."

The silence in the stadium stopped all interviews as Guy's face and voice was on the huge video screens in each end zone. "I have a beautiful five-year-old daughter named Annie, who lives with Alex and Sally, just a couple of blocks from me. I see her almost every day, and she has twin cousins just a year older that are like a brother and sister to her."

The media crowd was now whipped into a frenzy, shouting out questions about

Annie's mother. Guy put up his hands to calm the crowd.

"Yes... OK... I hear you." Guy put his hands through his hair and looked down for a moment. It seemed like the time to set the record straight without revealing any details. He owed that to Anna, and besides, he knew that Berker Assante was watching, and he needed to get the message. "Her mother died when Annie was born. She was a dear person, a mentor to me, heroic in many ways, someone who was very close to me." He hesitated for a moment. "To be honest...it took a while to get over her death. I was pretty young at the time. Now I know things will be taken care of about that chapter in my life. Winning a third championship contest in a row will be the crowning achievement for this team, to be the greatest team in one hundred years of professional football." Guy sat back as a billion people watching or listening took a deep breath. "Now, does anyone have any questions about how we're gonna beat Baltimore?"

Ron Roswell was sitting in a row in front of him, listening and taking notes. He was waiting for this nonsense about Guy's personal life to finish. With his head down and his right-hand scribbling, he lifted his left hand in the air.

Guy was relieved to see Ron's hand go up and called on him. "Yes, Ron Roswell-who I must confess is my father's favorite reporter from the *Washington Daily.* I hope you have a football question."

"Yes, I do, Mr. Finelli, but I am curious about one thing. Is "The Safety" just a football player for the Washington Potomacs, or is he really a superhero?"

"Well, Mr. Roswell, that sounds like a great title for one of your columns, but honestly, I have loved to play football ever since I was old enough to catch a football from my father. He taught me how to play and have fun. I stopped playing for a while in high school when it wasn't fun after Sean Taylor was murdered, but then Hank Harrison talked me into playing again. He's the best friend anyone could have. I got lucky to play with great coaches and players in high school, college, and now the pros. But really... I play football to have fun-being on the field, rolling in the grass, running, catching, tackling, being with great players. So when it gets to be not fun, maybe I'll consider being a superhero when I grow up!"

The press spent the next hour barking out questions like they were filling their plates at an all-you-can-eat seafood buffet, never knowing if they would ever get such a chance again. Talking football, like playing the game, came natural to Guy Finelli. His knowledge about offenses and defenses would surpass any player and most coaches in football. The history of the game, dating back to the first college game in 1869 and the first professional season in 1920, was also very important to him. During the press conference, he left enough quotes to be used for the hours of shows leading up to the M2C2-I. He made it clear that he was confident in a Potomacs win but did say that stopping the "Freeze" offense might be impossible. Guy remarked with great clarity, "We will have to throw out all of our defenses and come up with something new to stop the Banner offense. There is too much motion before the snap count, too much speed in wide receiver Russell Jones, too much arm in quarterback Rocky Falcone, and of course, there's Emmitt Excel." He smiled with such delight that it disarmed the press and sent them home satiated with irrelevant information about his private life but a great story about his abundant personality. "It will be nice to run into my former teammate again."

A GAF official stepped forward and called an end to the conference. Guy quickly hopped over several rows behind him and ran up the aisle, jumping over three steps at a time. Quickly, he found the exit to the back halls of the stadium and a cherished sanctuary from his hour-plus with the media. His charm and apparent honesty had sunk the Clark Battle story back to the bottom of the ocean once again.

It was now time to take care of his final preparations to take on his opponents. As for the Banners' high-powered offense, he knew exactly what his defense had to do to stop them, but it would take the best performance of his career to make it work. He would take over the middle of the field with a little help from Day and Night and some clearing out from Black and Blue. It meant almost being in three places at one time, something not out of the question for "The Safety."

· · ·

He drove home straight through DC, making it past Georgetown before rush hour, and headed up MacArthur Boulevard to his secret townhouse to meet with Mach. He drove around several blocks before heading through a maze of alleys to get to his garage behind his house and away from any possible tail.

Mach was staying very comfortably in the finished, windowless basement apartment that Guy had built to hide from the world. He had not left the five-hundred-square-foot basement since he had arrived with an FBI escort. When Guy walked in from the garage, he saw several computer screens set up in the living area that had several of Guy's accounts showing vast amounts of money.

Mach had spent several days setting up many steps and accounts to minimize the attention of divesting $10 million from Guy's investments, at least for a week or two. He needed to acquire $1 million in cash and another $9 million ready for a complex bank transaction.

"So, how is life working with the FBI for you and Farand?""

It is quite simple...really...our contact with people is limited, but we are very happy together, thanks to you, Guy, my friend." Mach's eyes were moist as he continued to type away, writing code on a black screen. Guy put his arm around his very thin shoulders.

"Well, hopefully your life will get back to normal pretty soon if we can get this plan to work."

"We will get the money to him, but this is a very dangerous man, Guy, as you know. You are foolish to do this, my friend." Mach turned away and walked into the bedroom. He was sitting on the bed with his glasses off, blowing his nose. When Guy walked in, he turned away and picked up his glasses to clean them.

"Mach, this is the right thing to do. We have him ... trust me. My role is the least dangerous part of it. The FBI will close this thing out. I am just getting the final piece of evidence to nail him."

"Yes, of course, my friend...and in the meantime, you will win this extraordinary third championship contest and bring a million dollars in cash to him and another..."

Guy held up his hands and stopped the argument with a big hug. Mach's tears rolled down Guy's shirt as his head barely made it to Guy's chest. "I know there is some danger, but it has to be done this way." Guy pulled away and held him at arm's length. "Winning the game will be a piece of cake," he added as he winked, "so stop complaining and get me some cash. Oh yeah, just make sure that the money transfer works."

Mach cracked a smile as he nodded, but he was still trembling when he said, "Thank you, my friend, but please be careful."

Chapter 46

THE NEW THIRTY-TWO-STORY Marriott Parker Hotel was the tallest building in DC, almost doubling the mandatory ceiling height of buildings throughout the city. The top two floors were occupied by a new world-class restaurant with panoramic views of DC. To the west, the US Capitol, the Mall, the Washington Monument, the World War II Memorial, the Reflecting Pool, and the Lincoln Memorial sat in a straight line. The hotel was built on reclaimed land from the Anacostia River just east of the new stadium, with the top two floors in a long, angled, oval shape like a spaceship just blasting out of stadium.

Looking north, upstream on the Anacostia, it felt like being in the middle of the river. In the east you could see the Chesapeake Bay through binoculars set up on the viewing decks. To the south was a majestic view of the Potomac River, the historic town of Alexandria, and the National Airport giving a daily show of jets landing and leaving.

Burton Parker built and owned the structure as a part of the development package he negotiated with the city. He was given an exemption to the ceiling height because he convinced the DC Council that the height of the new stadium would block most of it. He had not mentioned that the oval top could be seen from all around the beltway. No one complained after the completion of the two projects. It would become the twenty-first-century gateway look to the nation's capital and the jewel of the new 2024 Olympic Village being planned around it. By 2025, the village would be converted into condominiums, shopping, and a world-class golf course for the city.

The opening of the hotel had been coordinated with the WSS for the M2C2-1. But to Mr. Parker's delight, both projects were: finished well before Thanksgiving, with the hotel providing accommodations through the holidays and the stadium giving daily tours.

Burton Parker held back the opening of the restaurant for the night before the championship contest, counting on his team making it to M2C2-1 to be first to use it. He had reserved the top ten floors of the hotel for the same purpose, including team employees and special friends.

Walking into the restaurant for the first time, players and coaches were stunned by the luxury and the omnipresent views. They immediately felt special to be the first group to see the nation's capital from such a vantage point. It felt heavenly and gave certain team members the feeling of being a team of destiny.

The defense sat at three tables thrown together, with three guests from the offense: Hank Harrison, Amos Enos, and Albert Christian.

The main course of rock: fish stuffed with crabmeat was surrounded by asparagus and mashed sweet potatoes. The days of steak and fries at pregame meals had come and gone.

Guy Finelli had snuck in two small boxes under his seat. Just before the main dish was served, he opened them up and passed out two dozen, twelve-ounce bottles of Don Shula's Hot Sauce to every player at his table. He'd had them specially made with extra-hot peppers just for this meal. Each one had the player's name on the bottle.

"I want to make a toast...to the offense, minus my three special friends that I kidnapped for my table, you need to eat your meals and sleep well for tomorrow, because you will play a flawless game. But my boys over at this table will play with extra-crazy power from my special hot sauce that I had custom-made for them. As you all know, I am "The Safety," and I have superpowers!" The room of players erupted with laughter and applause.

Marcus McNeil III stood up and raised his glass to silence the hooting and hollering. "Well, well, let the defense and the three traitors have their special hot sauce from the great Guy Finelli." Mac III then put two boxes of his own on the table and pulled out a jar of cocktail sauce.

"Back in Texas, we eat a lot of shrimp, crab, and fish. This special cocktail sauce has been in my family for a century. Now, it ain't hot like that killer stuff, Mr. Finelli is making you fools tear up you-all's insides with, but it is sweet, and for damn sure it's sssspicy!" The offense banged the table in agreement like hungry gladiators. "Now, the defense may play with fire in their stomachs, but we on offense like to score with a lot of sssspice!"

The special chef and serving crew, brought in from NYC just for this occasion by Burton Parker, served the main meal to the offense and the defense. The Middle Eastern-looking crew and their chef noticed the defense table using their little bottles of hot sauce over the gourmet food and wondered how these American football players could ruin such a special meal.

• • •

The pregame pageantry for the M2C2-1 included the opening of the roof to see a flyover of four stealth bombers, followed by a single F-35 jet fighter that stopped in midair over the stadium, spun around to face the opposite direction, fired his engines like a dragster, and, in the blink of an eye, disappeared into the night. A parachutist then timed his descent into the stadium as the roof was closing, using a blue parachute adorned with fifty stars and dressed in red-and-white stripes as country star Bobby Gentry sang the National Anthem.

The teams gathered around their head coaches for one final pep talk. For the Banners, head coach Neville Chambers was fiery, spitting out f-bombs every other word as his eyes bulged out from their sockets. "This is it... there is no tomorrow...no second place...bring it home to Baltimore!"

Coach Gerry Williams had been here before and trusted his players to be motivated. He was emotional but calm, like a father shipping his son off to college. "Remember, this is just a game. Play it like you did as a kid; fly around; have fun; be creative. The sun will come up no matter how this turns out." He paused for a moment and looked at the circle of players huddled around him for the last time as a professional coach. He felt a rush of happiness and accomplishment that forced him to crack a smile. "But just remember one thing...it will be one hell of a party if we win this fucking thing!"

The team broke from the huge huddle and split into offense and defense groups. Coach Furrey Favarro had some choice words for his defense. They had worked on a special alignment to force Baltimore to throw and run up the middle. The middle linebacker was replaced with a third safety, who, along with Mark Pelligrini, would play deep outside coverage. Comers Collins and Hall would bump receivers off the line of scrimmage, sometimes pinching inside to hit the men in motion and stay short on most patterns. The four linemen and the two outside linebackers were going to rush almost every play, forcing quick throws or knocking down passes, and of course, when possible, sack or knock down Rocky Falcone.

The middle of the field would be left to Guy Finelli. At times it would appear to be wide open, but Finelli would be at two or three places at one time, or at least he would appear to be. They expected some big plays against them early in the game, but they expected Guy Finelli to guess correctly on most plays, causing some fumbles and interceptions for the defense.

Coach Favarro spoke calmly. "It will take some discipline to stay with our game plan, but it will pay off in the long run. We'll make adjustments at halftime, but the constant blitzing will wear them down, slow down their motion, making them cautious. That's when we'll get some big plays.[11] He turned to Guy and said, "You got a lot of room to cover, but stay with your instinct, be aggressive, make them pay for each run or completion."

Coach Joe Finelli stepped in the middle of the circle, still big enough and mean enough to compete on the field with his players. *"Remember, we play tough football."* He

286

looked around, seeing heads nodding. "If we *bloody* their noses, they'll be *crying* on the sidelines, *asking* for tissues, *scared* to come back into play."

Players were smiling now, still nodding, and now clapping.

"*Remember,* on each and every play, we have to beat them up, to dominate our man, to get to the middle and back up Guy, whenever possible. *Remember,* you should be dog-tired after every play, but we'll *have* two months to rest."

The players were now answering with "Yeahs" and "All rights."

Joe paused to let the players get louder, but he boomed his voice to be heard. "*Remember,* we *have* been here before."

"That's right." "Oh yeah."

"Right on, Coach."

"*Remember,* this is *our* turf, *our* stadium, *our* city." "Hell yeah... *our* city... *our* turf... *our* home."

"And *remember...we are the champions!*"

Guy Finelli and Marcus McNeil III walked out to the center of the field as the Potomac captains to meet the Banners captains: Rocky Falcone, the veteran QB, and linebacker Eadgar Engauge, a fan favorite with a French rugby background, nicknamed "Picard" by his teammates. The record crowd of 132,000 was already in peak cheering form, exchanging chants-"Bal-ti-more Ban-ners, clap, clap, clap" and "Po-to-macs...*rock* ... *Day* and Night"-from one shaking and packed end zone to the other.

This was not your normal "just get in your seats before kickoff" championship contest. It was a war. On one side were the blue-collar baby boomers that had survived the Colts' loss in 1984 and the professional, millennial Banner babies. On the other were the lifetime DC-area residents, both black and white, and the DC power elite, all with the expectation of championships in their blood, pumping as one big heart.

Falcone and Eadgar exchanged man hugs and "good lucks" with Marcus, but Finelli silently shook hands with both Banner captains, keeping them from any further contact with his forearm and stopping them in their tracks. Marcus called "heads" as the one-hundredth- anniversary coin was flipped, and the Potomacs won the toss. Guy turned quickly without shaking hands and returned to the sidelines. About halfway back to the sidelines, Mac III stopped and bent over while holding his stomach. It was just a moment, but when he returned to the sidelines, he blew his lunch while the offense gathered around him. His skin lacked its normal, healthy, dark- brown color when he stood up, but he just tried to shrug it off as anxiety. "I guess I'm more nervous than I thought."

The offense took the field as the kickoff flew through the laser uprights and out of the end zone. Amos Enos took the first carry and ran around blocks from Albert Christian and Hank Harrison for fifteen yards and a first down. From the shotgun, Mac III was sharp as he hit Harrison on a seam rout over Engauge into Banner territory. Hank felt an extra knee up his ass on the tackle and a "Feel good?" from the Banner linebacker. As Harrison fired the ball at Engauge's face, he responded with, "That feels even better!"

Within seconds, Eadgar was plowing Hank into the ground, followed by Albert Christian and Amos Enos lifting him off and holding him down with their knees on his throat. Banner players pushed Hank away as the officials arrived a little late to the melee. No penalties were thrown, and both players made it back to their huddles, with Eadgar rubbing his throat and Hank pulling his pants out of his crack.

Mac III ran the zone-read option and gave to Amos, who bolted over Eadgar down to the Banner thirty-five.

Next snap, Mac III faked the zone-read and fired again to Hank Harrison to the twenty for another first down. Macs fans in the end zone were shaking their whole section as a score seemed certain. Mac III took the next snap from the shotgun, ran around right end, and made a great cut back to the fifteen and then the ten. Suddenly, he was blindsided by Eadgar Engauge, who knocked him sideways like a rag doll. The football came free and bounced to Engauge as he rolled off his target. The Frenchman got up after being tackled and headed to the sidelines, holding up the football to the crowd and yelling like a macho man, "See what came out of his ass!"

Mac III was on his feet in a hurry but then felt wobbly as he gasped for air. His stomach was rumbling like a volcano ready to explode as he made it to the bench. Mac III and every offensive player were bent over on the bench, holding their stomachs. Only Harrison, Enos, and Christian were standing on the sidelines, watching the Banners head down the field with their high-powered offense. Behind them, it looked like a scene from a frat party after a night of drinking.

The Banners took the lead on a deep post thrown by Rocky Falcone to Russell Jones down the middle of the field over the outstretched arms of Guy Finelli. It was a spectacular catch, followed by a run by Emmit Excel for the conversion to make it 8-0.

As the offense finished losing their lunch and breakfast, Mac III picked up his helmet and commanded his offense to follow him out to the field. Reluctantly, they followed.

Amos Enos ran into a host of Banners in the backfield on first down. Mac III was sacked on second down. On third down, he found Hank Harrison downfield for a first down. Then Amos Enos broke outside and ran for twenty yards over midfield for another first down.

Mac III jogged up field, feeling almost delirious as he made it to the huddle and heard the next play in his helmet. It was a quick screen to the left side. He came to the scrimmage and barely remembered the play. In the shotgun, he caught the snap from center, quickly spun right, and threw toward a target, but it lacked the blue, gold, and burgundy jersey. Instead, a defensive back wearing a white jersey with blue numbers and playing in a short zone who had shrugged his man came up and picked it off against no one. It was an easy TD, highlighted by a backward somersault into the end zone without a Potomac within thirty yards of him. A pass to Excel out of the backfield for the extra point made it 15-0.

Coach Gary Williams huddled with his offensive players. They were a sorry-looking group, with most of them on one knee ready to keel over. Six of the starters were already in the locker room getting IVs to replace fluids. Mac III was looking straight down at the ground as Coach Williams asked him if he could go back in. He put on his helmet for the last time and headed toward the field, but before he took ten steps, he fell down and was taken to the locker room.

The backup QB was already in the locker room, and by now, there were just barely enough players left for the offense as Guy Finelli took over as QB. The hot-sauce crew of Harrison, Enos, and Christian looked fired up and ready to continue playing. Only some backup offensive linemen were left to be on the field along with the Sprint offense.

Surprisingly, all the coaches seemed to be free of the stomach pain-possibly distracted by the frenzy of trying to figure how to fix this disaster.

Finelli's first series as QB went nowhere. The snap went high on first down and trickled back on the ground on second down. Two handoffs to Amos Enos were awkward and slow developing. The blocking seemed comical as assignments were missed. On third down, the rush descended on Finelli like a surging flow of lava, and only a great effort got him back to the line of scrimmage. Guy's punt on fourth down went too high in the air and faded like a bad golf drive, traveling only twenty yards downfield but thirty yards out-of-bounds.

The Banners took over on the Potomacs' forty-three and quickly ran a screen pass to Excel for twenty yards, and then Jackson sliced a post-flag pattern between Mark Pelligrini and Duran Hall for another touchdown. Falcone passed for the extra point, making it 22-0 late in the first quarter.

Besides losing most of the moving parts for the offense, the special teams were missing pieces as well. Coach Joe Finelli assembled a patchwork unit for the impending kickoff return. He followed his unit onto the middle of the field as if they were at a practice, yelling instructions on positioning and blocking assignments. As he rushed to get off the playing field and turned around on the sidelines, he saw the Banners go into an onside kick formation. Before he could call a time-out, the ball was topped and rolled perfectly past the forty-yard line to an inattentive Potomac front line running away to set up blocking. The timely strategy by the Banner coaches gave them a recovery near midfield.

The defense had been victimized for two TDs but finally made three stops for no gain on this series. But the Banners took advantage and kicked a 57 yard field goal through the laser-lights extending up from the goal line to extend the lead to 25-0 at the end of the first quarter.

In the three minutes between the first and second quarters, the team doctor reported to Coach Williams that every offensive player except for the "Hot-Sauce Trio" was now dealing with severe food poisoning and could not function on the football field. Coach Williams gathered Guy Finelli and Coach Favarro and asked who could play offense from the defense.

"Let's move Albert Christian from tackle to center; he snaps on special teams and knows all the calls. Guy can work out the snap calls with him even if he can't hear a thing. Black and Blue can play the tackles, while Day and Night can play the guards. Hank's at tight end, Amos at running back with Cary, and Duran and Mark at the wide receiver spots. Remember, Cary is big enough to play some tight end if necessary." Coach Favarro reported the facts of the situation without showing any emotion.

Coach Williams stared for a few moments after receiving the assessment and turned to Finelli. "Guy, you need to run some of your plays that you do with these guys when you play seven-on-seven against the offense at the end of practice. Otherwise, run the Sprint offense package whenever possible. The best thing you can do is make it a street game, like a chaotic battle. You may not have much time to run real plays unless you can get them to back off. They'll be sending blitzes until you burn them once or twice. We don't have time to go over the blocking schemes until halftime, so be careful with the ball."

"Don't worry, Coach; it will be the 'pick-a-man' blocking. You know, hit whoever's in front of you." Guy was almost giddy at the challenge. He thought of the Turk, who was already so proud of himself for pulling the most outrageous act of game-fixing for a football game in history. He was not going to make it easy for that son of a bitch to win the chess match.

"Listen, Coach, the roof's open, the sky is awesome, the weather is perfect for football, and these guys are in shape to play all night. They'll love it, and they're ready to crack some heads."

"Well, just get us to halftime not any worse off; we'll tighten things up with adjustments and some tricks up my sleeve." Coach Williams smiled, realizing he was in now a backyard brawl, his kind of football game. He remembered to send his favorite and best player one more message. "Hey, Finelli, this game ain't over yet!"

"No shit, sir!"

The second quarter was a battle of pure masculinity. The Potomac offensive line seemed more intent on beating the shit out of the Banners' defensive linemen on blocks than moving the football. They were like kids in a candy store, coming back to the huddle boasting about their latest takedown. Guy tried to settle things down with a basic running attack from the shotgun formation. Either Amos Enos would grind out tough yardage behind his line of Black, Day, Christian, Night, and Blue, or he would cut outside if Harrison and Collins sealed the defensive ends. Guy scrambled effectively for good yardage, running over tacklers like they were little children. Together they gained 120 yards rushing on three drives in the second quarter, but they had no TDs to show for it. Two drives were stopped on fumbles and one on downs because their field- goal kicker was a backup tight end on offense and was still puking his guts out in the locker room.

One of the fumbles by Amos Enos was returned for a TD, and the Banners scored on a horrendous pass interference call on a Hail-Mary play at the end of the half. The ball was placed on the one-yard line for one more play. Unbelievably, they ran a reverse by Russell Jones for the TD. The passing extra point made the halftime score 39-0.

As the undermanned Potomacs headed to the locker room after the stunning ending to the first half, they held their heads high, knowing they had outplayed and outmuscled their counterparts in the second quarter, even though they had nothing to show for it. Without saying a word to each other, they knew that the second half would be different. The odds of winning were infinitesimal, but the Banners were going to pay a price with their bodies to wrestle the Thorpe Trophy away from the defending champions.

The halftime show was introduced by the popular president of the United States. She received a long-standing ovation from the fans, who were thanking her for saving organized American football in the world. Since she was running for reelection in the fall, her appearance for some pundits was controversial, but most Americans agreed that it was appropriate for the president to make an appearance at the first Mars Mission Championship Contest (M2C2-1) in Washington, DC. Her remarks were brief as the stage for the musical talent was being assembled.

Finally, the scene was set for the group that had taken over American music with four number-one albums since 2016. Apparent Boarders had three girls and four guys hailing from North Korea, Seattle, LA, New Orleans, NYC, Atlanta, and Nashville. They had met in Austin in 2012 and formed a sound that combined Asian techno beats with country music-type harmonies and soulful rock melodies. You could sing to it, dance to it, get stoned to it, or just sit back and listen to the emotion of the lyrics. It took popular music by storm with twenty-five top-ten singles. Baby boomers, Gen Xers, millennials, and Zero- Gens were all drawn to the inclusive music. Topics from immigration and human rights to love and joyful dancing were all a part of their message. Their latest single, "From Earth to Mars," seemed appropriate to start off the concert. The two-decade race to our sister planet seemed to be off to a great start.

In the Potomacs' locker room, Coach Williams and the offense had streamlined twelve plays that they could run without a huddle. Guy Finelli had hand signals for six additional pattern changes for his three receivers. They organized three running, extra-point plays, which were mainly controlled scrambles for Finelli to score with his feet. Their strategy was to score five TDs and make five running extra points to get to forty points. If they could score on defense or punt returns, that would be a bonus.

On defense, Coach Favarro knew he had the "Freeze" offense figured out. Their physical play had knocked the intricate offense off its skates. In other words, the smoothness and flow was gone from their patterns and motion. They had turned the hesitation that the "Freeze" was supposed to put on the defense into their heads on offense. Guy Finelli would continue to be the main factor on defense. He had successfully clogged the middle in the second quarter. The rush from Black, Blue, Day, and Night had taken the deep pass away from the Banner offense.

Special teams coach Joe Finelli was only concerned with punt returns. There would be no kickoffs in the second half from the Banners. If there were, the game was over. He stressed to his team to get no penalties on the returns and to just get good field position after each punt return. They needed five possessions to score and maybe a sixth to win, if they got that far.

Field goals were out of the question for two reasons: they had no one very competent to kick, and they needed TDs. Guy had the best leg on the team but only kicked in the old-fashioned, straight-on style in practice for fun at times. That style had not been seen in football in thirty-five years.

Guy would punt if necessary. Joe went over the "Rouge" scoring just for clarification. In the GAF, a team was awarded a Rouge (one point) if they did not return a kick that stayed in the end zone, caught or downed by the defense. Punts or kickoffs that went out of the end zone were not Rouge-worthy. Being down by thirty-nine points, it seemed a bit extravagant to be concerned about how one point could be scored. But the coaching staff was confident that the Macs would make this game competitive. Meanwhile, the rest of the world believed the game to be over, but they stayed tuned to their giant televisions to watch the Apparent Boarders concert. The volume was turned down on most sets after halftime as the partying took over most venues. Eating and getting drunk or stoned became the main priorities. Most Banners fans left their seats and partied in the massive decks of the stadium with great views of DC, unconcerned with the score of the game. Only the Macs fans seemed interested in how their decimated team would start the third quarter. They found out in a hurry.

The Potomacs had only twenty-two players able to play the second half-three from the offense and nineteen from the defense. Of the coaching staff, only Coaches Williams, Favarro, and Finelli were left. The rest had fallen to the food poisoning. Those three had been too nervous with game preparation to eat at the team dinner and had left early. They had forced their assistants to stay and enjoy themselves.

Coach Favarro's strategy on offense was to play his first team defense for the first three plays on each possession. If the Banners made a first down, the linemen would be rotated out, and then the corners after six plays. Luckily, the defense played only nine plays in the third quarter, stopping the "Freeze" offense each time. There were three sacks, three running plays for loss, and three incompletions.

The Potomacs Radio Network summed up the third quarter of play as the Macs had the football for their third drive of the second half. "Ladies and gentlemen, for those of you just turning on the radio or coming back to check on the score of the game, or for most of you with us the entire game, here it is: the Potomacs are the best team in football. They have shut down the famous Freeze offense cold as a glacier. More importantly, quarterback Guy Finelli-yes, I said quarterback-will not be stopped as the Banner defense is looking beaten and bruised, trying to tackle him and Amos Enos. He has not thrown a pass yet this half, as they have powered over and through this defense for two scores and are about to score again as we come close to ending the third quarter.

"Pardon me, fans, for my enthusiasm, but a time- out was called by the Banners after Guy Finelli ran up the middle for forty-four yards to the Banner twenty- three-yard line on the last play. It looked like an old-time maul-ball game. Finelli seems possessed, running with the football, punishing players as they try to get ahold of him. His line, now centered by three-hundred-twenty-five- pound Albert Christian and flanked by guards Horace Day and Clarence Night and tackles Chester Blue and Braxton Black, have been terrorizing the Banner front seven, like they were rushing the passer. I'm not sure they would know how to pass block-except for Albert, of course. You may want to ask, why are these defensive players blocking and running on offense? Two words: food poisoning!"

After a splendid recap, Gilbert Herzog Martin, better known as Gil, took a moment to drink in the scene from his booth, high above the playing field. His thirty-seven years broadcasting Washington football would come to an end after this final game. He was an icon to fans in the DC area, having broadcasted every winning Washington

293

championship since 1982. At age seventy-eight, with fifty-five years of broadcasting football on the college and professional levels, he had seen it all. Or so he thought, as he readied himself to broadcast the last quarter of his career.

"Here we go, ten seconds left in the third quarter. First down on the Banner twenty-three, and Banner fans are finally back in their seats, starting to make noise from their end zone. The Mac fans have been on their feet the whole quarter, yelling their hearts out...Finelli is in shotgun, a fake to Enos on the option...heading right... no, no, he steps back in the pocket...looking to throw...for the first time. Cary Collins is wide open over the middle... Finelli throws...holy Mother of God! He's walking in with the score... keep saying your prayers, folks; we have a ballgame!"

The fourth quarter started with a Potomacs kickoff, featuring Guy Finelli kicking straight ahead with his toe. Now in his fourth kickoff, his leg was finally making solid contact as he bombed it down to the goal line. The Banner players looked passive as they tried to form a blocking unit for a return. The Macs kick coverage took little time surrounding the kick returner like a SWAT unit, arresting him as he reached the fifteen-yard line. The Macs end zone of fans were abusing their rows like seesaws, flying up and down and screaming at top decibels as the Banners tried to run their offense.

Baltimore had run nine plays in the third quarter, gaining a negative six yards of offense. Coach Neville Chambers tried to change the momentum of the last three drives by shelving the motion of the famous "Freeze" offense, coming out in two tight ends with QB Rocky Falcone behind the center and Emmitt Excel in the "I" formation to reassert some domination over the Macs front four.

It turned out to be feeding meat to caged lions. Tackles Black and Blue hardly gave Emmitt time to receive the handoff on first and second downs, together meeting the star running back five yards deep in the backfield. On third and twenty, Falcone tried play-action with a fake to Excel and set up to go across the middle to Russell Jones for a first down. Unfortunately, Day and Night flashed before his eyes and put him down for a brief nap in his own end zone for a safety.

Horace Day asked his fellow sack mate if Falcone was still breathing as he eyed his victim, face down on the ground. "Hey, Night...is that Italian still suckin' in that oxygen?"

"Oh, Day... I just don't see no breathin' there...oh, maybe a little bit...yeah, he movin'...oh yeah, he movin'. We better do better next time!"

As they ran off the field laughing and celebrating, Day said, "Hey, Night...guess what...we get to play 'dat o-fence' again!"

"All day and all of the night!"

"Yes, we are ... my brother...now, let's show them how to block on offense and kick some ass."

"I feel you, Night...let's protect *our* Italian!"

Gil Martin, a devout Catholic, had the rosary out, seeing the possibility of a miracle comeback happening. "Mr. Everything, Guy Finelli, will receive the free kick after the safety. It will be a punt...high into the open sky and deep. Finelli at the twenty...straight ahead to the thirty... sidesteps a Banner to the thirty-five, cuts left to the sidelines...there are some blockers...up to the forty, forty- five... cuts inside, bowls over a defender to midfield. Hit at the forty-five...but spins away...hit again and keeps his feet to the forty...caught from behind by two Banners, and finally, Finelli falls at the thirty-six-yard line. What a forty-four-yard return...my friends, you may not believe this, but I did not see Jim Thorpe run the football. But my Lord, I have seen a lot of football, and ladies and gentlemen, this is something I can barely describe."

Gil Martin collected himself during the television time-out, quietly working the beads on the rosary. "Now Finelli continues...how much longer can he do this, folks? He's in shotgun...the handoff to Amos Enos...no, another fake... he fires to Harrison across the thirty inside the twenty-five for a first down. Hank was wide open in front of the safety...Finelli quickly gets to the line. Now behind the massive center, Albert Christian, calling an audible to Hall on the right side, he fakes again to Enos and runs right, bulls over the linebacker like a weak sampling, stiff-arms the corner back, and goes out-of- bounds at the thirteen-yard line. He's unstoppable, fans... unstoppable! Walking slowly back to the huddle, Finelli looks exhausted, surrounded by his linemen, Christian, Day, Night, Black, and Blue... Harrison takes him by the shoulders, holding up his helmet, patting him on the back. This is like a prize fighter, knowing he needs a knockout to win, never giving up. Do they have enough left in the tanks, fans? I'm staying to watch, my friends. I can't take my eyes away from it. Stay with me, fans; nobody's leaving this beautiful stadium. The Potomac fans are standing and stomping with encouragement. The Macs break the huddle, and Finelli is deep in the shotgun back on the twenty-five. Takes the snap from Christian, good protection, looking to throw...waiting, waiting...out of the backfield, it's Pelligrini open at the ten ...to the five and dives to the two. First and goal! They run to the line, Finelli quickly behind center, calling a play with Banner fans screaming in his face from the end zone. He steps to the right and to the left, screaming the play. Baltimore's defense jumping up and down the scrimmage line, now Enos in motion to the right, empty backfield, Finelli stands to throw, fakes to Enos, and turns left to run, Harrison and Black in front of him, knocking over defenders...he walks in for the TD... Finelli scores...the Macs are within seven, thirty-nine to thirty-two! Holy Mary of God... folks...I need to sit down."

The Potomacs missed their first extra-point conversion as Amos Enos was stopped on the one-inch line on a two- point try. They still needed a TD and an extra-point pass to tie, a run to win. On the sidelines, Coach Brown looked at the clock with ten minutes to go in the game and then at his players sitting on the bench-dead tired after the last TD celebration. He would have to play his second-team defense on the next series and hope for a miracle.

Finelli boomed the next kickoff out of the end zone. He was really getting this kickoff thing down. His cousin Joe was his tutor, giving him tips on the sideline after every kick. He remembered his dad kicking to him straight on as well. For years he had tried soccer-style kicking and just could not do it, but straight-on kicking seemed easy to him. Even drop-kicking like during the old days was a fun challenge. He would do laps after practicing with his dad, run with the football, and then drop-kick it and chase after it.

The Banner offense finally found some success against the second-team defense and moved into Mac territory with five minutes to go in the game. Coach Brown used a time-out to rally his troops. His first defensive line of Black, Blue, Day, and Night looked ready to play, along with Collins, Hall, and Pelligrini. They would join Finelli, who had stayed in the game and looked like a soldier on the front line of a long battle.

The Banners had caught a rhythm on offense as Falcone sat in the shotgun against the Mac defense. Coach Favarro had called an all-out blitz, like the Seattle game, but it was mistake. Falcone stepped away from the pressure and flung a deep pass downfield. Russell Jones had run by Finelli after a fake turn-in pattern at ten yards, caught the ball on the ten-yard line, and coasted into the endzone for the TD. But Finelli looked back at the video as he walked back up-field and saw the flag. He smiled with delight and clapped as he heard "offensive holding." Jones flipped him the ball as he headed past him. "You know I got you on that play, Mr. Safety!"

"What play was that, Russell?" asked Guy as he carried the ball back to the referee, who announced, "First and twenty."

The defense kept up the blitzing without Collins and Hall, who covered the wide-outs. Blue knocked down a pass on first down. Finelli came up to make the tackle on a draw play for a loss on second down. On third down, Day and then Night broke through the middle of the Banner protection and crashed into Falcone like a tornado touching down.

Baltimore punted on fourth and twenty-seven from their own forty-three. Finelli stood on his own fifteen and watched as the punt boomed over his head, seemingly out of the stadium, but it landed in the end zone, eleven yards deep, jumped backward, spun around, and rolled to the back of the end zone before stopping an inch before the end line. Finelli's stomach felt sick as he watched the football in horror and scrambled back to pick it up in a U- shaped route. He efficiently scooped up the football while trying to keep up his speed as he headed out of the end zone. As he turned up-field, he saw a half-dozen Banners crossing the goal line to surround him. He accelerated straight up the middle, but three linebackers met him like a brick wall, reinforced with almost a half-ton of linemen just behind them. Guy realized that he had no chance to escape the end zone and would pay a price for it, as the linebackers grappled him to the ground, surreptitiously landing punches to his ribs and groin. The trio of linemen piled on top of them as icing to the Finelli cake.

It was the first Rouge ever scored in a championship contest, and for the Macs a very costly one. The single point for the Banners increased their lead to 40- 32 with less than four minutes to go in the game.

The eleven Macs stood anxiously around their own ten-yard line, waiting for the last major three-minute television time-out run its course. At $15 million in advertising revenue, the major corporations were getting their money's worth-the buzz on the Internet about the Macs comeback had brought almost two billion people to television screens all over the world.

Guy Finelli was on one knee in the huddle, picking out grass from the field to clear an area for his finger to draw a play in the dirt. Hank Harrison was kneeling next to him, listening to his voice, which was almost reduced to a whisper from barking signals on offense and defense since the first quarter.

"OK, Hank, we got the quick out and up the seam over the linebacker or the turn-in off it in front of the safety if the backer blitzes or clears out...but I want you to run the split off a fake turn-in after we set it up. Can you cut like that without tearing your knee up?"

"Could Jerry Smith do it?" "You betcha!"

"Did you just think of that in the dirt?"

"Kinda...their safety has been inching up all day, really pissing me off. Thinks he's some hot shit over there..."

"Oh, you mean...like you?"

Guy had enough energy for a smile as the referee's whistle started the play clock. "Don't worry, Guy; we all know you're the man, or pardon me, The Safety," Hank laughed as the nine others in the huddle intently focused on their leader.

He called six plays, which they ran flawlessly to get to midfield with less than three minutes left and counting- two runs by Amos Enos, two scrambles by Guy Finelli, and two passes to Hank Harrison, the second being a turn-in in front of the safety.

"I got him in my back pocket, if we want the split," Hank reported as they huddled for the first time on the drive.

"Gotcha...we need at least twenty yards to run the split, so let's go, backs out, and then an out to the thirty to Cary if we need it. Then huddle at the two-minute warning."

Gil Martin was trying to broadcast with the volume at the stadium at an impressive 13 5 decibels. He was close to screaming to hear himself. "The clock is at two thirty- two and counting. They break the huddle, split backfield, single wide-outs on both sides. Harrison tight on the left side. Pinelli back in deep shotgun, takes the snap from Christian, big rush, he waits...he waits. Now hits Enos over the middle at the forty-five...with room to scamper... to the forty...the thirty-five...cuts right...trying to get out-of-bounds at the thirty...didn't make it. Clock running... two-twenty...Guy brings them to the line...barking out to Collins on the right...behind the center...two-ten to go... barks to Amos behind him...how can they hear anything? It's like a tornado in here...holy Mother of God...two oh two...finally the snap...fakes to Amos... three-step drop... fires to Collins at the twenty-five...and out-of-bounds at the twenty-two. One fifty-five left...second and two. Time- out, folks...take a breath...have a drink...listen to the crowd!"

Guy barely had energy to walk to the sidelines. His ribs were aching, his groin felt like a knife was in it, his hamstrings were tightening, his right toe was aching, and his right arm was on fire every time he threw.

Coach Brown came out to the field to meet him alone. "What are you gonna run, Mr. Finelli?"

"I'm going to run Amos up the middle twice to run some clock, and then we got them set up for the split with Hank. Then I'm running in the two-pointer if it takes me a minute to scramble back there!"

"Well, just get me eight points so we can get to overtime...and you better win the goddamned toss!"

"I got it, Coach."

As he had predicted, Amos ran up the middle twice, picked up the first down on the twenty-one-yard line, and then ran two yards to the nineteen. In the huddle during a time-out, Guy quickly went over assignments on the "split" pattern. "Cary on right side out at five, Mark in motion to the slot on the right side, and then run the clear out straight to the end zone. Duran outside left, and bring your safety left with a flag or something. Amos, I need a block on the weak side. Hank, do your split and make the catch. Let's go, break."

Gil Martin picked up the call from there. "Folks, second and eight from the nineteen with less than a minute to go, Guy brings them up to line; he drops into a deep shotgun. He's back at the thirty-two...Pelligrini in motion to the right...sets up in the slot, Collins right, Hall left, Harrison tight right...there's a perfect snap from Christian, Amos with crushing block on the left, Finelli pumps over the middle...looking right...floats a pass into the deep corner...Harrison dives...the ball...the defender, Hank roles out of the end zone, the referee turns and bends down...holy Mother of God...he has the ball, he has the ball, he has the ball. I can't hear myself, folks. It's bedlam in the end zone. Hank has the ball for a touchdown. They mob him at the goal line...the Macs are down by two with fifty-two seconds left. Can they make the two-point conversion and get this to overtime? I don't know, folks, but I'm still here to see..."

The referees confirmed the touchdown and placed the ball on the three-yard line. In the huddle, Guy made the play clear. "Listen, we have no play; I'm just running it in. They know it, I know it, America knows it...we need two points. No penalties, just knock somebody senseless."

After two minutes of complete silence, Gil Martin calmly announced the extra-point play. "Guy Finelli in shotgun...he takes the snap and stops and reverses his field and heads left...running to the corner, he backs off and stops, fakes a throw to the right, ducks under a defender, heads back right, and cuts toward the middle... there's an opening...he's at the five... the three...he dives and lays out the ball...he's hit ...I don't know, folks...the ball is loose...the ball is loose...the Banners recover... he didn't make it...can that be? Oh, my Lord...it can't be!"

Guy Finelli was on the ground with dirt in his face and grass stuffed in his helmet as he waited for the pile to untangle. The replay was clear. The football was short by a centimeter before he lost control.

It was 40-38 with fifty-two seconds left and two time-outs. An onside kick seemed to be the only option, but Cousin Joe argued against it with Coach Brown. "We can pin them back and force a punt with fifteen seconds to go. The onside kick is virtually impossible with who we have left, and Guy has no idea how to kick it."

Coach Brown agreed and told Guy to kick it as far as possible. He complied with a low liner out of the end zone. The Banners ran two plays, losing three yards and six seconds off the clock. It was third and thirteen with forty-nine seconds. They decided for Falcone to run a sneak on third down for no gain. Now the play clock returned to thirty seconds based on the new rules in 2018. The game clock ran down to thirteen seconds and a

Banner time-out.

The punt was high but not deep to the Macs forty- three-yard line. Finelli put up his hand for a fair catch and cradled the ball and stopped the clock.

They huddled, and Guy called two plays. "OK, trips right, Duran, Mark, and Cary, in that order. Three out- patterns at the forty-three, the thirty-three, and the twenty-three. Duran, yours last, with a top of the house starting at the twenty-seven to the twenty and back to the twenty-three...got it?"

They all nodded in silence. "Hank, tight left, hook at the forty inside...catch and fire it to me outside left. I'll try to get out-of-bounds, but I'm going to Duran if I can."

Guy looked at his guys in the huddle one last time. "Listen, I need four seconds before I throw the ball."

"No problem, Guy," spoke Albert Christian for the first time in the huddle today. "Just knee somebody in the balls if you have to!"

Everybody laughed. "Any questions?"

"Yeah, Finelli, what do we do if we get it to Duran?" Clarence Night asked.

"Don't worry, my friend; just line up on the ball. I'll let you know."

"Dig it, brother...yeah, all day and all of the night!"

Gil Martin was in deep prayer, trying to finish his last Hail Mary on the rosary, realizing it was exactly what the Potomacs needed to win the game. "The Macs come out in trips right, Harrison tight left. Finelli is back on his thirty for the snap. Here we go, folks just hang on for one more miracle, there's the snap, good protection...Guy waits...and waits...he throws deep right. Hall is open and a catch at the twenty-three-yard line. He's out-of-bounds with five seconds left. What a pattern! What a pass! Now what, one last toss into the end zone? Holy Mother of God, we need a miracle, fans...Finelli is running to the line of scrimmage...yelling out a play and formation. He is lining them up...Collins tight right, Harrison tight left, Pelligrini and Hall on wings...and my goodness, Amos is in motion to the right...nobody is out there to cover him. Throw it, Guy quick! Oh, pardon me...Guy Finelli is taking his time at the line of scrimmage and finally retreats to the deep shotgun again. Now he moves up to the thirty-two. He looks left to see a Banner safety is finally running after Amos...Oh lord!

Well, here's the snap...Finelli catches. There is no rush up the middle...perfect blocking...he takes a step, now... oh, my Lord...he's dropping the ball in front of him ...and kicking it? Can it be from the thirty-yard line? It's up over the linemen...end over end...straight down the middle... is it long enough? Holy Mother of God... oh, my Lord...The colors explode! He's done it...Finelli has done it...Finelli has done it...the kick is good...the kick is good...the kick is good...the Macs win ... the Macs have won...the Macs win forty-one to forty...it's a miracle, folks...it's a miracle from the heavens!

The greatest comeback in professional football history led to a massive explosion of fans storming the field from the opposite end zone. Security and police held them back at midfield to form just a peaceful celebration as the players mobbed Guy Finelli at the thirty-yard line.

The twenty-two players and three coaches still functional by the end of the game stayed on their backs after falling to the ground in a massive pile over Guy Finelli. They were left facing the open roof and the moonlight above, wondering what planet they were really on.

Chapter 47

T HE FRIVOLOUS PRICE of $20,000 was the answer for the peace of mind to secure his deal. How to transfer $1 million from an investment account into cash and then set up the wire transfer to complete a $10 million payment was the question. Guy Finelli was a rich man, with ready cash assets at his beck and call.

The Turk wanted the cash delivered personally to him by Guy Finelli, early on Monday morning, while America would be waking up to a hangover celebration after watching the greatest championship contest in history. Berker Assante was in business to dominate people, mainly by taking their money and having them serve him. The millions lost when Guy Finelli drop-kicked the winning field goal from thirty yards out, sealing the third football championship in a row for the Potomacs, would be wiped from his books and memory when he received the $10 million from the football MVP and American sports hero. And all for a stupid gun!

Mach had been in touch with an ex-league security person friendly with Guy, who put him in touch with a New York guy specializing in cash movement. The $20,000 gained valuable information and an attaché case recommended for carrying the $1 million in cash. The case was impenetrable without blowing up the money and could not be opened without an hourly updated combination from a security company.

Without sleep, Guy Finelli had been home less than an hour from the all-night partying after the historic victory. He knew of his perilous morning meeting, but he wanted to enjoy every minute with his healthy teammates, especially his Sprint DMC boys.

It started with the surviving healthy twenty-two players partying together walking down East Capital Street from the stadium and scattering to every night spot on Capitol Hill.

Horace Day and Clarence Night each drank a beer on every block from people partying on their front porches. After meandering for twenty-four blocks, they both passed out in a crowd at Staunton Park on Massachusetts and C Streets. Chester Blue and Braxton Black lost them when they turned to Tenth and D streets, where they accepted invitations to a private party with two beautiful French interns working at their embassy in DC for their last semester of college. Both had watched their first American football game and had lots of questions for the two-star players. Black and Blue did not leave until the parade on Wednesday morning.

Amos Enos, Hank Harrison, and Andrew Christian found New Orleans jazz music playing and Cajun food cooking in one backyard near Fifth Street. It was a diverse crowd that paraded in costumes around the block around four in the morning, throwing beads to those still hanging out on their porches. They all found beds in the grand row house, passing out after sunrise.

Guy, Cary, Mark, and Duran found free drinks at a dozen bars. They developed an entourage from the first few bars and ended up with thirty people on the porch of a Supreme Court justice who lived on the Hill. She was a huge Potomacs fan and invited them all in after the last bar closed. She brought out her best cognac for a toast and then led them in singing "Hail to the Po-to-macs!" After serving sandwiches, she found cabs for all her guests to bring them safely home by five in the morning.

The parade in DC would come in a couple of days, and Guy was expected to be in various studios to discuss the victory on every sports show possible by seven in the morning. All of these activities were based on one thing: Guy being alive in a couple of hours.

The plan was to transfer to the white van somewhere in the little town of Catonsville just southwest of Baltimore. The drive there, in the dark morning of a cold February Monday, was soothing for his tired eyes. His adrenal glands were pumping out fumes, hoping to get a much-needed fill-up. He had been following a blue Ford Escape since the exit for MD 32 on I-95 to Baltimore. They joined in a two-car caravan, after he left I-95 for five minutes. He had been instructed to pull off the exit and wait. Quickly, the Ford SUV pulled in front of him and blinked its lights three times.

The seven-year-old Ford Escape was now leading him to the town of Catonsville. They peeled off onto the BWI Airport exit but headed west, bypassing the University of Maryland-Baltimore County (UMBC) on Rolling Road. The two-lane country road rambled by a private golf course on the right and then through several blocks of beautiful, century-old houses on large, tree-lined lots, set back from the road, before reaching Old Frederick Avenue. The classic avenue became Main Street in Catonsville. It was the original route from Baltimore that headed west through the Maryland cities of Frederick, Hagerstown, and Cumberland.

As the caravan headed east into Catonsville, the shops and restaurants were still dark, waiting for another week of business to start. Guy knew that the avenue, which was a straight shot into downtown Baltimore, was just a few miles and a couple turns from the Turk's compound in West Baltimore.

They turned into an isolated parking lot. It happened to be behind a great seafood place that Guy had enjoyed previously in Catonsville. He quietly remembered that in spring 2008, not the best of times for him, his family had visited the UMBC campus for Grace to consider their engineering program. Afterward, they drove through the neighboring town of Arbutus to the south and then to Catonsville in the north before settling for the convincing smell of Old Bay seasoning at the Catonsville seafood restaurant. As that same smell emanated from the back of the restaurant now, he recalled how his juvenile missteps had led him to this present situation. Was it all worth it? *Hell yeah,* he thought-besides, it was the only way to cope, and honestly, it was so much fun that it seemed harmless at the time.

He finally concluded that this situation was far more complicated than that memory. If he could pull this trade and bring down the Turk and his empire, then everything he had experienced would have been for a purpose. As a smile came to his tired face, it seemed to peel off the mask of fear and extended warm feelings of confidence down through his aching muscles. Guy honorably believed that he was meant to be in this situation and righteously accepted his position to finish the play, to take down their best player, and to win the game. After all, he was "The Safety!"

It occurred to him that Berker Assante might own this property in the sleepy town that bordered the Baltimore Beltway and UMBC. That would make this an easy meeting place for situations like this-plus, it was a great place to eat.

The FBI did not concern Assante. He concluded that Guy was flying on his own with his offer, and therefore, the FBI had no reason to follow him. He knew that the trail to his empire had grown cold over the years after Anna Cobb had been shot to death seven years ago. The gun trail had never been found, and selling it was a fortunate bonanza for him. The current Baltimore drug connection into Montgomery County was getting Assante richer every day. Since hard liquor had become a big sell to high school and college-age kids in the last decade, cocaine had become resurrected as a drug of choice for the well-to-shots of hard liquor. It was simple-alcohol was a downer, and cocaine was an upper. It made for a perfect harmony or just a great, continuous buzz.

Guy knew it would be twenty to thirty minutes before the white van showed up. It gave him a chance to listen to the endless football postgame coverage that was no won rerun at five in the morning. After a couple of minutes, he turned the XM radio to the sixties channel to help him relax and think about his dad. It soothed his distress and sadness about his dad's condition. If this plan was a success, he knew that his next project would be to bring his dad back to good health.

304

The Beatles' "A Day in the Life" was just finishing with a long piano chord sounding into eternity, followed by the brilliance of Donovan's "Hurdy Gurdy Man." It seemed like an omen. He turned the volume way up and closed his eyes for the first few lines:

Thrown like a star in my vast sleep To find that I was by
the sea Gazing with tranquility

Then his head fell back with the explosive guitar chord that sunk him into his next adventure:

'Twas then when the Hurdy Gurdy Man Came singing songs of love

After surviving the depth of the Hurdy Gurdy refrain, he realized the answer:

Thrown like a star in my vast sleep
I open my eyes to take a peep
To find that I was by the sea
'Twas then when the Hurdy Gurdy Man
Came singing songs of love!

Fully recharged with a purpose, Guy was wide awake as the white van pulled up, with a different pair of thugs this time. He followed their procedure without incident, and twenty minutes later he was standing in front of his opponent.

"Please untie our guest. He is an important person and a national hero...yes, my friend?"

Guy smiled with confidence. "Thank you, Berker." He stood up and took a step forward. Guns appeared as the Turk held up his hand.
"Please show some respect; this man is unarmed."
"Thank you, Berker...please, thank you...may I say something. please?"
Berker sat down and nodded with a sense of accomplishment and recognition that this famous man was asking permission to talk. He thought to himself that Guy possessed the manners of a gentleman.
"You have been my toughest opponent for almost a decade now. I entered the business as a boy, and now I ask to leave after many mistakes. I have decided that I do not need the gun to complete this transaction." He opened the case with $1 million dollars

305

in cash to impress his opponent. "The rest of the money will transfer to you as I drive home. When it is done, your van will leave my trail. Can we agree to this arrangement?"

Sitting upright, Berker felt strong from the honor he was receiving from a worthy opponent. He felt respect for this honorable, trusting young man. He could steal the $10 million and dump him somewhere off I-95, but that would not be worthy of this relationship. He again felt the same intimacy from their last meeting. It was warm and appealing. "No, my friend, a deal is a deal. I want you to have the gun; it is yours. It was an unfortunate acquisition that should not have happened. It was a sign of disrespect that my men showed. I took care of it for many years because I knew it was very special to you."

Guy stepped forward, extending both hands to Berker, kissed him on both cheeks, and walked back with a bowed head and his hands together in prayer against his chest. He only needed to play out the charade to receive the prize that he was desperate for to avenge Anna and to change West Baltimore.

He was numb to the kind words from his opponent, because he could only hear in his head, "'Twas then when the Hurdy Gurdy Man came singing songs of love!"

Chapter 48

(Five years later) *Washington Daily,* May 15, 2025, front-page
headlines:

West Baltimore: A $300 Million Youth Sports Center

Film-Making Team Alex Santucci-Guy Finelli Donate By Ron Roswell

A spokesman for former baseball MVP Alex Santucci and his half-brother, former football MVP Guy Finelli, announced at a press conference in Baltimore City that a program will build the following facilities on blocks of abandoned row-house properties in the western part of Baltimore City: athletic fields for youth football, soccer, baseball, and lacrosse; indoor facilities for basketball, volleyball, gymnastics, and swimming; and a community center for town meetings, family counseling, tutoring, and drug treatment on fifty acres of land that has been razed by the city over the past few years in hopes of attracting an investor to the location.

The area has been destroyed by the violence of drug wars and the ongoing use of illegal drugs. Finelli Films has produced two movies, *The Big Train* and *The Tackler,* in the past two years that have grossed over $1 billion worldwide / both adapted from novels written by their father, Phillip Finelli.

The spokesman, former assistant FBI director Brooklyn O'Malley, will be the director of the project, including the building of the facilities, the hiring of staff, and the establishment of a community board to oversee the development and running of the programs.

"Brooks" O'Malley worked undercover in Baltimore for fifteen years, leading to the arrest of the drug boss known as "the Turk," or Berker Assante, in February of 2020. The block of row houses that were used to run his illegal empire will be the future building of the outpatient drug treatment and family counseling center. The project is set to open in spring 2026.

W HAT AWARD-WINNING REPORTER Ron Roswell witnessed at the announcement / but did not include in his article, was the heart and soul of Director

O'Malley's comments that came at the end of his speech. Roswell was the only individual on the planet, outside of the Finelli family, that understood the real story behind O'Malley's comments. He was sworn to never tell in his lifetime, but he thought that it might make for that great novel he'd never yet gotten around to writing.

O'Malley, as the only speaker at the event, made the announcement with the famous brothers on either side of him. He finished the event with an emotional plea: "To defend against the 'atomic bomb' of drugs in the next decade, the idea is to stop this escalation of the new offensive weapons that have arrived on the scene. A new defense is needed to bring sanity to this conflict of drug abuse. A balance is necessary to return the power of the community to dominance. A beacon of hope to even the playing field of despair, something bigger, faster, smarter, and bolder than before-a super-community place that breeds heroes, not dealers; a place of safety that gives the community a chance to be nurtured and protected."

As tears crested in the corners of his eyes, the seventy- three-year-old Brooks O'Malley-a public servant to his core-paused, seeming to nurture a feeling for his final words. The crowd was silent, patiently waiting for the powerful emotions of hope to pass through them. Then came a quiet question from an African-American teenager standing in the rear of the packed room. Tall enough to be seen and making certain to be heard, he was there covering the event for his high-school newspaper.

"Mr. O'Malley... sir ...what will the center be called?" Brooks looked down. He knew the answer in his heart, and even though he had never discussed it with the brothers, it was his decision. As the director, he would be in charge of the project, and he knew that the name had to be something special-inspirational and unique.

He felt the powerful presence of Alex Santucci to his left-a true sports hero and a supportive brother to the man on his right, Guy Finelli, whom he first met as a boy who was trying to find the right path to greatness. Brooks realized he had become his "guardian angel," protecting him while overseeing his journey to reach this moment.

Guy had become something more than just a sports hero. Retiring from the GAF after his amazing victory in the M2C2-1, he became an actor and a community leader, eventually starring in the two movies that he produced with his brother Alex Santucci. He had raised above great adversity, leading his team to victory while flourishing in his role as a defender without fear, a challenger of evil, someone to make right out of wrong. In this day and age, he was a superhero whose real identity as a crime fighter would never be revealed.

Reliving the story in his mind brought a smile to Brooks's face and released the pressure of his emotions. He felt relief as the exterior lines of experience in his face ebbed to expose a natural, youthful face. Announcing the name of the project would cap off years of pursuit and patience, bring meaning to the months of isolation and inaction, and dampen the days of fear and ferocity in pursuit of peace for this community.

As he looked up to answer, Brooklyn O'Malley felt his high-tech voice box and cleared his throat. "It will be quite simply known as 'The Safety'!"

Epilogue

January 19, 2043

PHILLIP FINELL! WAS in his Parkwood home, the house of his youth, enduring January for the first time in years. The comforting heat burning out from a stone fireplace made the outside cold tolerable. He had made his last trip home from Cape Canaveral after witnessing another successful Mars Mission blast- off before Thanksgiving and was not feeling well enough to travel back after the New Year. His cardiologist, Dr. Scarlett Williams, who still looked youthful as ever at the age of seventy, had made good on her promise to keep him alive until at least eighty-five. Now nearing ninety, he was still reading the *Washington Daily* every morning, now on his handheld tablet, which was as light as a newspaper and opened up in thin sections that felt like stiff sheets of paper to read the different pages. It even oozed the artificial smell of an old-time printed paper.

His oldest grandchildren, twins Phillip II and Philly II, were approaching thirty, married, and living in the nearby houses on Everett Street. Alex Santucci and Sally Keegan had sold their mansion in Bethesda and rebuilt on the two lots above them on Oldfield Drive with a commanding backyard view of Rock Creek Park. Grace and Guy Finelli had purchased the two houses on Parkwood behind their parents and below Alex and Sally over the years for their families and two kids each: Annie (now twenty-eight) and Anthony (twenty-two), and Laura (twenty) and Walter (eighteen).

There were no fences between the seven lots, just steps and worn-out walkways. On most days while growing up, Phillip II, Philly II, Annie, Anthony, Laura, and Walter would sprint out their back doors after school and fly down the hills to see Grandma the gardener and Grandpop the writer in the afternoons. On the weekends, they would join the rest of the families for Sunday night dinner at their grandparents' house.

Phillip could still throw the football and shoot hoops with the grandchildren until their junior-high years, when friends became important, and less time was available for others. Phillip and Carol understood the cycle and enjoyed every moment they had with them.

As Phillip sipped his coffee, he felt more of the pain creeping up from his back and through his chest. All the pain patches were becoming ineffective, and morphine would be the next option. His heart was becoming inefficient, and a transplant was too late at this point. Phillip had fought open-heart surgery for over forty years and was not about to give in to the possibility now.

After watching another oak log transform into a final burnt ember, he decided to head to his bedroom, take a narcotic to ease the pain, and lie down. As he walked by the hallway, he paused to look at his favorite photograph of his grandparents, Geraldo and Philomena, taken in 1911, two years after their wedding. Geraldo Finelli looked like a handsome, young John Wayne at age twenty-four, ready to start a family in America. Little did Geraldo know at the time that it was the first picture of Philomena carrying his son, Guy I.

On this date, a federal holiday celebrating Martin Luther King's birthday, Phillip thought about his grandfather, Geraldo, who had died ninety years ago on January 19, 1953.

Even though that had been five months before Phillip was born, somehow, he could always feel his touch every time he saw his picture or thought of him. Spiritually, it penetrated his being and gave him strength, even now as he moved to his bed for some rest.

After turning a few pages from a novel he was reading, he curled up on top of the made bed and felt the pained state of his body relaxing as the medication started the magic of pain relief.

In his dream, the noises in the room were gentler than a whisper, but it moved him to wake from a thirty- minute nap. Phillip II and his spouse, Chahna, joined Philly II and her husband, Malak, to see if Grandpop was awake. Chahna and Malak were brother and sister from an Asian-Indian family that had met the twins in the School of Engineering at UMD. All four now were engineers in the electrical, structural, civil, and computer areas of the profession. Their houses had been rebuilt with great precision, simultaneously next to each other, with their expertise. They stood with excitement, wanting to share some wonderful news with Grandpop Phillip.

Carol, his wife of fifty-six years, had just heard the news and was following the foursome into the bedroom. She took the lead, a little concerned about Phillip back in bed and resting already.

"Dear... the twins are here. I thought you were awake already...are you feeling OK?"

"Oh, just a little nap...I think this book puts me to sleep. Everybody come in, please. What a nice surprise![11]

Philly II was first to hug her grandpop, with an extra squeeze this morning. Chahna was next, unable to show her normal cautiousness with public displays of affection, to find warmth in the grasp of Phillip's hug. With his large, strong hands, Phillip held the hands of both of them for a moment while Phillip II and Malak waited patiently for their hugs. He closed his eyes and felt spiritual strength, an intuition that had propelled his life for so many years. That skill had helped him to write his three novels, the last one full of shocking honesty about his life-a project that had haunted him for years until he finally finished. It became a masterful ending to his trilogy of novels.

He suddenly felt that a great spirit-perhaps his grandfather-was telling him something about his hands. It said, "Feel them now, and pass it on.[11] He gently extended his hands on Philly's II and Malak's abdomens and felt the spirit of greatness pass through him into their wombs. With tears in his eyes, he looked at the two couples and said, "Your news is so wonderful...! can feel them."

A stunned Philly II led his hand without delay under her sweater to touch her slightly protruding belly at four months of pregnancy. Chahna felt the warmth of his hand and did the same.

"They will be very strong and healthy. Please bring them my love and all your family's love, each day that you love them...forever and ever...[11] They both brightly beamed with fulfillment as their faces flushed red, in contrast to their normal dark features and jet-black hair. Phillip laughed to himself as he remembered that Phillip II had not succumbed to the Finelli redhead gene.

Carol called his cousin Philly in New York and put her on speakerphone to share the news. Phillip loved every minute of the conversation with his dear cousin and the excitement of his grandchildren.

Now his pain was gone as they said their good-byes. His life felt complete. He lay back down and was about to enter into a final, wonderful dream. It was that moment just before the state of sleep finally takes over, like the second before the football reaches your gut, and you know a victory is certain. Curled up on the ground, holding on to that final catch, he saw a circle of friends and family above him hiding a cloudless sun, stretching to reach him and lead him to eternity.

And as a writer, he knew there was no better way to end a story.

312

About the Author

P. EDMUND FISCHETTI is a life-long Washingtonian living currently in the suburb of Silver Spring, Maryland with his wife and two children. He graduated from the University of Maryland with a BA in criminology and an MS in family studies. Playing and following sports has always been a big part of his life.

The Safety is his second novel following *Big Train's Backyard* published in 2013. Each novel follows a great athlete in the Finelli family; Alex Santucci in *Big Train's Backyard* and his half-brother Guy Finelli in *The Safety.* Fischetti plans on a third novel, a prequel, involving the father character, Phillip Finelli.

Writing has come late to P. Edmund Fischetti after three previous careers over a thirty-five-year span. For the last seven years, he has spent many days in Cape Canaveral walking the beach and swimming in the ocean, -ing ideas and writing stories.